OECD Studies on Water

Towards Sustainable Water Services in Estonia

ANALYSES AND ACTION PLAN

OECD

BETTER POLICIES FOR BETTER LIVES

The activity "Analyses and action plan towards sustainable water services in Estonia" was co-funded by the European Union via the Structural Reform Support Programme REFORM/IM2020/004. This publication was produced with the financial assistance of the European Union. The views expressed herein can in no way be taken to reflect the official opinion of the European Union.

Please cite this publication as:
OECD (2022), *Towards Sustainable Water Services in Estonia: Analyses and Action Plan*, OECD Studies on Water, OECD Publishing, Paris, https://doi.org/10.1787/b82d71c6-en.

ISBN 978-92-64-71372-7 (print)
ISBN 978-92-64-68351-8 (pdf)
ISBN 978-92-64-54845-9 (HTML)
ISBN 978-92-64-36985-6 (epub)

OECD Studies on Water
ISSN 2224-5073 (print)
ISSN 2224-5081 (online)

Photo credits: Cover © kavalenkava/Sutterstock.com.

Corrigenda to publications may be found on line at: www.oecd.org/about/publishing/corrigenda.htm.

Foreword

The Estonian Ministry of Environment called on the OECD in 2020 to facilitate a national policy dialogue focused on aggregation of utilities as a condition to set water supply and sanitation services on a sustainable path. The OECD is grateful for this invitation to support an ambitious reform agenda.

The report captures the main analyses and policy discussions, which informed the policy dialogue on water in Estonia. The analyses were initially clustered in several project outputs, compiled here as chapters of the report. Some analyses and policy discussions are likely to be relevant for countries considering options to enhance the performance and financial sustainability of water supply and sanitation services.

The active and constant support of the Ministry is acknowledged. Special thanks go to Karin Kroon, Raili Kärmas, Liisi Arm, Tatjana Rõõm for the time and expertise allocated to this project. The Ministry was particularly successful is in engaging with a range of stakeholders, through co-presence or virtual meetings. The active engagement of the Competition Board – most particularly Aurelie Grenman - was much appreciated.

The project was undertaken in collaboration with – and with the financial support of – the European Commission DG Reform. This collaboration and support have been particularly fruitful. The OECD Secretariat thanks Mauro Sibilia for a pragmatic and problem-solving attitude throughout the process.

The project was undertaken by the OECD Environment Directorate (Tatiana Efimova), with substantial contributions from the OECD Centre for Entrepreneurship: Oriana Romano shared her understanding of the governance of water utilities and Maria Salvetti contributed her extensive knowledge of aggregation processes in Europe and beyond. Tim Keyworth (Keyworth Consulting) plaid a pivotal role, in particular in relation to tariff policy and the role of economic regulation to enhance the performance of water utilities; the OECD Secretariat benefitted from most inspiring discussions on these and related issues. Ain Kalme (Attorney-at-Law, Triniti Estonia) provided robust legal analyses and options. The OECD Secretariat thanks Andres Aruhein, who shared his vision early in the process. Xavier Leflaive, the OECD Environment Water Team Leader, co-ordinated the process and contributed his vision on consolidation options and sustainable water services. Ines Reale provided impeccable support to the project. The work was conducted under the overall supervision of Walid Oueslati, Acting Head of the Environment, Transitions and Resilience Division of the OECD's Environment Directorate.

Table of contents

Tables

Figures

Boxes

Executive summary

Water supply and sanitation services have remarkably improved in Estonia, in terms of share of the population connected to a service and quality of service provision. Over the last two decades, investments to achieve the current level of quality benefitted from significant financial support from the European Commission, of which the Estonian government was able to make the best use.

The services are now facing new challenges: additional investments are required to keep up with social expectations and environmental and health regulations; additional funding is needed to operate, maintain and potentially renew assets financed through EU grants. These needs must be met at a time when downward demographic trends will affect revenues from utilities. Moreover, EU funding for water supply and sanitation services will be gradually be phased out.

It is clear that current and future investment and financing needs can only be met if substantial efficiency gains are achieved, in a sector that remains highly fragmented (177 water companies were operating in Estonia in 2018; 44 local governments are serviced by more than one water company). Business-as-usual is not an option, as delaying reform can only lead to decaying of assets, jeopardising service quality and dramatically raising the cost of rehabilitation and service provision later on.

The Estonian Ministry of Environment called on DG Reform and the OECD to contribute to making the case for reform, while exploring practical ways forward. The process included in-depth analyses of a series of issues, in particular in relation to tariff setting, economic regulation of the sector, and legal provisions. The process entailed recurrent consultation with stakeholders as well, including national authorities (the Competition Board, the Ministry of Finance), local authorities and utilities, and national experts. The project was informed by lessons from similar endeavours in Europe and beyond.

Consolidation of utilities is acknowledged by all stakeholders as a practical way forward to deliver substantial efficiency gains, for operations and investment. However, over the last decade, efforts in this direction have been hampered by concerns that i) smaller municipalities will not have their voices heard in merged utilities, and ii) customers of well-managed utilities will lose, as they would have to pay higher water bills to absorb less cost-effective ones. These concerns are serious. They need to be addressed, if the Estonian ministry favours a voluntary dynamics towards consolidation.

The recommendations developed in the course of the project allow addressing both concerns, in line with the Ministry's preference for a voluntary approach. First, consolidation can take several forms. Merger on a geographical basis is only one of them. Discussions with stakeholders have made the case for the mutualisation of functions as a practical way forward that can build trust across service providers and lead to more ambitious coordination, all the way towards coordinated development and investment. Governance arrangements were discussed at utility level, which support both the capacity to make decisions and the need to hear the voices of diverse local authorities.

Second, several actions are required.to make the best of existing opportunities to incentivise – including financially - municipalities and utilities to move towards some form of consolidation. One set of actions consists in providing financial incentives to utilities. In the Estonian context, this can be done in two ways: i) accelerated depreciation of assets under conditions to be agreed upon by the economic regulator and the Ministry of Environment; and ii) reward utilities that explore ambitious options to enhance the efficacy of development plans, including through some form of consolidation. Stakeholder consultations have explored practical options, including through the Estonian Environmental Investment Centre.

Another set of actions relate to reviewing and assessing the opportunity of investments and expenditure programmes developed by local authorities and service providers.

Benchmarking can play an important role, to set performance objectives and review performance of water companies. In the course of the project, a benchmarking process was proposed, which goes beyond the comparison of costs and includes the comparison of levels of performance and the ambition of development plans in terms of efficiency gains. More broadly, transparency of performance can support a consolidation process, while contributing to stakeholder engagement.

Implementation of these recommendations requires strong coordination between the Ministry of environment, which sets policy objectives and levels of ambition, and the economic regulator – the Competition Board – which defines the tariff setting methodology and can arrange the adequate combination of benchmarking and reward. Stakeholder consultations throughout the project also emphasised the role of other government agencies (Ministry of finance), local authorities and utilities (individually and collectively). Training material was developed on issues discussed in the course of the project, to further strengthen capacities of the key partners.

It is noteworthy that the Ministry has the capacity to set targets and a deadline for a move towards some form of consolidation. Should such targets not be meet ahead of the set deadline, a more top-down approach could be considered.

On these and related issues, experience sharing among Baltic states and across Europe can be a source of inspiration. An international workshop in the course of the project revealed the breadth and depth of experience with forms of consolidation for water supply and sanitation service provision, both in terms of end point and in terms of processes for getting there. Estonia has a lot to share, building on recent experience and the on-going reform. This confirms the distinctive value added of peer learning supported by DG Reform.

1 Report with a robust analysis of the state of play

Guided by a questionnaire drafted by the OECD Secretariat, Estonian authorities collected data and information on the state of play for water supply and sanitation in the country. That background information provides the common knowledge on which to identify pending issues and areas for further work.

1.1. Background and objectives

The Ministry of the Environment of Estonia jointly with other governmental authorities (the Ministry of Finance, the Minister of Public Administration), the European Commission –DG Reform, and the OECD are partnering to enhance the sustainability of water supply and sanitation services in Estonia. The Project will support the preparation of a roadmap for the consolidation of the water utility sector, a requisite for a sustainable and socially acceptable financing strategy and a broader water sector reform in Estonia. See the Detailed Project Description, for more information on background, scope and process.

The specific objectives of this Project are:

- to support the initiatives of national authorities to design their reforms according to their priorities, taking into account initial conditions and expected socioeconomic impacts
- to support the efforts of national authorities to define and implement appropriate processes and methodologies by taking into account good practices of and lessons learned by other countries in addressing similar situations
- to assist the national authorities and water utilities in enhancing the efficiency and effectiveness of human-resource management, inter alia, by strengthening professional knowledge and skills and setting out clear responsibilities.

The report presents background information compiled by Estonian authorities on the state of play, previous attempts to agglomerate water utilities in the country. Data and information were collected on the basis of a questionnaire developed by the OECD Secretariat (see Appendix). The questionnaire covers the following areas:

- Legislation, institutional and regulatory framework
- The organisation of service provision
- The performance of service providers
- Tariff setting
- Inter-agency co-ordination and cooperation for WSS service provision
- Mapping WS service coverage and recent trends in service provision
- WSS strategic policy making and financing water supply and sanitation
- Experience with consolidation of municipalities and/or service providers.

Propositions unfold, on key issues that deserve further analysis in the context of this project. The analyses are meant to document possible courses of action and options to facilitate agglomeration of water utilities in Estonia. They define the proposed programme of work in the context of this project for the next 12 months (in line with the Detailed Project Description). The proposed course of action will be discussed with Estonian stakeholders at the kick-off meeting. The outcome of the discussions will be reflected in an Issue paper.

1.2. The state of play

Estonia has implemented a massive investment programme over the past two decades to catch up with EU standards for water supply and wastewater collection and treatment. Recently built assets now need to be properly operated and maintained, to ensure lasting service provision and performance and avoid costs related to premature decay of existing infrastructures. More than 90% of the population is connected to safe water supply across the country, reflecting a high level of compliance with the Drinking Water Directive (DWD). However, there is room for improvement as regards the Urban Wastewater Treatment Directive (UWWTD).

The institutional and regulatory frameworks are in place (most notably the Water Act, the Public Water Supply and Sewerage Act). They have been recently strengthened (e.g. set up of the Competition Authority, under the Ministry of Justice; extended accountability of local governments for communal infrastructure).

Diverse forms of contractual relations to operate WSS assets, including PSP (e.g. Tallinn) take place. Regionalisation of WSS services have been implemented in selected localities. These developments indicate the sophistication of service provision and the capacity to adapt modalities to local conditions in Estonia.

1.2.1. Access to water supply and sanitation services in Estonia

Estonia has undertaken significant investments to reach compliance with the EU water *acquis* on water supply and sanitation (WSS). As a result of investments made in the last decade, 87.3% of the population in Estonia is connected to the public water supply and 83% to the public sewerage system. The constructed public water supply and sewerage systems require consistent maintenance and new investments. Unfortunately, the present fragmentation of water companies, where the majority are micro-companies, prevents access to the funds required for investments and the qualified workforce for maintenance of equipment while offering water services at affordable tariffs.

One of the most important strategic documents of the Estonian environmental policy is the *Environmental Protection and Use Programme for 2020-2023*. The important goal set in this programme as regards water use is sustainable access of the residents to a safe drinking water, collection and treatment of wastewater, and provision to the service at an affordable water tariff. The following performance indicators, among others, are set in the programme:

Table 1.1. WSS services in Estonia

Indicator	Initial level (2018)	2020	2021	2022	2023
Population connected to public sewerage system	82.9	83.8	84.1	84.4	84.7
Share of consumers receiving safe drinking water from public water supply system, %	99 (2017)	100	100	100	100
The average tariff of the water service and its share in the average income of a household does not exceed 2.5%	Yes	yes	Yes	yes	yes
Share of wastewater collection areas of over 2000 p.e. that comply with wastewater collection and treatment requirements, %	94.7	95	98	100	100

Source: Environmental Protection and Use Programme for 2020-2023.

1.2.2. Institutions in charge of policies that affect water supply and wastewater management

The Ministry of Social Affairs develops policies and legislation in issues related to public health, incl. about the quality of safe drinking water. The Health Board, which is an institution of the Ministry of Social Affairs, performs oversight of the quality requirements for drinking water and the obligations of drinking water operators. You can read about the goals of the Ministry of Social Affairs and about public health in English here: https://www.sm.ee/en/environmental-health and about the Health Board and the safety of drinking water here: https://www.terviseamet.ee/et/keskkonnatervis/inimesele/joogivee-ohutus .

The Ministry of the Environment is developing the water economy and public water supply and sewerage policy. The Environmental Inspectorate, which is an institution of the Ministry of the Environment, also performs oversight of the compliance with the regulations of local governments concerning on-site treatment and removal of wastewater and checks the compliance of the activities of water companies and the clients of water companies with the requirements for handling hazardous substances. The activities of the Environmental Inspectorate can be found here: https://www.kki.ee/et/eesmargid-tegevused/keskkonnakaitse .

The Environmental Board is an institution of the Ministry of the Environment which, in addition to issuing environmental permits and registering activities that pose a risk to the water environment, approves public water supply and sewerage development plans and the formation and alteration of wastewater collection areas. The activities of the Environmental Board can be found here: https://www.keskkonnaamet.ee/en/activities/water .

The Ministry of the Environment also develops support measures for the development of the public water supply and sewerage service. The Environmental Investment Centre is an institution of the Ministry of the Environment, which is the central financier of environmental projects in Estonia as the implementing agency of support policy. You can read about the Environmental Investment Centre here: https://kik.ee/en/kik .

The Competition Authority is an institution of the Ministry of Justice, which is responsible for the regulation of the tariffs of public water supply and sewerage services. You can read about the Competition Authority here: https://www.konkurentsiamet.ee/en/water-district-heating/water/overview .

1.2.3. Legislation and regulatory framework

Legislation is developed in cooperation of the institutions above. The drafts of legislation must be officially approved by the parties concerned. The Health Board and the Environmental Board also approve the public water supply and sewerage development plans, which must be prepared by each local government. Communication about other issues takes place as necessary.

Training and meetings for water companies and local government employees are also organised in cooperation. For example, the Ministry of the Environment organises training for wastewater treatment plant operators, the Partner Day (where we introduce our priorities, answer the questions of partners and organise discussions on WSS in a workshop), quarterly meetings with the Environmental Investment Centre (an overview is given of how to apply for support, the problems that have emerged in the grant or application for support), etc. At the start of every year, the Ministry of the Environment also sends an overview of its annual work plan, incl. planned legislative amendments etc., to its partners (NGOs).

The main pillars of the legislative and regulatory framework are the following.

The Water Act

This Act provides for:

- grounds for planning and organising the use and protection of water, the implementation of which will promote sustainable water use;
- water protection requirements which will ensure protection of water resources in the long term;
- rights, obligations and liability of persons in water use;
- state supervision over compliance with the requirements for the use and protection of water;
- liability for an infringement of the requirements provided for in this Act.

The English version is available here: https://www.riigiteataja.ee/en/eli/511052020001/consolide .

The Public Water Supply and Sewerage Act

The Act regulates the organisation of supply of registered immovables with water and the collection and treatment of wastewater of the registered immovables, rain water, drainage water and other soil and surface water through the public water supply and sewerage system. It provides for the rights and obligations of the state, local governments, water undertakings and client. The Ministry of the Environment started developing the new Public Water Supply and Sewerage Act in 2015 in order to remove vague definitions and harmonise the text.

Pursuant to the Public Water Supply and Sewerage Act, a local government establishes the rules for use of public water supply and sewerage, which must include:

- the procedure for measuring the water taken and the wastewater to be discharged
- the limit values of the wastewater and rainwater discharged into the public sewerage system based on the consideration that the wastewater flowing out of the public sewerage system must comply with the requirements established on the basis of the Water Act and the wastewater discharged into the public sewerage system must not disrupt the functioning of the system
- the procedure for checking the pollutant content
- the procedure for payment for the public water supply and sewerage service
- the definition of unauthorised extraction of water and unauthorised leading off of wastewater, rainwater and drainage water, and other soil and surface water, and the procedure for determining their volume and value.

The English version is available here: https://www.riigiteataja.ee/en/eli/529082019006/consolide .

Regulation of Minister of Environment (08.11.2019) No 61

The regulation sets the requirements for discharging treated effluent, storm water, mining water, quarry water and cooling water into recipient bodies. It sets the methods for assessment of the compliance of discharged water and limit values for pollutant concentration in discharged water.

Regulation is only available in Estonian, here: https://www.riigiteataja.ee/akt/112112019006.

Regulation of Minister of Social Affairs (24.09.2019) No 61

The regulation sets the quality standards and inspection requirements and the methods for analysis for drinking water. It is only available in Estonian, here: https://www.riigiteataja.ee/akt/126092019002 .

Local Government Organisation Act § 6 (1).

The Article stipulates that the functions of a local authority - in the rural or urban environments - include the organisation of the provision of a range of social and cultural services, housing and utilities, including the supply of water and sewerage. The functions also include waste management, spatial planning, and the construction and maintenance of roads or city streets unless such functions are assigned by law to other persons.

1.3. The organisation of WSS services

Local governments are mandated to organise the collection and treatment of urban wastewater before it is discharged into the receiving water body as effluent (industrial or other production wastewater, which is treated in an industrial wastewater treatment plant, is not included in urban wastewater). Local governments make proposals to the Ministry of the Environment for the formation or alteration of a wastewater collection area. A wastewater collection area is an area that has enough residents or economic activities for the collection of wastewater via a sewerage system and for discharging wastewater to a wastewater treatment plant or effluent receiving water body pursuant to the Urban Waste Water Treatment Directive 91/271/EEC. Pursuant to the requirements established in Estonia, wastewater collection areas in Estonia are formed on the basis of the level of protection of the groundwater layer and the load of the wastewater collection areas, considering socioeconomic criteria, the status of surface water and water protection goals. The size of a wastewater collection area must be at least five hectares.

Households' capacity to pay for public water supply and sewerage service must be taken into account when a wastewater collection area is formed. The money spent by a household member on the water supply and sewerage service may not exceed four per cent of average annual net income in the country of residence according to the data of Statistics Estonia. If the establishment of a public sewerage system in a wastewater collection area brings about unreasonably high costs, leakage-proof collection tanks may be used for wastewater collection in wastewater collection areas where the load is 2,000 p.e. or more.

Building a public sewerage system in a wastewater collection area whose load is less than 2,000 p.e. is not mandatory, but any existing public sewerage system and wastewater treatment plant must be kept in good technical order to guarantee that wastewater is collected and treated according to requirements. The local government establishes the regulations for on-site treatment and removal of wastewater in their administrative territory.

Pursuant to the Public Water Supply and Sewerage Act, the public water supply and sewerage system may be in public or private ownership. The provisions of § 158 of the Law of Property Act are applied to public water supply and sewerage[1]. In practice, assets belong to water companies, but the majority of water companies belong to local governments. In a few cases, the assets belong to private persons (there are four private companies in WWCAs of over 2,000 p.e.). Non-profit co-operatives, which serve small settlements of up to 200 people, also operate as water companies here.

WSS is a fragmented industry in Estonia. The 2018 annual reports on water use indicate that there are 177 water companies in Estonia and 44 local governments have more than one water company (local governments that have more than one water company are listed in Annex 6). These 177 water companies have declared themselves as water companies, but the number of water companies that comply with the definition of water company given in the Public Water Supply and Sewerage Act is actually bigger. There are companies among said undertakings for whom the provision of water services is not the principal activity (e.g. peat mining and processing company Peat Mill OÜ), but that still provide water services by giving water to some settlements from their drill wells or treating wastewater in their treatment plants.

Changes in the water business occurred after the administrative reform when local governments merged and water companies were merged as well. For example, Alutaguse Haldus OÜ was formed in Alutaguse Municipality after the administrative reform, which provides other utility services in addition to the water service. Regional water companies have also been formed to increase the probability of receiving support from the national environmental programme of the Environmental Investment Centre (KIK).

An example of a water company is Emajõe Veevärk AS, which characterises itself as a company established by local governments on the initiative of the Ministry of the Environment in 2004. The company provides water services in 106 settlements located in five counties. The shareholders of the public limited company are 12 local governments:

Elva	Luunja	Põltsamaa
Jõgeva	Mustvee	Räpina
Kambja	Nõo	Tartu
Kastre	Peipsiääre	Vinni.

Regional water companies are established in cooperation. If the assets are operated by regional water companies, then each local government owns assets proportionally to the local government. Water companies are mostly commercial undertakings, which means that they are free to use their assets as they see fit.

1.4. Concerns about the sustainability of the state of play

While the quality of WSS services markedly improved over the last couple of decades, stakeholders share concerns about the sustainability of the current level of performance.

First, demographic trends affect the financing needs and capacities of water utilities. On the one hand, urbanisation drives investment needs in urban settlements. On the other hand, a decreasing population can affect the revenues of utilities and lead to oversized infrastructures, which will be costly to operate. These contrasted trends need to be properly reflected in infrastructure and service development.

Second, the economic and fiscal situation deteriorates. It is unlikely that public funds, which account for a lion's share of investment finance in the country, can be sustained in the long run. This calls for a revision of financing models, which need to harness other sources of finance, including (but not limited to) revenues from tariffs.

Another source of concern is the complex devolution of responsibilities across institutions involved in setting policies, monitoring performance and providing support to the sector. Blurred responsibilities or lack of accountability can undermine performance of the sector.

Finally, cause and consequence of the concerns above, the performance of water utilities seems to be very fragile. Financing sustainability, in particular is an issue Other potential weaknesses reflect the lack of technical and financial capacities to cope with a range of operational and strategic issues (such as efficient use of water resources, or energy efficiency).

As a result, there is a risk that performance of the service to the population (or selected settlements) deteriorates in the coming years/decades. As an early signal, it is noteworthy that compliance with the EU acquis on water is lagging, in particular as regards the Urban Wastewater Treatment Directive.

1.4.1. Demographic trends

The country has 1.3 million inhabitants. Approximately 1.2 million people will be living in Estonia in 2080 according to the population forecast of Statistics Estonia made in 2019. The population will decrease by 11% in the next 60 years, by 35,800 people in the next 25 years and by 145,200 people by 2080. The demographic trends affect the revenues of water utilities. They also drive investment needs (where population grows) or lead to some infrastructures being oversized and costly to operate (where population decreases).

Urbanisation is increasing. Young people tend to live in cities while aged people mostly stay in rural areas. The population of rural areas also changes seasonally, because more people move to the countryside for summer. More people moved to the countryside during COVID-19 as well.

The type of settlements has been the basis for the definition of rural and urban population in Statistics Estonia until 2018. This classification was recently adjusted, to better monitor increasing suburbanisation. The population of settlements around cities was growing, while being still classified as rural population. The working group on regional statistics under the Ministry of Finance decided to start defining rural and urban population in line with an internationally recognised methodology. However, the internationally used criteria do not meet the needs of Estonia for the determination of rural and urban areas, as the thresholds are too high. This is why the working group developed the following thresholds fort Estonia: urban (type 1), small urban (type 2) and rural (type 3).

On the map below, one can see urban regions are red, small urban regions (i.e. the transition territories of rural and urban settlements) are green and grey marks rural areas.

Figure 1.1. Urban, small urban and rural settlements in Estonia

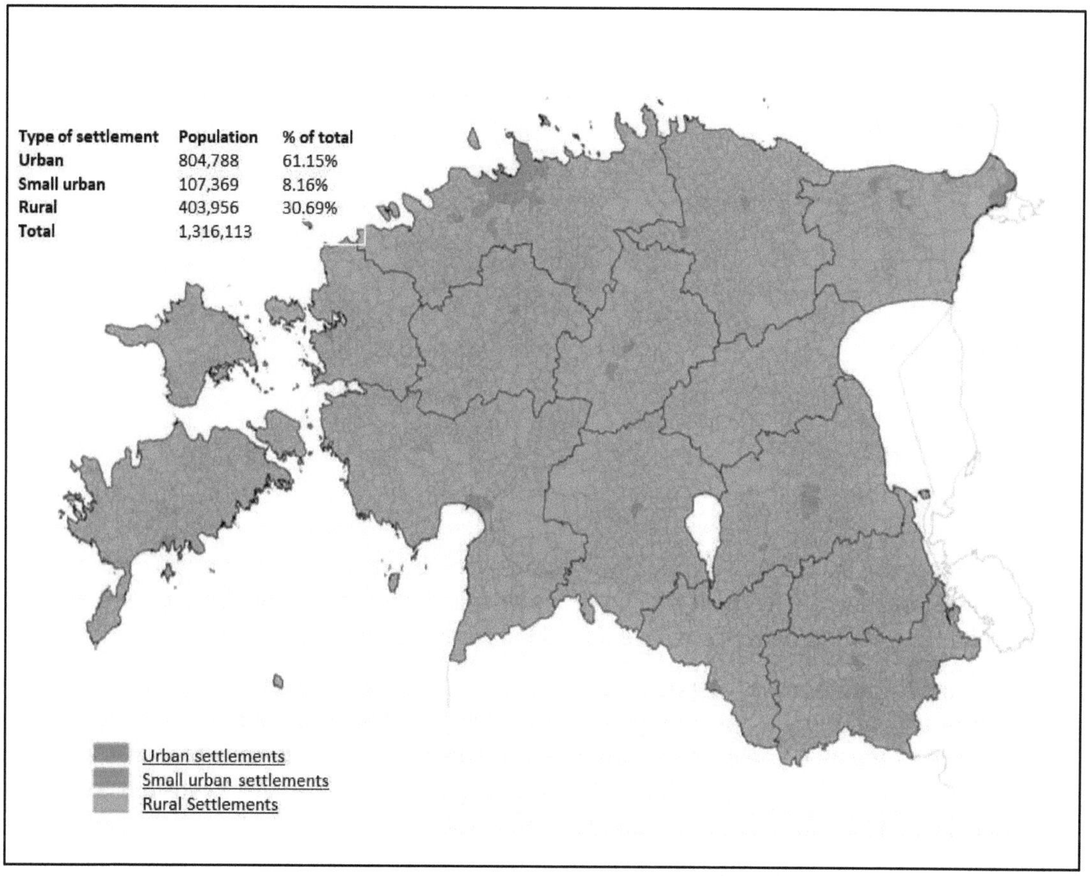

The population of Estonian cities, towns, small towns and villages as at 1 January 2019 was published in the map application of Statistics Estonia on 28 May 2019. There are 4,712 settlements in Estonia. They include 73 villages without permanent residents. The map is accessible here: https://estat.stat.ee/StatistikaKaart/VKR

Number of residents in settlements:

- up to five residents in 344 settlements
- 6–10 residents in 349 settlements
- over 1,000 residents in 102 settlements

These figures have not changed much in two years. For example, the number of villages not populated all year round was 71 at the same time last year.

The number of unpopulated villages was the biggest in Võru County with 23. There are 16 of them in Saaremaa and eight in Hiiu, Harju and Pärnu counties. Unpopulated villages are usually small with an area of less than 2 km2, and only consist of a couple of farms. These villages are often located far from important roads. There were no unpopulated villages in Lääne, Rapla, Jõgeva, Viljandi, Valga and Põlva counties.

From 2017–2019, population increased the most in Harju and Tartu counties, more specifically in Tallinn and Tartu with their neighbouring settlements. Among these, the increase in population was the biggest in Tallinn City Centre. The population of Haabersti and Lasnamäe districts also increased by more than 1,000 people. There are other green areas on the map as well, but they are mostly close to county centres and larger roads.

Narva City was the biggest settlement with a decreasing population – it lost 1,881 people in two years. The population of Järve and Ahtme, the largest districts of Kohtla-Järve, and of Sillamäe also decreased by more than 500 people.

In general, population decreased the most in county centres and other small towns, and settlements in the peripheral regions of counties. However, the change in population was small in most settlements, ranging between -4 to +4 in 66% of them.

Table 1.2. Population by type of settlement

	Number of dwellers	% of total population
Urban settlement region	804,788	61.15%
Small urban settlement region	107,369	8.16%
Rural settlement region	403,956	30.69%
Total people:	1,316,113	100.00%

Projected trends

Birth rate is an important component through which population increases. The current trends suggest that the birth rates will continue growing. According to the baseline scenario of the forecast, we assume that by 2080, the birth rate will increase to the level of 1.86 children per woman on average.

The life expectancy at present is 74 years for men and 82 years for women. These indicators have increased year over year and will continue growing according to forecasts – life expectancy will increase to 83.5 years for men and 89.0 years for women by 2080. The increase in the case of men is slightly faster than in the case of women, as a result of which the gender gap in life expectancy, which is extraordinarily large in Estonia in comparison with other European countries, will decrease to 5.5 years.

The forecast indicates that natural growth is the main factor that will shape the population. There will be fewer births and the number of deaths will start growing after some time. The way the age structure of Estonian residents changes is important in terms of the changes in population. The forecast indicates that working-age population (aged 15–64) will decrease by 8.6 percentage points by the 2060s, which will be followed by a small increase. The share of people aged 65 and over in the population will increase evenly from 20% to 30% by 2060. The share of children (aged 0–14) in the population will decrease from 16% to 14% in 20 years and will be followed by a small increase. The natural growth will remain negative, as the birth rate is below the recovery level.

Figure 1.2. Age structure of forecast populations, 2020–2080 (proportion of people aged 0-14, 15-64, over 64)

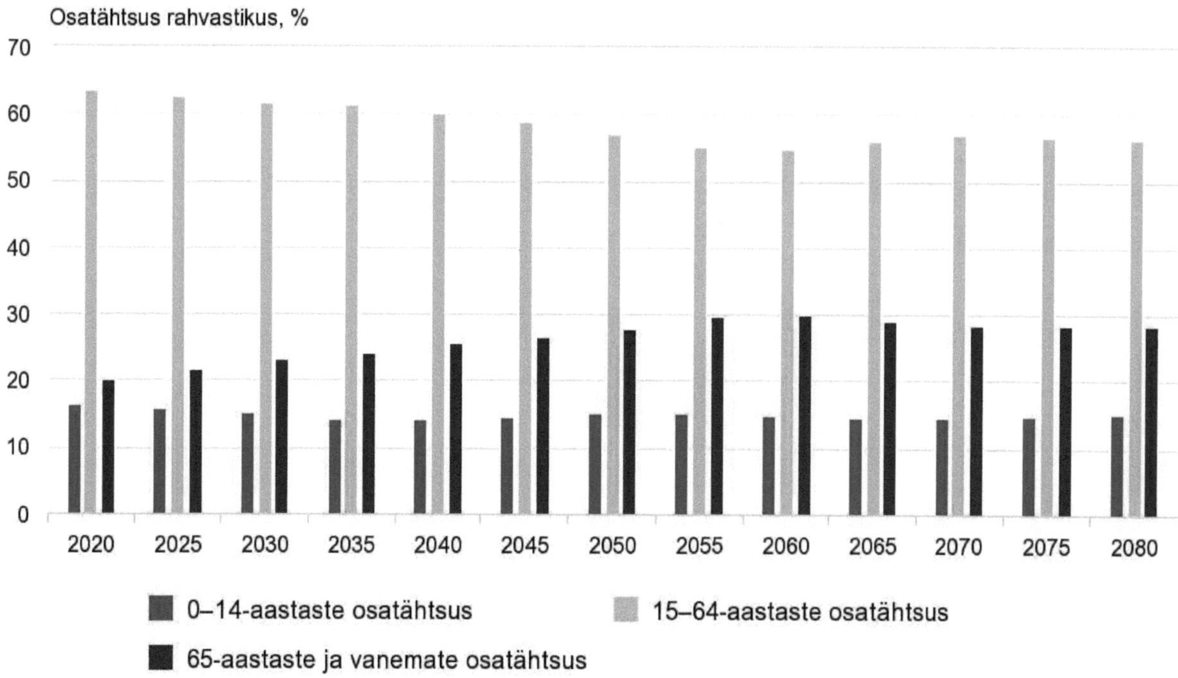

Source: Statistics Estonia

The forecast was also prepared about counties until 2045. Changes in rural areas are occurring differently: whilst the total population of Estonia decreased 2.7% by 2045, the population of Ida-Viru, Järva, Valga and Jõgeva counties decreased by a third. The people living in counties with decreasing populations are older on average and the population in them is mainly shaped by the number of deaths. The population is growing the most in Harju County, including Tallinn. The population of Tartu County is also growing to a small extent.

Population forecasts are prepared according to the existing trends by extending them into the future. However, the future is actually difficult to predict. Even stable progression always entails alternative possibilities of how trends will change, not to speak of unexpected turns.

Statistics Estonia completed four population forecasts by 2080. In its press release, Statistics Estonia introduced the baseline scenario. In addition to the baseline scenario, there is a scenario where the birth rate and migration are bigger, a second one where the birth rate is lower, mortality higher and migration balanced, and a third one where the birth rate has risen to the recovery level by the end of the period.

On 12 September 2019, Statistics Estonia wrote that thousands of people leave Tallinn every year. We're used to thinking of the capital as a strong magnet. However, when we look at the movement of the people living in Tallinn from another angle, it's also the local government with the biggest number of emigrants in Estonia.

21,185 have moved abroad from Tallinn in the last four years, which is considerably more than the number of residents in Pirita at the start of this year. 33% of the population of Estonia lives in Tallinn. People leaving the capital comprise 44% of the total emigration from Estonia.

Figure 1.3. Emigration of residents of Estonian counties and Tallinn to foreign countries, 2018

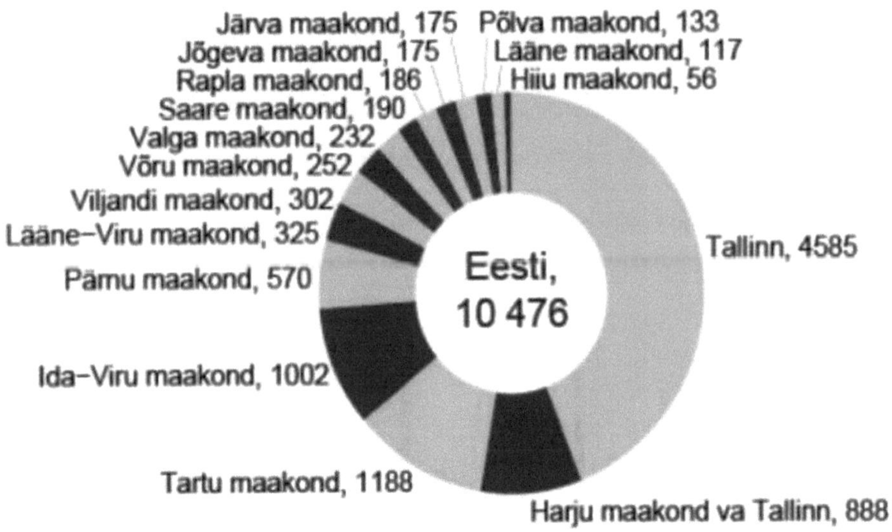

Allikas: Statistikaamet

2,571 men and 2,014 women, i.e. 4,585 people in total, moved abroad from Tallinn in 2018. There were more emigrants than Tallinn residents who passed away. 4,474 residents of Tallinn died in 2018.

Most of the people who leave Estonia are young: the biggest group of emigrants are 20–39 years old. Thus, every person who leaves affects the size of the working population and the subsistence of households. This can mean babies not born, jobs not filled and companies not established in Estonia. [https://blog.stat.ee/2019/09/12/igal-aastal-lahkub-tallinnast-tuhandeid-inimesi/]

These trends are consequential for WSS service provision. The changes in the population of densely populated areas (increase or decrease) change the provision and development of the water supply and sewerage service significantly (it affects the productivity of infrastructures and the efficiency of work). Population ageing does not change the water supply service. However, legislative changes in the maximum levels and requirements concerning drinking water and/or wastewater change the service considerably.

The introduction of stricter drinking water and/or wastewater provisions in legislation of any level bring about additional work and resources, We have to start thinking about changing, updating, reconstructing and financing the existing technologies. It's particularly bad if the changes are significant and require massive changes in technologies and cannot be solved with simpler changes in the operation of drinking water processing/wastewater treatment plants.

1.4.2. Economic and fiscal situation

Four times a year, Eesti Pank publishes an overview that summarises the most important developments in the economy of the world and Estonia. The overview also includes an economic forecast for Estonia. The last overview was published on 10 June 2020. Two tables are reproduced below. The first table shows the economic forecast according to key indicators. The second table presents a comparison with the forecasts prepared by other institutions.

Table 1.3. Economic forecast by key indicators

	2019	2020	2021	2022
GDP at current prices in billion euros	28.04	25.41	27.95	29.34
GDP at constant prices**	4.3	-10.0	8.5	2.3
Private consumption***	3.2	-7.9	9.5	3.7
Consumption by government sector	2.8	3.4	-1.7	-0.5
Total capital investment in fixed assets	13.3	-18.8	13.5	4.1
Export	5.2	-13.9	9.3	5.9
Import	3.9	-15.6	8.7	7.2
GDP gap (% of potential GDP)	4.5	-6.9	0.6	1.2
Consumer price index	2.3	-1.1	0.0	2.1
Harmonised consumer price index	2.3	-0.9	-0.1	2.1
GDP deflator	3.2	0.7	1.4	2.6
Unemployment rate (% of workforce)	4.5	9.5	8.8	7.3
Employment****	1.3	-4.4	0.7	1.4
Average gross monthly wages (euros)	1,407	1,393	1,395	1,478
Average gross monthly wages	7.5	-1.0	0.1	5.9
GDP per worker at constant prices	3.0	-5.8	7.8	0.9
Current account balance (% of GDP)	2.2	2.6	2.9	2.7
Balance of the government sector budget (% of GDP)	-0.3	-10.3	-4.3	-2.2

* The indicators are presented as annual change in percentages, unless otherwise noted, ** The GDP and its components are presented as chained values. *** Includes non-profit institutions serving households. **** Covers resident production units. ***** The forecast of the revenue and expenditure of the government sector considers the impact of the measures known to sufficient detail by the time the forecast was prepared.
Sources: Statistics Estonia, Eesti Pank.

Table 1.4. Comparison with forecasts of other institutions

	Actual GDP growth, %				Change in consumer prices, %			
	2019	2020	2021	2022	2019	2020	2021	2022
Eesti Pank	4.3	-10.0	8.5	2.3	2.3 (2.3*)	-1.1 (-0.9*)	0.0 (-0.1*)	2.1 (2.1*)
Ministry of Finance	4.3	-8.0	8.0		2.3	0.6	2.1	
European Commission	4.3	-6.9	5.9		2.3*	0.7*	1.7*	
IMF	4.3	-7.5	7.9		2.3*	1.5*	2.0*	
Consensus Economics	4.3	-7.1	5.7		2.3	0.7	1.7	
SEB	4.3	-9.8	6.5		2.3	0.4	2.8	
Swedbank	4.4	-7.0	5.0		2.3	0.4	1.3	

* Harmonised consumer price index.
Sources: June Forecast of Eesti Pank, 10.06.2020; Spring Economic Forecast of the Ministry of Finance, 09.04.2020; European Commission. Economic Forecast. Spring 2020. 07.05.2020; IMF, WEO, April 2020, 14.04.2020; Eastern Europe Consensus Forecasts, May 2020; SEB, Nordic Outlook, May 2020, 06.05.2020; Economic Overview of Swedbank 13.05.2020.

In 2020, Estonia is going through a health crisis with far-reaching economic effects, because of which the total annual production is projected to decrease by 10%. Unemployment is expected to rise to over 13% by the end of 2020. The average wage is falling. As this crisis is more acute for population with lower incomes, the government ensures adequate social protection measures. As a consequence, COVID-19 created further stress on public budget expenditures.

The budget deficit of previous years has made it more difficult for the government to help the economic sectors. This affects provision of public budget guarantees and/ or direct financing of new investments in infrastructure.

Over the last decades, investment in WSS infrastructure and household connection has been largely financed with EU support. Infrastructure development was essentially financed through international support (70% of funds came through the EU Cohesion and Structural funds or grants). New financing capacities are required to operate and maintain existing assets, adapting services to changing needs, driven by more stringent environment and health regulations, or a changing climate.

1.4.3. Accountability of local governments for local infrastructure

Decentralised ownership for local infrastructure creates issues with accountability for service provision. The allocation of tasks and responsibilities across institutions is blurred, on some issues. Water companies and local governments are responsible for the provision of water services in cities and settlements; the Ministry of the Environment is responsible for sustainable access to WSS services in the state as a whole. The situation raises a few questions:

- Are these responsibilities equally clear and understandable to each party?
- Do all of the parties agree to the performance of the functions and obligations assigned to them?
- How are some obligations and functions financed? Is this allocation fair from the viewpoint of all parties and does it treat all of them equally?

There may be disputes and misunderstandings between the Ministry of the Environment, the local governments and water companies about who should be responsible if a policy goal is not achieved. For example:

- Who should guarantee the WSS access in areas of over 2,000 p.e. to the sewerage system?
- Who should pay the fine for non-compliance with the EU directives, should it occur?

Questions also arise when major disruptions and problems occur in the provision of the water service in a densely populated settlement. For example, if a major problem occurs, and drinking water no longer complies with requirements, so that an advanced water treatment is to be put in place; or if treated wastewater does not comply with norms, and a solution requires major investments, and minor operational improvements cannot solve the problem. Who bears responsibility to the citizens and/or the Ministry of Environment – the local government or the water company?

In that context, the utilities boards' roles, responsibilities and capacity to deliver on the tasks devolved to them seem uneven across the country.

1.4.4. The performance of utilities

As 70% of the infrastructure of the water sector has been built with the help of grants, the challenge is to guarantee the sustainability of the systems as well as the quality and consistency of the service in the future and, by achieving all this, eliminate the dependence on grants, but by guaranteeing affordable tariffs to consumers at the same time.

The constructed public water supply and sewerage systems require consistent maintenance and new investments. Unfortunately, the present fragmentation of water companies, where the majority of them are micro-companies, is unable to guarantee the funds required for investments and the qualified workforce for maintenance of automated equipment when offering water services at reasonable tariffs. It is estimated that only three or four water companies in Estonia that service larger cities are able to operate sustainably today, but there are more than 150 water companies in Estonia in total. The Environmental Protection and

Use Programme for 2020-2023 states that a vision for the policy regarding the provision of public water supply and sewerage services will be developed in order to guarantee the sustainability of the public water supply and sewerage service and ensure the continuity of the service in all regions.

Financial sustainability is not the only challenge water utilities face in Estonia. The efficiency of using water resources is an issue. This means that water leakages from the pipeline must be reduced and various water saving and reuse technologies must be implemented in regions where wastewater must be redirected to reduce flood risks, extract natural resources or for other economic activities. Nature-based solutions could be further deployed, together with incentives for people to use rainwater more efficiently; they include green areas, ponds, drenches and other solutions, which make it possible to manage rainwater via landscaping at the place where it occurs, thereby avoiding the pollution of rainwater.

The adequacy of the groundwater resources is a problem in some regions, which is why the use of groundwater must be managed in a manner that would primarily cover the water needs of people. It is also important to guarantee that water suitable for drinking is used expediently and the resources of clean water are preserved for the future as much as possible.

Another challenge is to make urban wastewater treatment plans work as required by making the necessary investments or improving the competencies of operators. Five treatment plants in wastewater collection areas whose load exceeds 2,000 p.e. do not meet the maximum limits and 90 treatment plans in areas where the load is smaller than 2,000 p.e. do not meet said requirements.

Energy efficiency is also a challenge. The Study of Resource Efficiency of water companies was completed in 2019, to support action in this domain. The objective of the study was to analyse the resource efficiency of Estonian water companies.

1.4.5. Compliance with the EU acquis on water

Coherent implementation of the EU *acquis* on water would help to enhance cost effectiveness of new water investments. A comprehensive monitoring of water quality and setting treatment standards based on expected environmental impacts can better inform investment decisions by features of the receiving water body. A robust cost-benefit analysis (particularly, in case of diffuse pollution) can support agri-environmental actions to improve the ecological status of rivers.

Compliance with UWWTD, in particular, needs to be analysed in more details. Distance to compliance may depend in the size of the settlements and the status of receiving water bodies. In this context, prioritisation of new investment, taking into account the total cost for O&M costs over the lifetime of the investment, is to be done.

1.5. Pending issues

This section sketches issues that need to be analysed to address the concerns listed above on the sustainability of water supply and sanitations services in Estonia.

The institutional and legal framework is one. In particular, Estonia is completing a major reform of its administrative structure, which lead to a significant diminution of local governments. The consequences on water services remain to be seen.

Second, a robust and effective framework to drive performance improvements of water utilities is missing. While some utilities report on selected indicators, a systematic list of performance targets, indicators, and a performance monitoring and benchmarking capacity are lacking.

Third, tariffs for water supply and sanitation services have a critical role to play to generate the revenues needed to enhance the financial sustainability of water utilities, and to drive operational and resource efficiency. It is not clear how prevailing tariff setting process and tariff levels combine cost recovery and affordability. This enhances financial challenges of current and future development plans for water services.

Ultimately, previous attempts to urge utilities to agglomerate and benefit from economies of scale have reached limited results. Lessons can be learned, that can inspire further policies and incentives in this domain.

1.5.1. The institutional and legal environment

Legal framework

The existing framework limits the range of arrangements that can be considered for ownership of assets and operation and maintenance of WSS services. More work is needed to characterise the options to combine local ownership with a wider range of arrangements for the operation and maintenance of WSS services.

In line with the regional and local government policy reform, the Ministry of the Environment of Estonia jointly with other governmental authorities (the Ministry of Finance, the Minister of Public Administration) is working towards the enhanced sustainability of WSS services in the country. Modalities of the reform implementation, including options for consolidation of the water utility sector, have to be further considered and included into the proposal to the Government. It also relates to further improvement of the Shareholder Agreement framework for regional companies. The agreement could be further strengthened to reflect on responsibility and obligations of the local governments as shareholders.

The context of the administrative reform

In Estonia, municipal and local governments own WSS infrastructure and water companies. They bear most of the cost of providing water supply and sanitation services and operating and maintaining existing systems. They face a severe financial challenge. On the one hand, the small size and low density of population make the unit cost of WSS services provision high. On the other hand, most of the Estonian municipalities lack professional staff to properly operate the existing water supply and sanitation infrastructure. Creating such competences would further increase the operation cost of services.

The administrative reform took place in Estonia in 2017. The total number of local governments decreased from 213 to 79 as a result of the administrative reform. The average number of population and the average area of a local government almost tripled. After the reform, the share of small local governments with a population of less than 5,000 decreased from 79% (169 local governments before the reform) to just a fifth (15). 47 cases of voluntary merger were approved and 160 local government participated in them. Thus, the majority of the mergers (86%) occurred in the stages initiated by the councils themselves and in the manner that was locally agreed. Pursuant to the Administrative Reform Act, the Government of the Republic initiated merger proceedings in respect of local governments with fewer than 5,000 residents, i.e. the local governments that did not meet the minimal population criteria.

Figure 1.4. Number of local governments in Estonia from 1995-2018

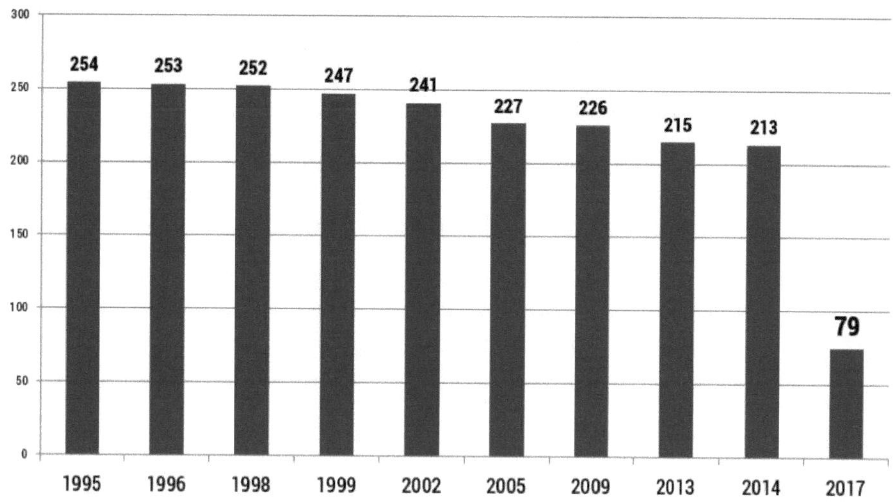

There are 15 counties and 79 local governments in Estonia. Local governments are divided in 15 cities and 64 municipalities, which decide on and organise the matters concerning local life independently. Irrespective of their size, local governments must perform the same functions and offer the same services to residents throughout Estonia. The territory of local governments, i.e. administrative units, divides in settlements: cities, towns, small towns, villages. Local governments decide on and organise all matters concerning local life and act independently. The state may assign obligation to them only on the basis of law or by agreement with the local governments.

Figure 1.5. Changes in counties borders and population (%) after the administrative reform

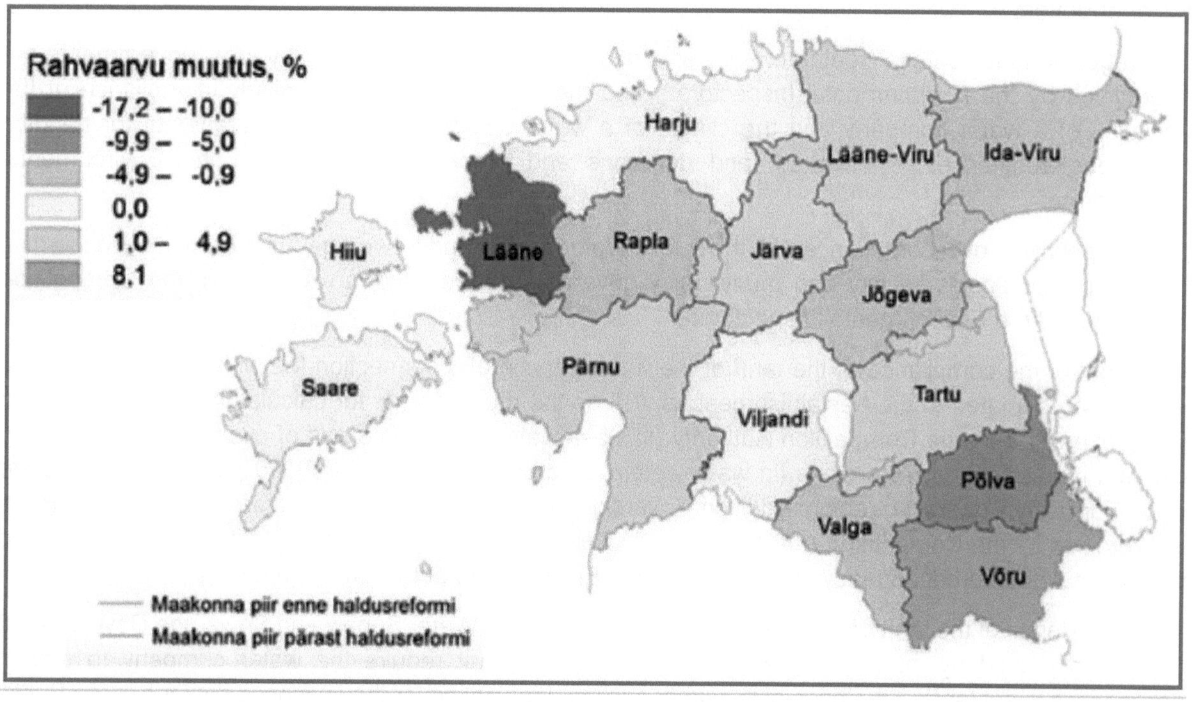

Table 1.5. Local governments before and after the administrative reform

	Before mergers 01.01.2017	After the administrative reform of 1 January 2017	01.01.2018	02.01.2019 (after the Population Register was updated)
Under 5,000 residents	169 local governments	15 local governments	17 local governments	17 local governments
5,000–11,000 residents	28 local governments	36 local governments	34 local governments	36 local governments
Over 11,000 residents	16 local governments	28 local governments	28 local governments	26 local governments
Average number of residents	6,349	17,118	17,152	16,835
Median number of residents	1,887	7,865	7,739	7,558
Average area	204 km^2	550 km^2	550 km^2	550 km^2
Median area	180 km^2	512 km^2	512 km^2	512 km^2

Source: population according to the Population Register.

Completion of a large scale administrative reform is in progress. Further analyses would characterise what is in it for WSS (capacity and financial sustainability of municipalities; synergies with other services). Some utilities can operate sustainably; however, most utilities are unable to secure the technical skills for the operation of existing assets.

After the administrative reform, many of the merged local governments agreed that no structural changes will be made in the local governments until the results of the local elections of autumn 2021 are announced. In particular, they agreed that water companies will not be merged until then.

1.5.2. Performance monitoring

The Health Board supervises the quality requirements for drinking water and the obligations of drinking water operators.

The regulations for on-site treatment and removal of wastewater established by local governments are supervised by the Environmental Inspectorate and the local government. Similarly, compliance of the activities of a water company and the clients of a water company with the requirements for handing hazardous substances is checked, and decisions and precepts are made by the Environmental Inspectorate.

State supervision over compliance with the Public Water Supply and Sewerage Act is carried out according to their competencies by city and municipality governments (i.e. local governments), the Competition Authority and the Environmental Inspectorate.

Oversight of the compliance of the tariff of the water service and connection fee with legislation and the requirements related to their establishment as well as the methodology for calculation of the connection fee is exercised by the Competition Authority (in wastewater collection areas of over 2,000 p.e.) and by city and municipality governments (in wastewater collection areas of under 2,000 p.e.) according to the water company's operating region. Additional oversight of the connection fee and tariff of the water service is exercised by the Competition Authority at its own initiative, on the basis of a justified request received from a local government agency, the Ministry of the Environment or the Environmental Board.

The compliance of the tariff of the water service with the Public Water Supply and Sewerage Development Plan is inspected by municipality and city governments (that require the water company to submit applications to set tariffs if the price of the water service does not cover the expenses set forth in the Public Water Supply and Sewerage Development Plan). The state and local governments are responsible for the oversight of the activities of water companies. For example, the state supervises compliance with the terms and conditions of environmental permits. In addition, local governments are interested in how the population is served – are there any leaks, has water been shut off, what is the quality of the tap water, whether and how fast the queries of clients are addressed, etc. No major changes has occurred in the allocation of responsibility over the last 10 years.

City and municipality governments exercise oversight of the compliance of a water company's activities with the Public Water Supply and Sewerage Act, local government legislation (including the rules on connection to public water supply and sewerage and rules on the use of public water supply and sewerage) and the public water supply and sewerage development plans.

Water companies disclose a report on their own website or on that of the local government once a year within 30 days after approval thereof by the water company. This obligation arises from the Public Water Supply and Sewerage Act. The report must include a summary of the financial year, an overview of the investments made in the last year, quality of drinking water, wastewater treatment, future development trends and the investments planned for the development of public water supply and sewerage.

Performance management and benchmarking of utilities may help to attract more effective and efficient business arrangements. However, performance is not systematically benchmarked across utilities. For instance, there is no information on the rate of water losses and recent trends. Collection of information on water leakages started in 2019 with annual reports on water use, but the submitted information is still too incomplete for making summaries. However, leakages and water losses have been discussed in section 2.4.3 "Share of Leakages and Breakdowns" of Part 2 of Stage II of the study "Development of a Strategy Towards a Sustainable Water Sector", which was completed in 2018. The analysis in the study was prepared on the basis of the data for 2016. However, considerable investments have been made in infrastructure in the last four years and the number of leakages has certainly decreased even further as a result of this.

Incentives to improve performance and sanctions for poor performance are lacking, not enforced or not effective. The independent regulator is not involved in performance definition, monitoring and enforcement.

The City of Tallinn established the Tallinna Vee-ettevõtjate Järelevalve Sihtasutus (Tallinn Foundation for Oversight of Water Companies), which checks the compliance of the quality of drinking water and wastewater treatment with norms and assesses the performance of the service agreements entered into with the city. The Foundation also checks the adequacy of the investments made by water companies, adherence to construction volumes and deadlines, protects the interests of the consumers of the service and also solves consumers' problems. However, this remains a local solution and an exception rather than the rule.

1.5.3. Tariff setting and tariff levels

Water supply and wastewater services are regulated by Public Water Supply and Sewerage Act (Water Law) in Estonia. According to the law, water tariffs must be cost based – including a reasonable rate of profit - and approved by the regulator. The Estonian Competition Authority (ECA) is a multisector regulator, established in 1993. ECA regulates prices in district heating, electricity (network) and gas (network) sectors and has supervisory functions in area of airport, railway and postal communications, as well as supervising overall competition at state. ECA has been the regulator of water companies since 1st November 2010, when the Water Law was amended. Since then, ECA approves prices for water service and methodologies for calculating connection fees to public water supply and sewerage systems. In accordance with the Water Law, ECA also issued recommendations on calculating the price for water services. In addition, the Competition Authority has oversight of the tariff of the water service and the revenues from connection fees.

ECA is not an only regulator approving prices of water companies. If the territory of operations of a water company is situated in the wastewater collection area with pollution larger than 2000 p.e., prices (or methodology for calculating connection fees) are approved by ECA. If the territory of a water company is situated in the wastewater collection area with pollution smaller than 2000 p.e or outside a wastewater collection area, prices (or methodology of connection fees) are approved by local government. In case a water company provides the water services in several different wastewater collection areas and intends to set uniform prices for water services in these areas based on its total costs, ECA approves prices (or methodology of connection fees in that area).

WSS tariff regulation process:

The WSS tariff regulation process goes through the following four phases:

I. Submitting price application by water company
II. Evaluating the price application accordance to the requirements (by regulator)
III. Analysing the price application, a water company can be contacted for further clarifications.
IV. Decision on price approval or disapproval made by regulator. In case regulator does not approve the price application, a water company can provide comments on the decision.

For further clarification - prices are set for indefinite period of time and are in force until new prices are approved by regulator (ECA or local governments, depends on competency of a regulator). Approval takes place upon water company`s application. Water company's rights to submit an application to set prices for water services are not restricted.

Table 1.6.Average service tariffs of EVEL members as at the end of 2019

Water tariff €		Sewerage tariff €		Water tariff €+VAT		Sewerage tariff €+VAT	
resident	company	resident	company	resident	company	resident	company
1.10	1.23	1.57	1.75	1.32	1.44	1.89	2.05

Source: http://evel.ee/teabepank/infomaterjalid/

The water tariff regulation was revised in 2010. However, the reinvestment component is not part of the tariff formula for most water companies. The cost of replacing decaying assets is not properly reflected in the tariff-setting process. Therefore, most utilities are unable to generate the revenues to renew and upgrade (where appropriate) existing infrastructures. Capital is not being amortised adequately.

Concerns about the financial sustainability of water companies are serious, because the capital component included in the tariff of the public water supply and sewerage service according to the effective methodology is not sufficient for the modernisation and maintenance of their assets.

Another issue is that, according to the regulator's model, the calculation of capital expenses is linear and calculated according to the acquisition cost, and the average useful life of the fixed assets belonging to water companies is 30–40 or even more years. The capital expenses calculated according to the guidelines ignore the time value of money and the fact that the cost of the investments made today is considerably higher than the investment made in equivalent assets at the time. Also, there have been several monetary reforms since some of the assets of water companies were acquired. The regulation would serve its purpose and it would be possible for the companies to make the necessary investments if the capital component covered the amount required for the investments, e.g. considering the indexed value of fixed assets instead of the replacement value. The actual investment needs are considerably bigger.

A proper maintenance and operation of the WSS system in Estonia would require a significant increase of WSS tariffs, possibly beyond the affordability level for most of the municipalities. Currently, an average affordability rate is estimated by Estonian experts about 2.2 -2.5% of household disposable income, reaching 4% for low-income households.

An affordability check is not a part of the tariff setting procedure in Estonia. Here, the issue of affordability of the water tariff is solved at the level of the local government (e.g. income support etc.) by granting social support to specific people. In practice, the water tariff is less than 2.5% of the income of a household member, which is why affordability is not considered yet. However, it may have to be considered in the future when the proper functioning of the infrastructure has to be guaranteed.

1.5.4. Financing for WSS

Recent trends in financing for WSS and emerging issues

The Investment Plan of the Water Management Infrastructure prepared in 2019 can be found here: https://www.envir.ee/sites/default/files/Vesi/Uuringudjaaruanded/veemajandustaristu_investeeringute_kava.pdf . Possible funding sources have been discussed in the aforementioned Investment Plan of the Water Management Infrastructure.

Public budget allocations and EU finance of new investments were driven largely by the need to connect more households to WSS service. The Ministry of Environment - Environmental Investment Centre (EIC[2]) can support three activities associated with the provision of water service:

- Water Economy Programme (Environmental Programme) to support drinking water supply and wastewater management. Support is provided to achieve goals stipulated in the General Part of the Environmental Code Act. The EP of EIC started in 2000 when the EIC was founded, and the programme still funds the largest number of environment projects every year. There is a specific sub-programme for WSS investments under the EP of EIC. The WSS sub-programme covers a wide sector of water management starting from construction of water treatment infrastructures to specific R&D projects. The main beneficiaries of the sub-programme are water service companies of municipalities. Over the last ten years, the annual budgets of WSS sub-programme of EP have varied from seven to twenty-four million, depending on the receipt of national pollution charges and political priorities.

  The funds of the programme come from environmental charges and the money is distributed within the scope established by the Act between local governments. The Ministry of the Environment allocates an amount for the implementation of the Environmental Programme every year, the size of which corresponds to the amount of money received by the state budget from the issuing of special water use rights. Over the last ten years, the annual budgets of WSS sub-programme of EP have varied from seven to twenty-four million, depending on the receipt of national pollution charges and political priorities.
- Development of water supply and sewerage infrastructure (European Union Cohesion Fund). The support is provided to ensure access of population to sustainable drinking water supply and wastewater collection and treatment services within wastewater collection areas approved by the Minister of the Environment.
- Development and reconstruction of water infrastructure (European Union Cohesion Fund) in wastewater collection areas with a pollution load of over 2,000 consumers, and the reconstruction of public water supply systems that serve over 2,000 people.

The last two measures are part of the operational programme of the Structural Support Act for 2014–2020 under the partnership agreement between Estonia and the European Commission. The operational programme of cohesion policy funds was prepared on the initiative of the Ministry of Finance on the basis of the partnership agreement.

The intention is to plan the use of the structural funds of the 2021-2027 period of the European Union Cohesion Fund on the basis of development needs, targets and reforms to be defined in the long-term strategy Estonia 2035 that is currently being prepared.

The WSS programme of EIC covers a wide sector of water management starting from construction of water treatment infrastructures to specific R&D projects. The main beneficiaries of the programme are water service companies of municipalities.

Local governments form a significant part of the government sector. They cover 25% of the total expenditure of the government sector. Local governments have independent budgets, which are prepared according to the basis and procedure set forth in the Local Government Financial Management Act.

The tariff of the water services is determined on cost-bases and it must cover all of the justified expenses required for the provision of the service. The local government may give support for covering certain activities (e.g. rainwater expenses), which will then be subtracted in pricing (i.e. the expenses compensated by the local government are not included in the tariff).

Cross-subsidies between other services exist at local level, but do not bridge the gap between revenues from tariffs and O&M costs. The losses of water companies tend to be accepted on the account of the profitability of other services, as smaller companies often provide other public services of local governments as well, such as district heating, maintenance, street cleaning, street lighting, asset management, etc.

The support granted to the drinking water supply and wastewater treatment strand from the Water Management Programme are shown in the table below.

Table 1.7. Support to WSS granted by the Water Management programme

Strand / €	2011	2012	2013	2014	2015	2016	2017	2018	2019
Drinking water supply	4,562,794	3,677,737	3,267,494	2,300,233	2,835,028	797,164	873,390	1,071,805	5,837,876
Wastewater treatment	15,747,727	14,190,003	5,487,279	6,178,351	12,329,719	10,347,575	8,168,245	14,410,331	

Of note: whilst many water companies have managed to modernise their old assets with the help of state aid, the state has established restrictions due to which Tallinna Vesi is the only one in Estonia that has not qualified for state aid. Namely, a condition of state aid is that only water companies that belong fully to one or several local governments and own the water management infrastructure in the region are eligible for support. As Tallinna Vesi is a public limited company listed at the stock exchange and whilst the City of Tallinn is one of its shareholders, it does not meet the rule emphasised above.

WSS sector development plans and expenditure programmes

The strategic planning of WSS generally takes place at local government level. National goals are set at the level of the state, e.g. achievement of compliance for settlements over 2,000 p.e. and consistent maintenance of this compliance. Various programmes for supporting the development of the area are also developed at the national level for the achievement of national goals and those set by local governments. At the national level, goals and programmes are developed by the Ministry of the Environment. The issues related to the budget and grants are to be approved by the Ministry of Finance, the Government of the Republic and the Riigikogu.

The main functions of the Ministry of Finance are to advise the Government of the Republic on the budget, taxation, macro-economy, spatial panning, financial, administrative and regional policies, the implementation of regional administration and the economy. Every year, the Ministry of Finance prepares the state budget, the state's budget strategy and the stability programme in cooperation with other ministries (including the Ministry of the Environment) and constitutional institutions.

The Ministry of the Environment proceeds from the Estonian Environmental Strategy 2030 adopted in 2007 (which establishes the framework of environmental protection and use until 2030) and the Environmental Protection and Use Programme for 2020-2023 when providing input for and cooperating with the Ministry of Finance, and when preparing its budget. The environmental strategy stipulates the goals and measures of the area (lines of action). Programmes are established for the implementation of the strategy and have been prepared for the achievement of the goals set in sectoral development programmes, through which the measures, activities and services required for the development plans are planned, budgeted and implemented, and reports are prepared. The on-going Environmental Protection and Use Programme that defines the development directions of the water service has been prepared for 2020-2023.

Sector development is planned by local governments. Local governments prepare the Public Water Supply and Sewerage Development Plan for the development of public water supply and sewerage, which is prepared for at least 12 years and reviewed at least once every four years, and adjusted if necessary. The data of the wastewater collection area (boundaries, pollution load) must be checked when the Development Plan is reviewed and an application for approval of the wastewater collection area must be submitted to the Minister of the Environment. The Development Plan must be approved by the Environmental Board and the Health Board before it is approved by the local government. The guidelines for preparation of the Development Plan were set by the Ministry of the Environment.

1.5.5. Lessons from previous attempts with agglomeration of utilities

Consolidation of WSS services is not envisaged in the legal or regulatory frameworks of Estonia. However, the Ministry of the Environment claims that the potential for consolidation of water management exists in Estonia, as the service quality has improved, water infrastructures have been renovated and the water quality has become better in the regions where regional water companies have been established or where the water companies of local governments have been merged after the administrative reform.

The position of the Ministry of Finance is that the consolidation process should be voluntary. So far, attempts have been made to implement a voluntary consolidation through the establishment of regional water companies. The term *regional water company* was introduced in the regulations on granting support to water companies in 2018. A regional water company is a company that provides its service to more than 5,000 residents in at least six wastewater collection areas (WWCA), one of which is a WWCA of over 2,000 p.e. Until now, getting support on more favourable conditions has been an important incentive for the formation of water companies (and the merger of smaller water companies with larger sustainable water companies).

Well-performing utilities have been reluctant to agglomerate with poor-performing ones, as this may affect their overall performance and capacity to deliver over the long term. What kind of incentive, support or compensation mechanism may address this concern?

A study in 2018 considered four alternatives of WSS consolidation, aimed at developing strategies towards a sustainable water sector. The study analysed the situation after the implementation of the aforementioned administrative reform in Estonia. It considered a business as usual scenario (rural municipality, or city-based water companies) and 3 main alternatives: county-based, regional and country-wide water companies. According to the sustainability criteria (service quality, affordability, company's investment capacity, dependence on state aid and feasibility to implement the model on a voluntary basis), the options of regional and country-wide water companies can be considered as sustainable solutions. In terms of affordability, the optimal solution is the country-wide model including Tallinn. However, establishing a country-wide water company on a voluntary basis, i.e. involving all local governments as shareholders, is quite complex. The local government-based model cannot be considered sustainable as it would require state support to ensure affordable tariffs in all regions.

Previous attempts have focused on agglomeration, looking for a blanket solution at national level based on the geographical scale (local; county; regional; national). Additional options could be considered, that may promote different types of agglomeration (e.g. ownership and operation being arrangement at different scales; organising different functions at different scales), and a dynamics that may evolve differently in different parts of the country (at least in the short and medium term).

Of note: the largest Estonian network company Elektrilevi, which has covered 93% of Estonia with an electricity network, has contacted the Ministry of the Environment and shown interest in the management of the water network. Analysing the merger of services (e.g. network management service, centres of excellence, etc.) is an alternative that could certainly be considered.

Rules for the connection and use of services vary between municipalities, complicating agglomeration. Each local government establishes its own rules for the use of and connection to the public water supply and sewerage system. This is particularly an issue for regional water companies, as the rules for the use of and connection to the public water supply and sewerage systems of local governments are different and thus, there is no common approach in the service area of the regional company.

Points to be considered include the following:

- Particular attention needs to be paid to multi-purpose utilities: how would consolidation of the operation of water services affect the capacity to deliver other services (district heating, or else)?
- There seems to be a legal issue with the ownership of the assets and the utilities. What are the options to combine – and legal consequences of combining - ownership at municipal level and bundling assets at a larger geographical scale?

One observer notes that, according to the constitution the central and local level functions are and should be clearly separated. As water service is mandatory local function of local governments and the service property (as well as service companies) belongs to municipalities, there are limited possibilities for compulsory consolidations. Consolidation policy could focus on regulatory aspects (e.g. competencies, water management, separation of operation and infrastructure, etc.) and mechanisms to stimulate voluntary consolidation providing at the same time consulting, guidance, monitoring and other motivation packages.

1.6. Suggestions for further work

Background information on the state of play and preliminary understanding of concerns about its sustainability and pending issues help characterise a list of topics that deserve further attention, as they can support reforms that effectively encourage agglomeration of water utilities and put water supply and sanitation services in Estonia on a sustainable basis.

The proposed topics for further investigation are listed below. This list is destined to ignite a discussion with Estonian authorities and stakeholders. A fine-tuned programme of work in the context of this project will unfold, in line with the detailed project description and with the experience and ambition of Estonian counterparts.

Preliminary list of topics for further analysis:

- Make the case for change. Explain that business as usual is not an option and the national and local governments and water users will be affected by the unsustainable management and operation of WSS services.

- Consider a range of options for agglomeration, which are flexible and can adjust to local contexts. They are not only based on geographical scale only. They may vary according to functions (planning; programming expenditure; technical skills; relationship with users; billing and tariff collection).
- Address practical issues, such as the case of multipurpose utilities: how to secure proper operation of these utilities if water services are severed from them? What are the consequences for water supply and sanitation services (losing capacity, revenues and benefits of cross-subsidies, else)?
- Beef up the role for the economic regulator. Define a role for setting and enforcing performance targets; assessing the opportunity and efficiency of expenditure programmes; setting tariffs as a policy instrument to drive investment and performance. Offer options regarding the status, skills and governance of the economic regulator.
- Clarify and address legal issues related to asset ownership. Explore options to transfer ownership to entities operating at larger geographical scales, or to combine local ownership with operation at larger geographical scales.

Annex 1.A. The performance of water utilities. Selected cases

Annex Box 1.A.1. The performance of water utilities. The case of Tallina Vesi

Tallinna Vesi is the largest water company in Estonia that provides water supply and sewerage services to almost a third of the population of Estonia. The company serves over 23,600 private and corporate clients and over 450,000 final consumers in Tallinn and surrounding municipalities: Maardu, Saue and Harku.

The company must proceed from the terms and conditions of the administrative contracts entered into with local governments and legislation in its operations. For example, they must implement the Public Water Supply and Sewerage Act, the Water Act, the Emergency Act and the other legislation established on the basis of these as well as the environmental permits in which environmental obligations have been set for the companies in respect of water use, air pollution and waste handling. However, the administrative contract is the main operating document for a water company. For example, the company is obliged to guarantee service quality at the level of 97 according to the administrative contract entered into with the City of Tallinn in 2001. A similar administrative contract has also been entered into with the second largest local government, i.e. Maardu Town, which also sets service levels.

A contract entered into with a local government may include higher quality levels than specified by law or introduce more criteria if this is agreed between the parties, also in respect of reporting. In respect of the Tallinn service area, for example, the company must submit to the City of Tallinn within 90 days of the end of the previous calendar year a report on the compliance of its activities with the quality levels established with the administrative contract for services in the previous calendar year, where the achievement of the quality level and the emerged deficiencies are indicated with their reasons in comparison with the level requirements as well as the measures taken for the elimination of the deficiencies.

The requirements arising from environmental permits, the law or administrative contracts are used to assess service quality – did the company comply with these requirements or are there shortcomings in its activities.

For example, the company has agreed on an inspection plan with the Health Board, which is followed in terms of water quality. The administrative contract and the local government continuity regulation established on the basis of the Emergency Act also stipulate the permitted duration of water outages and what the water company has to do if the permitted duration is exceeded – guarantee water in another manner. Tallinna Vesi has water tank trucks for this purpose. The level of permitted leakage, which the company has tried to reduce year on year, is also regulated in administrative contracts. The number of sewer blockages, which is stipulated in the administrative contract, is also an indicator alongside many others.

The most important indicators that illustrate the company's results in guaranteeing service levels are disclosed by the company to its stakeholders on a quarterly basis. The information for six months in 2020 was as follows:

Annex Table 1.A.1. Performance indicators. The case of Tallina Vesi

Performance indicator	Unit	2020	2019	2018
Compliance of water quality samples taken from consumer's tap with requirements	%	100.0	99.5	99.9
Level of leakages in network	%	13.9	12.2	14.1
Average duration of water outage per registered immovable	h	3.05	2.63	3.28
Sewer blockages	pcs	227	302	295
Breakages of sewerage pipes	pcs	41	59	50
Compliance of treated wastewater with environmental requirements	%	100.0	100.0	100.0
Number of complaints	pcs	28	81	69
Client contacts about water quality	pcs	164	172	101
Client contacts about water pressure	pcs	149	154	183
Client contacts about blockages and rainwater discharge	pcs	473	542	516
Replying to written contacts in at least two business days	%	100.0	100.0	100.0
Cases of violation of promises made to clients	pcs	0	2	2
Notification of unscheduled water outages at least 1 hour before the outage	%	99.2	97.7	94.4

Annex Box 1.A.2. The performance of water utilities. Järve Biopuhastus (JBP)

The goals concerning the quality of the water service are established as follows in the acts adopted by the Riigikogu and the legislation based on these (the list is not exhaustive).

- The Public Water Supply and Sewerage Act regulates how supplying registered immovables with water, and leading off and treatment of wastewater, rainwater, drainage water and other soil and surface water from registered immovables should be organised, including definition of areas to be covered by the water service, development of the public water supply and sewerage, continuity of the provision of the water service, and use of the Development Plan in common interests.
- The Water Act stipulates the requirements for the organisation of water use and protection and the water protection requirements, which guarantee the long-term protection of water resources and the rights, obligations and responsibility of a person when using water.
- The General Part of the Environmental Code Act sets goals concerning the reduction of environmental nuisances, the promotion of sustainable development, the preservation and protection of natural diversity, the good state of the environment, the prevention of damage to the environment and the remedying of damage caused to the environment.
- The Atmospheric Air Protection Act stipulates the requirements set for affecting ambient air by chemical and physical pollutants and the measures for maintaining and improving the quality of ambient air.
- The Emergency Act stipulates the requirements for the continuity of water supply and sewerage.
- The Waste Act stipulates the organisation of waste management, the requirements for preventing waste generation and the health and environmental hazards arising from waste.

The requirements to the extent, water pressure, headwater level and continuity, construction, maintenance, repairs and inspection of the water works and sewerage of registered immovables, interruption and restoration of the provision of the water service, provision of the service in the case of breakdown, including provision of water in the case of a breakdown or repairs of the public water supply, and for the wastewater and rain water that is led off, which have been specified and adapted to the local conditions, are stipulated in the rules for use of public water supply and sewerage approved by the councils of Jõhvi Municipality, Lüganuse Municipality and Kohtla-Järve City.

Administrative contracts for the use of public water supply and sewerage in the company's operating region do not include agreements for the establishment of stricter conditions for the water service than the one established with effective legislation.

The investments necessary for guaranteeing the required quality of the water service are set forth in the public water supply and sewerage development plans approved by the councils of Kohtla-Järve City, Jõhvi Municipality and Lüganuse Municipality. In accordance with the approved plans, the shareholders of JBP approve the company's investment plan, in which the investments of JBP will be determined in terms of money and partly in terms of items by five-year periods.

JBP submits regular financial and environmental reports to the state. The quality indicators, flow rates and quantities of drinking water and wastewater are given in the environmental reports. The state can use these data to assess the performance of the water company. The companies belonging to the Estonian Water Works Association voluntarily monitor a number of key indicators.

Local governments control the activities of JBP mainly via the representatives of the shareholders and the supervisory board, the members of which are appointed by the local governments that are the shareholders of the company – Kohtla-Järve City, Jõhvi Municipality and Lüganuse Municipality

Annex Box 1.A.3. The performance of water utilities. Narva Vesi AS

The performance of Narva Vesi is checked by three to four control bodies:

- in everyday activities by the management board, which has one member, and middle managers (heads of departments)
- upon the implementation of major investments and decision of strategically important issues by the supervisory board, which consists of the representatives of shareholders (city councils); and
- the annual inspections of the company's activities in the year are checked and assessed by the company's supervisory board, auditor and shareholders (representatives of the city).

Both of the above consider and assess the production and financial results as well as the success and achievement of major goals (e.g. medium or major construction procurement or investments).

Narva Vesi uses different indicators to assess the success of its operations, which are checked and viewed according to the areas of operation (Narva City separately and Narva-Jõesuu separately), either:

- weekly – inspection of the quality of drinking water (route drinking water samples), routine inspection of appropriate treatment of wastewater treatment (routine wastewater samples, number of breakdowns in the water or sewerage network, customer complaints, orders for water and sewerage works, issue of technical specifications, approval of working designs and/or detailed spatial plans, occurrence of disruptions or breakdowns in wastewater treatment plants or drill well and/or wastewater pumping stations
- monthly – water losses in drinking water and filtration/infiltration in wastewater, change in the quantity of raw water pumped out (decrease/increase), scheduled repairs of the public water supply and sewerage network, number of people connected to the water supply and sewerage system, changes in the drinking water and wastewater volumes of the biggest consumers of water and sewerage services in the current month (increase/decrease), scheduled maintenance and/or repairs of the drinking water and wastewater treatment plants, inspection of the deliveries of chemicals; if there are any construction projects, routine monitoring of the progress of construction and compliance with the schedule and budget; monthly summary of the compliance of drinking water quality and performance of wastewater requirements, and summary of appropriate treatment of wastewater – the daily work of the plants will be made more efficient and/or adjusted according to the results
- semi-annually – aggregate summaries of monthly data are made and the operation of the most important infrastructures and the activities and expenses required for technical maintenance are primarily monitored; changes in water losses (decrease/increase), the actual fixed and variable expenses are compared with the expenses planned at the start of the year are monitored and based on the results, we either adjust our plans or make our daily operations more efficient
- annually – inspection of drinking water and wastewater treatment plants, the stock of spare parts for the water supply and sewerage network in departments, comparison of the financial indicators with the previous year, inspection of the results in the company's annual report

with the previous years; the success of construction sites is assessed in the case of construction projects, if any. Plans are made for the next year and goals are set in production and financial plans. In the case of major constructions (concerning external networks or stations or drill well pumping stations or wastewater pumping stations), the goals are set by the head of department, member of the management board and/or the supervisory board. The achievement of the company's financial results and correctness of accounting (incl. the correct recognition of revenue/expenses, profit/loss) are checked by an auditor. The sustainability of the company is assessed, among others, by the shareholders at the annual general meeting of shareholders.

The most important indicators and goals in Narva Vesi (for middle level employees, the management board, the supervisory board as the owners – representatives of Narva and Narva-Jõesuu – city governments) are guaranteeing safe drinking water for the population and wastewater treatment according to requirements, and the company tries to achieve both of these goals at optimal cost. Guaranteeing the smooth operation, good technical order and long life of the existing infrastructures (water plant, wastewater treatment plant, external water supply and sewerage networks, wastewater and drill well pumping stations) is extremely important to the company. In addition to the above, the management board and the supervisory board monitor the company's economic sustainability and annual economic results.

Annex 1.B. Questionnaire for data collection on the state of play

Legislation, institutional and regulatory framework

1. Please briefly describe the key pieces of legislation (e.g. water law/code, acts defining WSS assets ownership) and the regulatory framework (e.g. water quality standards, permitting/licensing) for WSS services provision.

2. Is the WSS services consolidation envisaged in the legal or regulatory frameworks? If yes, is it a mandatory or voluntary process, please describe the mandatory provisions and the legal forms that consolidation may take place.

3. Which institutions are in charge of setting WSS policies, development planning?

4. Characterise the main priorities (access in cities; access in rural areas; health or environmental standards; quality of service; adaptation to climate change; energy efficiency; connection to existing infrastructures; else).

5. Characterise the main drivers for change

- Demographic trends since 2000; projections to 2030, or 2050; regional disparities; urban/rural; trends in size of households, ageing;
- GDP growth since 2000; projections for the next 5 years.

The organisation of service provision

6. Which institution is accountable for service provision (central government; municipalities; other)? Has the WSS assets ownership been transferred from the central governments to municipalities? When? To what extent?

7. How is service provided?

- Please describe WSS services provision at local level. Please describe modalities of inter-municipal cooperation for WSS provision (e.g. agreements on cooperation between municipalities) if it takes place.
- Role and status of utilities, public or private (e.g. what legal forms (delegation, lease, management contracts) it can take between municipalities and water companies). In case of municipal public utility for WSS - are revenues from water supply and sanitation service earmarked for water-related expenditure only? Or any share of revenues accrue to other types of expenditures at local level?

8. How many municipalities exist in Estonia? Changes since 2010 (any trend towards consolidation)?

- Please provide a map of municipalities in Estonia
- Population by municipality.

9. How many entities/utilities provide services for water supply? For sanitation? Changes since 2010 (any trend towards consolidation)? Are there any municipalities with 2 or more WSS utilities?

The performance of service providers

10. Who sets objectives for service quality (e.g. continuity)?

11. How is performance measured (key indicators) and monitored?

12. Has the oversight of utility performance been a responsibility of central or local governments (municipalities)? Report any major change in the devolution of responsibility over the last 5-10 years/ or planned reforms in this area. Is an independent regulator involved in setting targets, monitoring performance, benchmarking service providers?

Tariff setting

13. Have a specific/dedicated tariff regulation for WSS services (or WSS and other communal services) been adopted in Estonia? When? By which part of the government?

14. Please describe the WSS tariff regulation process.

15. Have professional regulatory bodies regulating tariffs for WSS services (or WSS and other communal services) been established? When? What is their status vis-à-vis the government?

16. Please describe the access (if any) to water utility data, potential gaps in monitoring water utilities performance.

17. Are public budget subsidies envisaged to compensate water utilities for difference between tariff and cost?

18. Has an affordability check become a part of the tariff setting procedure for WSS? Please provide the information on the recent affordability ratio for different municipalities (if available).

19. How do water users participate in tariff revision (public hearings, consultations)?

20. How is information collected and shared, on the performance of service providers, and tariffs for services?

Inter-agency co-ordination and cooperation for WSS service provision

Please briefly describe and provide information on the following items.

21. Institutions in charge of designing and implementing policies that affect water supply and wastewater management (departments in charge of Health; Environment; Urban development; Infrastructure; Investment and finance; else).

22. Arrangements in place for co-ordination and co-operation among the institutions listed above.

23. Arrangements in place for ensuring effective multilevel governance (co-ordination and co-operation among different levels of government) involved in policies that affect drinking water supply and wastewater management (authorities at national, local or other sub-national levels, such as catchments or river basins).

Mapping WS service coverage and recent trends in service provision

24. Volume of drinking water produced and wastewater collected, treated (by municipality).

25. Share of the population with access to safe water and sanitation by municipality? Please describe distinction between urban/rural areas.

26. Age of assets and main periods for the construction of existing networks for water supply? For sanitation?

27. Rate of water losses and recent trends.

28. Please provide information on regional and social differences or disparities in WSS services provision:

- regional disparities: e.g. access, challenges, state of the infrastructure, performance
- social disparities: e.g. access, affordability; lack of access to water supply and sanitation services, wastewater and rainwater collection and treatment.

WSS strategic policy making and financing water supply and sanitation

29. Please describe roles and responsibilities for WSS strategic development and investment programming in Estonia.

30. Please indicate and summarise strategic planning documents (e.g. national financing strategies) for the WSS sector in Estonia. Are these plans backed by financing strategies? If yes, please characterise these financing plans:

- Investment needs, now and in the future
- Projected sources of finance (share of revenues from water tariffs; domestic public funds; EU financial support; else).
- Please describe public budget allocations to the WSS sector (if any). Are budget transfers from national governments earmarked for water supply and sanitation services?

31. If inter-municipal cooperation/aggregation of WSS services was considered in these documents, please describe key recommendations or planned actions. Is the WSS consolidation incentivized? If yes, please explain how?

32. Please characterise past (factual) WSS financing since 2000, and provide more specific information for the last 3 years:

- Levels of investment

Capital Investment in WSS (million EUR)	2017	2018	2019
Total investment			
Total investment in fixed assets for WSS			
as % of GDP			
Total investment in fixed assets for water supply			
Total investment in fixed assets for sanitation			
Sources of finance			
Public budget, total			
National budget (or government organizations)			
Regional budget			
Municipal budget			
IFIs, EU and donors[1]			
Water utilities own funds			
Private sources, total (incl. private operators)			

1. Please specify if development finance is channelled through public budgets, to avoid double counting

- Operation and maintenance costs (total)
- Any dedicated mechanism (such as a national water/environment/climate fund) in place or considered?

Experience with consolidation of municipalities and/or service providers

33. What are the key objectives pursued of WSS consolidation in Estonia (e.g. improvement of service provision, financial sustainability, economic efficiency, capacity, environmental benefits; else)?

34. Has consolidation/aggregation of municipalities already been considered for implementation of the EU Water Directives? If yes, how did it influence service provision, investment and WSS tariffs in those municipalities?

35. What are the key drivers and objectives pursued by WSS consolidation in Estonia, e.g. improvement of service provision, financial sustainability, economic efficiency, capacity, and environmental benefits?

36. Please describe key dimensions of consolidation under consideration, or already taking place:

- Geographical scale (administrative, watershed or regional boundaries)
- Functional scale (investment and service coverage; operation and maintenance; administration & customer relationships)
- Scope of service provision (provision of raw water; water supply; wastewater collection; wastewater treatment; pluvial and storm water collection; else)

37. Please describe:

- The potential for WSS consolidation in Estonia
- Possible scenarios (from a legal, financial, technical, social or political perspectives)
- The main challenges associated with implementation of WSS consolidation in Estonia.

Operational and financial performance of WSS operators

Please provide information by municipality/service provider (2019 or most recent year).

Municipality	Water Company/ Operator	Cost Coverage Ratio[1]	Total Debt (short term +long term liabilities) / Revenues	Non- Revenue Water[2]	CAPEX/ Total Costs
XX	...	%	%	%	%

1.Defined as the share of total costs covered by revenues
2. Defined as the share of water that is losses through leakages + bills that are not recovered

Please provide information on WSS tariffs rates, revenues from user charges and affordability ratio (2019 or most recent year).

Municipality	Water Company/ Operator	Household WSS tariff, applied by water operator (EUR/m3, on average)	WSS tariff for other consumer (EUR/m3 on average)	WSS tariff collection rate for households	Revenue from user charges (households) EUR	Revenue from user chargers (other consumers) EUR	Affordability[1] for households (if estimated)
XX	...			%			%

1. Defined as a share of disposal income

In 2017-2020 what was the level of public operational subsidies* to the utilities providing WSS services? (if relevant)

WSS, EUR	2017	2018	2019
Public operational subsidies to water utilities*			

Annex 1.C. Overview of resource efficiency survey of water companies

–	Type of site	Name of site	Type of measure	Measure	Description	Potential resource savings per year	Estimated cost	Estimated payback period	Comments	Risks and threats
1.1.	General	All	Immediate	Energy consumption KPIs	The suggestion is to develop indicators for assessment of the WTP and WWTP, which can be used to compare costs between sites (e.g. kWh/m3).	Not assessable	2,400	Less than a year	The cost of the investment is calculated on the assumption that it is not in the area of responsibility of any employee today. Payroll of €15/h and time for 160 working hours maximum for the development and implementation have been calculated. As the investment comprises 0.7% of the annual total energy costs, the payback time will certainly be less than a year.	- incomparable technologies and sites are compared in the case of indicators - documentation is not prepared, which means that validation of basic principles is impossible Solution: thorough preliminary work in the case of each site for the development of efficiency indicators and documentation of the work.
1.2.	General	All	Immediate	Training in SCADA data analysis	The relevant training will be carried out for the maximum use of the information saved with the existing IT solutions for optimising the operation of sites.	Not assessable	1,200	Less than a year	Time required *ca* 80 hours and payroll €15/h. The investment expense is very low and the payback time is certainly less than a year.	- people change, the people who have passed the training leave the company Solution: systematic approach, documentation and regular sharing of experience, not a one-off project.
1.3.	General	All	Long-term	Solar panels	Establishment of solar	6,500	52,000	8 years	The price of power	- the issue of maintenance

Type of measure	Measure	Description	Potential resource savings per year	Estimated cost	Estimated payback period	Comments	Risks and threats
and/or large-scale		park for covering own energy consumption. Savings, cost and payback time by the example of a plant of 50 kW output capacity if the support scheme is implemented (situation as at 01.12.2019). Installations with output capacity below 50 kW probably don't have an acceptable payback time as investments in the present condition.				purchased from the grid is €110/MWh, cost price of a PV plant €50/MWh, price of PV installation €700/kW, output 1,000 kWh/kW* per year excl. connection costs and plant size from 50 kW (solar plant, required area >0.16 ha). The payback time is based on financial calculations, not on simple payback time calculations.	should also be solved when the plant is installed and quality components from established manufacturers with references in Estonia should be used.
Immediate/ urgent	Monitoring the inside temperature of buildings	An option for reducing heating consumption is to reduce the temperature maintained in the rooms. Reducing the temperature in the rooms is possible, because most wastewater treatment plants have no staff permanently on site. The measure creates the possibility to constantly check the room temperature via the automatics system. Information on deviations from the desired temperature immediately reaches the administrator, who adjusts the work of	110	1,000	9 years	All small treatment plants with buildings (5) are classified as sites.	- the investment required for completing the project is bigger than presumed Solution: the measure is not cost-effective when ordered separately, must be done during the maintenance or repairs of the automation system. The measure must also be implemented when new PRP are planned.

_	Type of site	Name of site	Type of measure	Measure	Description	Potential resource savings per year	Estimated cost	Estimated payback period	Comments	Risks and threats
					the systems on-site if necessary. Reducing the temperature of heated rooms by one degree gives energy savings of 5–7%.					
2.1.	WWTP	Kullimäe	Urgent	Replacement of blowers	The SBR rotor blowers will be replaced with more energy-efficient screw blowers during the measure. The new blowers must have frequency converters and it should be possible to control them on the basis of the O2 indicator.	40,095	117,600	3 years	The new blower uses *ca* 85% of energy for doing the same work on the basis of specific power of kW/m3. The costs of replacement and installation of 4 blowers have been considered in the investment. The blowers have integrated frequency converters. The lion's share of the savings comes from control with frequency converters and according to an O2 sensor, and the savings resulting from the increase in energy efficiency are *ca* 10,400 euros (payback period 11 years).	- the resource savings described in the project will not be achieved Solution: inclusion of energy efficiency indicators in procurement criteria, routine resource savings inspection and correction activities where necessary. - the investment required for completing the project is bigger than presumed Solution: organisation of a procurement to find the best tenderer.
2.2.	WWTP	Kullimäe	Urgent	Aeration of the SBR block according to the O2 level	Control the sequencing batch reactor (SBR) according to the reading of the O2 sensor and installation of the	29,700	26,000	< 1 year	The investment is frequency converters for four blowers, i.e. 55 kW engines with installation and	- the resource savings described in the project will not be achieved Solution: routine resource

_	Type of site	Name of site	Type of measure	Measure	Description	Potential resource savings per year	Estimated cost	Estimated payback period	Comments	Risks and threats
					necessary frequency converter on the existing blowers. The dissolved O2 content in the SBR increases considerably higher than the optimal level of activated sludge: during the on-site inspection, DO=1.4 mg/L at the start of the aeration stage in an SBR processing tank and DO=8.8 mg/L in the second half of the aeration stage in the second tank. The existing blowers are equipped with frequency converters within the scope of the measure and the capacity of the blowers will be regulated according to the reading of the dissolved oxygen sensor.				connection to the automatics system.	savings inspection and correction activities where necessary - the investment required for completing the project is bigger than presumed Solution: organisation of a procurement to find the best tenderer.
2.3.	WWTP	Kullimäe	Urgent/immediate	Updating the SCADA interface.	Allow saving and monitoring of the main operating parameters, prepare extracts of data (tables and graphs) and analyse data (e.g. flows, cycle lengths, working hours of equipment, sensor readings (e.g. DO), quantities of chemicals, quantities of sludge and waste, etc.).	Not assessable	2,400	N/A	This is a supporting measure the implementation of which supports many of the discussed measures and the daily work of the company. In the opinion of consultants, the company already updates the SCADA interface today, but the	- the collected data are not used, resource savings are not achieved Solution: develop and document a systematic approach for analysing the collected data and implementing the corrective activities arising from the analysis. Include external knowledge in data analysis:

–	Type of site	Name of site	Type of measure	Measure	Description	Potential resource savings per year	Estimated cost	Estimated payback period	Comments	Risks and threats
									SCADA interface should support monitoring when energy consumption control is set up.	consultants, respective colleges and universities.
2.4.	WWTP	Kullimäe	Long-term and/or large-scale	Liquidation of aerobic stabilisation unit	Reconstruction of pipelines (connections of tanks and pipelines) to discharge excessive activated sludge directly to the sludge compactor and lose the aerobic stabilisation point in between. The aerobic stabilisation stage before compacting is completely unnecessary in the opinion of the consultant and the water company itself, as the sediment is later discharged into the methane fermenter for anaerobic stabilisation. The process has remained in the treatment scheme from the old solution (before the establishment of the SBR block and the new sediment handling complex). "Skipping" the stage required the reorganisation of the construction processes in the treatment plant.	9,900		3-4 years		The investment required for completing the project is bigger than presumed Solution: organisation of a procurement to find the best tenderer.
2.5.	WWTP	Kullim	Long-term	Reducing the	Reconstruction of the	17,900	Additional	The	The principle should	- the investment required for

–	Type of site	Name of site	Type of measure	Measure	Description	Potential resource savings per year	Estimated cost	Estimated payback period	Comments	Risks and threats
		äe	and/or large-scale	share of overflow discharged to the treatment plant	sewerage pipelines of Kuressaare City into a separate sewerage system, incl. use of combined solutions for on-site steeping of rainwater. The reconstruction of *ca* 20 km of canal pipe and 7 km of rainwater pipe in Kuressaare (stages I+II) is planned in the PWSS Development Plan that is being prepared, but this does not cover additional rainwater solutions of combined systems.		detailed analysis is required. We can use the investment of 1 million euros, which will be made to reduce the share of overflow by 21%.	payback period considering the energy savings alone is 56 years. The payback period may decrease significantly if we consider that flow rates will decrease when the wastewater treatment plant is reconstructed.	be applied to all new and reconstruction projects as a general approach. The share of overflow can be reduced by 21% in said case scenario was a result of the works (i.e. the share of overflow after the application of the measure will be 40%).	completing the project is bigger than presumed Solution: organisation of a procurement to find the best tenderer, a detailed preliminary analysis and consideration of all possible alternatives.
2.6.	WWTP	Kullimäe	Long-term and/or large-scale	Liquidation of BNR block, expansion of SBR	The additional analyses must clarify whether it would be reasonable to eliminate this in the future (when the BNR block becomes amortised) and expand the SBR.	Additional detailed analysis is required. The exact cost of the construction works will become clear after the preparation of the WWTP reconstruction project. The payback period may decrease considerably if the sediment processing solution is changed alongside the reconstruction of the WWTP.				The investment required for completing the project is bigger than presumed Solution: organisation of a procurement to find the best tenderer, a detailed preliminary analysis and consideration of all possible alternatives. The correct flow rates and pollution load are not taken into account when the WWTP is reconstructed.

–	Type of site	Name of site	Type of measure	Measure	Description	Potential resource savings per year	Estimated cost	Estimated payback period	Comments	Risks and threats
										Solution: Detailed surveys of the existing and future pollution load and flow rates must be carried out in the design stage.
2.7.	WWTP	Kullimäe	Long-term and/or large-scale	Strategic plan concerning anaerobic fermenter	Additional analyses must clarify whether and how the production of methane can be increased. If output cannot be increased with reasonable measure, an alternative case scenario should be prepared for when the useful life of the fermenter ends.	Increasing the methane output will reduce the need for diesel and could provide additional income when the generated products are marketed.	Additional detailed analysis is required.			Earlier surveys have proven that producing biogas from wastewater sediment alone is not economically justified. Agreements with bio waste suppliers must be achieved if the use of methane fermentation in sediment handling continues.
2.8.	WWTP	Orissaare	Long-term and/or large-scale	*Reconstruction of treatment plant (PWSS Development Plan 2020-2031)*	Reconstruction of the Orissaare WWTP is included in the short-term investment programme of the PWWS Development Plan, as the equipment and pipes of the activated sludge treatment plant have largely become amortised and must be replaced. The measures developed in this study, irrespective of priority, should be taken into account when reconstruction is designed. Using energy-efficient equipment must be included in the terms of	Energy consumption could be reduced by 7–10% by replacing the existing equipment with more energy-efficient solutions, and its monetary equivalent would be 500–700 euros per year.	The budget of the PWSS Development Plan is €80,000	10-15 years	The works are not directly related to increasing energy efficiency, but the need to reconstruct the plant. In terms of the energy-efficiency of the equipment used, cost-efficiency must only be calculated for the price difference between 'ordinary' and 'cost-efficient' equipment, and considering the planned life of the equipment.	- the investment required for completing the project is bigger than presumed Solution: cost control, organisation of procurements to take advantage of competition. - the water consumption of the reconstructed wastewater treatment plant will remain at the same level or increase. Solution: optimisation of the consumption of resources should be a part of the terms of reference of the design.

–	Type of site	Name of site	Type of measure	Measure	Description	Potential resource savings per year	Estimated cost	Estimated payback period	Comments	Risks and threats
					reference of the design. The scope and specific solutions of the reconstruction will be clarified during the design process.					
2.9.	WWTP	Valjala	Long-term and/or large-scale	Prevention of unnecessary repumping	The sludge solidification site should be eliminated (left as an emergency solution) and a sludge tank/compactor should be established instead, and the compacted sludge should be taken to Kuressaare similar to other treatment plants.	990	25,000	25	The works are not directly related to increasing energy efficiency, but compliance with environmental requirements.	Sludge is not removed from the compactor on time. Solution: Include the activity in the WWTP maintenance plan.
2.10.	WWTP	Eikla	Long-term and/or large-scale	*Reconstruction of treatment plant (PWSS Development Plan 2020-2031)*	Reconstruction of the unsuccessfully constructed treatment plant (replacement of the technological solution with an SBR pursuant to the PWSS Development Plan). The new treatment plant must be fitted with an O2 sensor and the adjustment of the aeration blower must be connected with this. The measures developed in this study, irrespective of priority, should be taken into account when reconstruction is designed.	Resource savings depend on the designed solution. The structure of consumption will change when the technical solution is replaced.	The budget of the PWSS Development Plan is €120,000	Not assessable	The works are not directly related to increasing energy efficiency, but the need to reconstruct the plant. In terms of the energy-efficiency of the equipment used, cost-efficiency must only be calculated for the price difference between 'ordinary' and 'cost-efficient' equipment, and considering the planned life of the equipment.	- the investment required for completing the project is bigger than presumed Solution: cost control, organisation of procurements to take advantage of competition. - the water consumption of the reconstructed wastewater treatment plant will remain at the same level or increase. Solution: optimisation of the consumption of resources should be a part of the terms of reference of the design.

–	Type of site	Name of site	Type of measure	Measure	Description	Potential resource savings per year	Estimated cost	Estimated payback period	Comments	Risks and threats
2.11.	WWTP	Tagavere	Urgent	Aeration control	Create the option to reduce air quantities with the installation of a frequency converter. Installation of a stationary oxygen sensor and connecting regulation to its readings. Introduce control with an O2 sensor if at all technically possible in the case of the existing system! Otherwise, provide minimal manual control of the frequency converter (energy saving are also smaller in this case).	440	4,000	9 years		- the resource savings described in the project will not be achieved Solution: monitoring of energy efficiency, routine resource savings inspection and correction activities where necessary - the investment required for completing the project is bigger than presumed Solution: organisation of a procurement to find the best tenderer.
2.12.	WWTP	Liiva	Long-term and/or large-scale	Optimisation of energy use of the building	Options for optimising the energy consumption of the building cannot be suggested without additional research (incl. the necessary measurements, thermography) during the heating period. Most measures for reducing the energy consumption of the building are very unlikely to be cost-optimal against the energy savings that can be achieved as separate investments (not by the complete	Additional detailed analysis is required.				- optimisation of energy use of the building is not cost-effective yet Solution: thorough analysis before measures are planned, cost control, organisation of procurements to take advantage of competition.

–	Type of site	Name of site	Type of measure	Measure	Description	Potential resource savings per year	Estimated cost	Estimated payback period	Comments	Risks and threats
					reconstruction of the WWRP), i.e. they would not pay off.					
3.1.	WTP	Unimäe	Long-term and/or large-scale	Optimisation of energy use of the building	A two-storey building is located by the Unimäe WTP, which has 540 m2 of heated space according to the register of construction works. As far as the consultants know, no employees are in the building every day. As the building is heated directly with electricity and there is no regular use, we should consider the possibility of transferring the activities to some other premises where the energy consumption is already optimal (e.g. an additional workplace at the company's head office).	1,980	1,000	Less than a year	1,000 euros is the approximate cost of the move and the creation of a new workplace. The maintenance costs of the building will be added to the savings side, but the consultant has no overview of them. 10% of the electricity consumption currently spent on thermal energy will presumably remain.	- optimisation of energy use of the building is not cost-effective yet Solution: exact mapping of the activities carried out in the building before the activity is kicked off, finding alternative use for the building.
3.2.	WTP	Unimäe	Long-term and/or large-scale	Reducing the share of leakages	Reconstruction of the water pipelines of Kuressaare City to minimise network leakages and consequently the costs of raw water processing. The reconstruction of *ca* 24 km of water pipe in Kuressaare (stages I+II) is planned in the PWSS Development Plan.	6,590	500,000	76	The efficiency of the measure depends on the accuracy of mapping the regions with the biggest leakages. The goal is to reduce the number of leakages with as few means as possible. Considered in the case scenario: leakages can be	- the investment required for completing the project is bigger than presumed Solution: cost control, organisation of procurements to take advantage of competition. - the pipeline with few leakages, where resource consumption will not

_	Type of site	Name of site	Type of measure	Measure	Description	Potential resource savings per year	Estimated cost	Estimated payback period	Comments	Risks and threats
									reduced by 7% with an investment of €500,000 (i.e. the share of leakages after the application of the measure will be 10%). The payback period is too long with the parameters of the case scenario.	decrease, will be reconstructed. Solution: pipelines will be presumably reconstructed where the need for this is the biggest (there are leakages).
3.3.	WTP	Orissaare	Immediate/ urgent	Optimisation of pumping	The energy consumption of a level 2 pumping station, i.e. transfer to the consumers, comprises a big part of the energy consumption of a WTP. During the analysis, it was clarified that one of the three pumps, which also has a frequency converter, operates for the majority of the time. The frequency is only reduced to *ca* 40 Hz due to the technical features of the pump, even when there is no load on the consumption side. It's also impossible to turn the pump off altogether, as constant operation is required for maintaining the pressure. This in its turn means that energy consumption is high even if there is no actual water	481.8	2300	3-5 years	The assumption is that there is no consumption at all for 8 hours a day and the capacity of the pump could be reduced by 50% during these hours. The existing pump is dimensioned on the basis of the maximum flow rate and it operates with an efficiency of ~26% for most of the time (the efficiency could be twice as much). The capacity of the pump that will be replaced is 3 kW. The investment includes the cost of the audit required for selecting the correct pump.	- the resource savings described in the project will not be achieved Solution: inclusion of energy efficiency indicators in procurement criteria, routine resource savings inspection and correction activities where necessary. An additional audit must be carried out before the investment is planned. - the investment required for completing the project is bigger than presumed Solution: organisation of a procurement to find the best tenderer.

–	Type of site	Name of site	Type of measure	Measure	Description	Potential resource savings per year	Estimated cost	Estimated payback period	Comments	Risks and threats
					consumption.					
3.4.	WTP	Kõljala	Urgent	Replacement of the reverse osmosis membranes and optimisation of membrane washing	According to the information received from the representative of Kuressaare water works, the equipment is not as energy-efficient as it should be according to the technical specifications. Kuressaare water works cooperate with the importer of the equipment to find the best possible configuration that guarantees good quality drinking water for consumers. Savings arise from smaller water consumption in keeping the osmosis device working, i.e. less water must be pumped from the drill well.					
3.5.	WTP	Eikla	Long-term and/or large-scale	Optimisation of energy use of the building	An estimated 2,508 kWh/year, i.e. 68% of the consumed energy is used for heating the building and drying the air, which is a disproportionately high quantity in comparison with the other analysed sites. Although the share of heating as a ratio is high and there is potential for saving energy, the heating	82.5	600	Approximately 5 years	The acquisition of an air dryer with condensation is an investment. A bigger procurement should be organised for selecting the air dryer, so that the unit price of the devices would be as low as possible. Energy efficiency should be an	- the resource savings described in the project will not be achieved Solution: inclusion of energy efficiency indicators in procurement criteria, routine resource savings inspection and correction activities where necessary. - the investment required for

–	Type of site	Name of site	Type of measure	Measure	Description	Potential resource savings per year	Estimated cost	Estimated payback period	Comments	Risks and threats
					consumption as an absolute value is *ca* 275 euros per year, which is why finding cost-optional energy saving measures is not easy. Replacing the drying device in order to reduce the energy consumption of air drying could be considered. The energy consumption of the building should be regularly monitored and additional measures should be considered if consumption increases additionally or the energy prices go up (e.g. additional insulation).				assessment criterion that is at least equal to the price.	completing the project is bigger than presumed Solution: organisation of a procurement to find the best tenderer.
3.6.	WTP	All water treatm ent plants	Immediate	Optimisation of pumping	The price of power is likely to go up in the near future, as the power generation capacity in the region of the Nord Pool energy market decreases and the price of CO2 increases. Therefore, it could be economically reasonable to configure the energy-intensive aeration and pumping processes in such a manner that the equipment could be turned on flexibly in certain periods of time. This would				The construction of the described operating regimes for these measures alone would certainly not be reasonable today in comparison with the benefits it would have, but the additional need for control on the basis of the input coming from the electricity market should be taken into account when equipment, controllers and remote	- the optimisation of work is not cost-effective. Solution: clarification of a mire accurate model for calculating the need for investment and the possible savings, which would make it possible to adapt quickly to the changing market situation or invest rapidly. - the necessary reserve of clean drinking water should be taken into account if the pumping of clean drinking

–	Type of site	Name of site	Type of measure	Measure	Description	Potential resource savings per year	Estimated cost	Estimated payback period	Comments	Risks and threats
					ensure that power is consumed during the hours when its price is as low as possible. The power system will need additional services to guarantee the parameters that are important to the system in relation to the synchronisation of the power system of the Baltic States with the Central European frequency area. One of the services for which a market is likely to emerge in the next 5–10 years is rapidly responding electricity output. This means that value will emerge on the electricity market for electricity output that can be turned on/off in a short time. At larger WTPs and WWTPs, pumps are the capacity that can participate in the market for system services.				control systems are selected. Thus, we should ask the supplier of the software and the hardware whether they are ready to carry out such interfacing.	water and the maintained levels were to be optimised. Solution: analyse the document the quantity of necessary drinking water (provided that the emergency reserve of drinking water can also be used, i.e. that the treatment of wastewater in an emergency is guaranteed). Probability of risk materialisation: average

Notes

[1] The English version of the Law of Property and the Commercial Code can be found here: Law of Property Act–Riigi Teataja and Commercial Code–Riigi Teataja

[2] The Estonian Investment Centre (EIC) was founded in 2000 by the Ministry of the Environment (MoE). For the last 20 years EIC has served as one of the main financiers of environmental projects in Estonia. With the support of various sources of financing, the EIC has helped to implement activities within the scope of different ministries in Estonia.

2 Summary of kick-off meeting

A kick-off meeting was convened, to inform stakeholders about the dialogue, its ambition and the working method. The agenda was designed to build a momentum and appetite for next steps.

2.1. General Overview

The Ministry of the Environment of Estonia jointly with other governmental authorities (the Ministry of Finance, the Minister of Public Administration), the European Commission DG Reform, and the OECD are partnering to enhance the sustainability of water supply and sanitation services in Estonia.

The kick-off meeting was co-convened by Estonian authorities and the OECD, on 27 October 2020, as a virtual meeting. The aim was to discuss the findings of the background report and the priorities for the remainder of the project. It was structured around four Agenda items (see Annex A). The meeting gathered approximately 25 delegates from national and local authorities, water utilities, the Estonian Water Works association, and international participants from the EC (DG Reform, DG Environment) and the OECD Secretariat (see Annex B for List of Participants).

This note captures the main messages of the meeting on the state of play of the water supply and sanitation (WSS) sector reform, OECD analysis and official and expert opinions expressed at the kick-off meeting.

2.2. Agenda Item 1: Opening and Welcoming Remarks

Participants took note of welcoming remarks from Mr. Kyriacos Kyriacou, Deputy Head of Unit of Growth and Business Environment, DG REFORM, who welcomed participants of the meeting. Mr Kyriacou underlined the value of evidence-based policy development and the benefit of cooperation programmes.

Mr. Harry Liiv, Deputy Secretary General, Ministry of Environment of Estonia, welcomed participants. He provided a brief overview of the most recent experience with water policy reform in Estonia. He emphasised the need for realistic, action-oriented recommendations, and affordability issues, particularly in small towns and rural areas.

2.3. Agenda Item 2: The state of play in the WSS sector of Estonia

The meeting took note of a presentation of Ms. Karin Kroon, Head of Water, Ministry of Environment. Ms. Kroon shared the experience with the administrative reform and its impact on WSS service provision in Estonia. The presentation reiterated the main objectives of national policy for water supply and sanitation:

- population connected to public sewerage
- share of consumers receiving safe drinking water from public water supply
- the average water tariff level
- share of agglomeration above 2000 p.e that comply with the requirements.

It also highlighted the key challenges faced by the sector:

- how to keep the compliance with the EU legislation in long term
- how to provide the service with affordable water tariff
- how to step out from state support (including EU money).

It also signalled the dynamic towards consolidation of local authorities and water utilities, induced by broader administrative reform in Estonia.

Mr. Vahur Tarkmees commented on the factors influencing voluntary inter-municipal cooperation for WSS service provision in Estonia. He shared experience with such cooperation in one particular utility. The following issues were mentioned:

- local governments may not realise financing challenges faced by water utilities

- There is no clear accountability or driver for change
- Local authorities scrutinise affordability of water bills in the short term
- How to deal with small, unsustainable utilities?

2.4. Agenda Item 3: Towards a greater sustainability of WSS in Estonia: further needs for the reform

Participants noted introductory remarks from Ms. Tatiana Efimova, OECD, reflecting the key findings of the background report.

The discussion highlighted:

- A massive investment programme implemented to comply with the EU Water Directives in Estonia
- Financing challenges associated with further needs to build new or rebuild existing assets
- A call for the reform of tariff policy and for mobilising additional sources of finance. Finance may not be an issue in the next 3-5 years, but will become more pressing very soon, as financing needs accumulate, potential EU funding are phased out, and affordability of water bills becomes is an issue for segments of the population
- The potential benefit for water users to benchmark the performance of service providers. The Water Works Association of Estonia is considering to resume benchmarking of water utilities; the Ministry of Environment collects data on water leakage. Incentives to improve performance through tariff structure or sanctions for poor performance are lacking, not enforced or not effective.
- Water utilities' need technical assistance, on both financial and technical issues.
- Local authorities would benefit from additional capacities to prepare Sector Development Plans and implement investment decisions. Some Sector Development Plans (e.g. Narva city) are actually developed by water utilities due to lack of capacity of local authorities.
- Practical issues can affect the possibility of agglomeration. For instance: what about loans contracted by utilities? Can tariffs remain different in agglomerated utilities?

Participants acknowledged the fact that the financial sustainability of water companies is an issue. The prevailing methodology for WSS tariff setting does not provide revenues for the modernisation and maintenance of existing assets.

Issues related to incentives for consolidation of service providers were discussed. While all water utilities should look for options to enhance efficiency of operations, consolidated ones get preferential state support (grants) for investments. Other utilities are facing difficulties to benefit from state grants.

Local authorities should systematically explore opportunities for inter-municipal cooperation.

Participants took note and endorsed the suggestions for further work under the project:

1. *Zoom-in on the issues* affecting sustainability of WSS services in Estonia
2. Consider a *range of options for agglomeration*: geographical scale *vs* functions (planning; programming expenditure; technical skills; billing)
3. Advance the role for the *economic regulator* for WSS:
4. Clarify and *address legal issues* related to asset ownership (options to transfer ownership to entities operating at larger geographical scales)
5. Develop an *action-oriented strategy* for a greater sustainability of WSS services in Estonia

Participants noted the feedback from Ms. Inese Kause, DG Environment, regarding the need to drive sustainable WSS models, keeping the environment and climate objectives high on the policy agenda.

Ms. Zinovia Tsikalaki, DG Reform, reminded participants about potential synergies to share practical experiences with neighbouring countries, most particularly Lithuania, where DG Reform launched a similar support programme.

2.5. Agenda Item 4: Next steps and priorities for the coming period

Participants noted the priorities of the project for the coming period introduced by Mr. Xavier Leflaive, OECD. It was noted that the analysis will cover opportunities for new business models to support improved sector operation; more attention will be paid to regulation, the inclusion of social issues and further consideration of the management of rural versus urban communities; and sustainable financing opportunities.

The Ministry of Environment thanked participants for their participation and informed that a next meeting of Working Group will take place in Q1, 2021, and closed the meeting.

Annex A. Agenda of the kick-off meeting

Chair: Mr Harry Liiv, Deputy Secretary General, Ministry of Environment of Estonia

14:00 ~ 14:15

Welcome and Adoption of the Agenda

Welcome by DG REFORM (Mr Kyriacos Kyriacou, Deputy Head of Unit of Growth and Business Environment)

Welcome by the Ministry of Environment of Estonia (Mr Harry Liiv, Deputy Secretary General)

Adoption of the Agenda

14:15 ~ 14:45

The state of play in the WSS sector of Estonia (led by the Ministry of Environment)

Status with the administrative reform and its impact on WSS services provision. Consolidation of WSS services: how did it work so far and what are the lessons learnt?

Factors influencing voluntary cooperation for WSS service provision.

Questions for clarification

14:45 ~ 16:15

Towards a greater sustainability of WSS in Estonia: further needs for the reform (led by OECD)

Issues related to the institutional and legal framework

Need for enhanced regulation

Financing of WSS services

Suggestions on further work under the project: milestones and key outputs

Discussion

---

16 :15 ~ end of meeting

Next steps and priorities for the coming period

Conclusions and a wrap up of the meeting.

3 Issue Paper

The issue paper derives from the Background report compiled by Estonian authorities and interactions with stakeholders. It sketches the key themes on which the dialogue focuses. Some of the key issues to be covered include: making the case for reform; scenarios for aggregation; incentives to foster consolidation of utilities; technical – including legal – issues; tariff policy and methodology; independent economic regulation for WSS.

3.1. Background and objectives

The Ministry of the Environment of Estonia jointly with other governmental authorities (the Ministry of Finance, the Minister of Public Administration), the European Commission – DG Reform, and the OECD are partnering to enhance the sustainability of water supply and sanitation services in Estonia. The Project will support the preparation of a roadmap for the consolidation of the water utility sector, a requisite for a sustainable and socially acceptable financing strategy and a broader water sector reform in Estonia. See the Detailed Project Description, for more information on background, scope and process.

The specific objectives of this Project are:

- to support the initiatives of national authorities to design their reforms according to their priorities, taking into account initial conditions and expected socio-economic impacts
- to support the efforts of national authorities to define and implement appropriate processes and methodologies by taking into account good practices of and lessons learned by other countries in addressing similar situations
- to assist the national authorities and water utilities in enhancing the efficiency and effectiveness of human-resource management, inter alia, by strengthening professional knowledge and skills and setting out clear responsibilities.

This issue paper presents a list of policy areas that requires further consideration to support reforms that effectively encourage consolidation of water utilities and put water supply and sanitation services in Estonia on a sustainable basis. The OECD Secretariat developed the issue paper building on i) a background report compiled on the state of play, ii) discussions at the kick-off meeting, and iii) interviews with select stakeholders in Estonia. Some features of the international experience with similar reforms have been reflected as well (e.g. on tariff reform); a more detailed review is on-going, which covers a broader range of issues.

Some of the key issues to be listed include:

- Making the case for reform
- Scenarios for the aggregation of water utilities in Estonia
- Incentives to foster consolidation of utilities
- Technical – including legal - issues to be tackled
- Tariff policy and methodology
- Independent economic regulation for WSS.

Propositions unfold, on key issues that deserve further analysis in the context of this project. The analyses are meant to document possible courses of action and options to facilitate consolidation of water utilities in Estonia. They define the proposed programme of work in the context of this project (in line with the Detailed Project Description). The outcome of the discussions has been reflected in this Issue paper.

The next steps of the project analysis will include:

- A review of international experience, with a particular focus on incentives, and on economic regulation
- Options to tackle legal issues, in particular at micro level (transfer of assets, accountability of local governments and water companies, etc.)
- Considerations for financial and non-financial incentives
- Modes of strengthening independent economic regulation (to set tariffs, benchmark performance of water companies, and assess expenditure programmes)
- A roadmap to manage the transition.

3.2. Issues to be covered in the project

3.2.1. Making the case for reform

Discussion on the reform of the water sector in Estonia has been going on for a couple of decades. A lot of research has focused that issue. Some experience has been gained, with several regional utilities already operating.

The long-term direction seems clear. Stakeholders seem to agree that the state of play is not sustainable and business as usual is not an option:

- Estonia has achieved a remarkable rate of construction of infrastructures for water and sanitation services, since its accession to the European Union, with multiple benefits for the population. These assets need to be properly operated and maintained. Failure to do so will need to a rapid decay and a need to rebuild existing assets, adding costs to the community.
- The fragmented industry has neither the technical nor financial capacity to operate and maintain existing assets. In 2018, 177 water companies were operating in Estonia. Some operate several services and the water service may be subsidised by revenues from other services. 44 local governments are serviced by more than one water company.
- The industry faces issues of compliance with the EU regulation. Five wastewater treatment plants (WWTP) of more than 2,000 pe (population equivalent) fail to comply with Urban Wastewater Treatment Directive (UWWTD) standard. Several WWTP of less than 2,000 pe (not covered by the UWWTD) do not meet required standards, potentially affecting compliance with the Water Framework Directive (WFD).
- Demographic trends will further exacerbate financial challenges for water services in the country. While the national population is projected to decline by 2.7% by 2045, population in four counties is projected to decline by 1/3, with negative consequences on the revenues for water services. This is an issue as a vast majority of the costs of operating water services are fixed.

In that context of high investment needs and projected decline of revenues, the prevailing financing model for water and sanitation services in Estonia is obsolete. The European Commission has indicated that financial support to the sector – which represents 85% of capital expenditures - will gradually be phased out. and the Estonian Ministry of finance confirmed that it will not be a substitute.

There seems to be a broad consensus on the state of play. Opinions vary on the direction for change and the pace of the reform. While some call for a rapid change, others argue that the current situation can prevail for 4-5 years, before the financial dead-end becomes more apparent and the case for change more pressing. This eventual grace period is best used to agree on a vision for the water industry in Estonia, and ignite change.

This project ambitions to support both the development of the vision, and the agreement on the course of action. The roadmap for the consolidation of water companies in Estonia will entail:

- A scenario for consolidation. For the moment, discussions essentially consider one model of agglomeration, on a geographical basis, where well-functioning companies gradually absorb smaller, fragile ones. This model can be discussed, and some nuance could be added. For instance, not all functions may need to be operated at the same scale: water supply could be operated at a different scale than sanitation; investment planning and procurement could be managed at a different scale than consumer relations and billing. Some competences could be available in regional centres, to support smaller utilities. These options (and more) deserve some attention, as for their relevance and feasibility in the Estonian context.

- A course of action. It is generally agreed that reform in Estonia should be voluntary only. Still, some staging may be required. One option may be to strengthen the operation of larger utilities first, so that they become able to merge with smaller ones, when appropriate. Another option might be to consider a pilot region, to test a number of options and accompanying measures; lessons could be learned, that inspire other regions. A range of actions need to be taken in parallel, such as the adjustment of the tariff setting methodology (if required), setting up capacities to review and assess the opportunity of investments and expenditure programmes (going beyond the assessment of eligible costs), organising benchmarking capacities to set performance objectives and review performance of water companies. Some of these actions relate to strengthening economic regulation. The roadmap will need to sequence these measures to ensure a smooth and effective transition towards the agreed-upon vision for a sustainable water industry in Estonia.

Mobilising local authorities to support the reform

Mobilising local authorities requires a clear case for the costs and benefits of the consolidation process. It also requires that a set of technical issues be tackled in pragmatic ways. Intense consultation is a must, with multiple opportunities for local governments to voice their concern – and support – and comment on the roadmap, the incentives being considered and the responses to their queries.

In case the roadmap foresees the possibility of a pilot water company or region, support needs to be provided for its establishment and initial operation. It may include the following accompanying measures:

- The creation of associations of municipalities to facilitate creation of regional utilities
- Support to contractual arrangements between such associations and the regional utilities. Performance-based management contracts could be promoted
- Water Operators Partnerships (WOP) consisting of reputable operators.

Partnerships with experienced operators would be critical to develop and strengthen the newly formed organisations. The consolidated utilities could provide specific support to rural localities that are not yet part of the association.

3.2.2. Technical – including legal – issues to be tackled

Preliminary discussions have highlighted a series of technical issues, which can explain why the reform of water companies in Estonia falters. These issues can create concrete and tangible obstacles to reform, even where the direction for change is not questioned. Some of these issues are legal. The project will endeavour to explore solutions in the context of the existing legal and institutional framework. More radical options may require changing the existing framework, making the feasibility more speculative.

Legislative and institutional issues

Clarification of the legal and institutional frameworks is the key issue to be addressed for successful implementation of the consolidation reform.

Several issues derive from the absence of a relevant and replicable contractual and institutional model for regional companies. According to the national legislation, local authorities collectively will remain the decision makers regarding the strategy and management of a common regional operator. Although the legislation stipulates the right for local authorities to associate with the objective of improving the quality of services of common interest, the regulatory framework is not as explicit about the legal forms and patterns of such co-operation.

A detailed review of the legal framework should therefore be conducted, to ensure its consistency with the considered institutional model. The next chapter will consider it with a particular focus on three aspects:

- Governance arrangements: how are voting rights allocated among municipalities
- Conditions required for joining and withdrawing from the association.
- Regime of assets: who owns the assets created under the association? In case of disbanding of the association, how are these assets returned to their original owner, and what happens with the assets built under the association?

Key features of the incorporation act of a regional service provider could be prepared to clarify the legal status and address some the pending issues listed above. The delegation contract would most likely be in the form of a concession contract (the operator is responsible for both operation and investment). It would need to address key questions that arise under such type of contract, such as:

- Who decides and finances investment?
- How are tariffs set and adjusted?
- How is the performance of the regional utility monitored?
- What happens in case of failure to meet its targets?

Accountability of local governments for local infrastructure

Decentralised ownership for local infrastructure creates issues with accountability for service provision. In Estonia, the allocation of tasks and responsibilities across institutions is blurred, on some issues. Water companies and local governments are responsible for the provision of water services in cities and settlements; the Ministry of the Environment is responsible for sustainable access to WSS services in the state as a whole.

The situation raises a few questions:

- Are these responsibilities equally clear and understandable to each party?
- Do all of the parties agree to the performance of the functions and obligations assigned to them?
- How are some obligations and functions financed?
- Is the allocation of responsibilities and resources fair from the viewpoint of all parties?

There may be disputes and misunderstandings between the Ministry of the Environment, the local governments and water companies about who should be responsible if a policy goal is not achieved. For example:

- Who should guarantee the WSS access in areas of over 2,000 p.e. to the sewerage system?
- Who should pay the fine for non-compliance with the EU directives, should it occur? Can the national government (which will be held accountable by the European Commission) ask non-compliant authorities to foot the bill? On which legal and financial basis?

Questions also arise when major disruptions and problems occur in the provision of the water service in a densely populated settlement. For example, if a major problem occurs, and drinking water no longer complies with requirements, so that an advanced water treatment is to be put in place; or if treated wastewater does not comply with norms, and a solution requires major investments, and minor operational improvements cannot solve the problem. Who bears responsibility to the citizens and/or the Ministry of Environment – the local government or the water company?

Operational issues

A range of operational issues need to be tackled, to overcome fair objections to the reform. Based on preliminary discussions, these include:

- How to deal with existing loans taken by a local government or water company, after agglomeration?
- In the case of multi-purpose companies, how to address implicit subsidies across services? Agglomeration of water services may shatter the delivery of other services in the community.
- What is the role of companies' Boards as regards investments and expenditure programmes?
- Should tariffs of the agglomerated company be harmonised, or can different tariffs exist?

3.2.3. Incentives to foster consolidation of water companies

Addressing the technical – including legal – issues listed above can go a long way to expedite agglomeration of water companies in Estonia. However, incentives will probably be required to ignite change.

Financial incentive is probably the most effective. One of the key drivers for consolidation could be easier access to funds. In that spirit, parts of government funds might be reserved for utilities willing to join the process. From that perspective, the Estonian Investment Centre – under the Ministry of Environment – may have a role to play: eligibility criteria and support on the ground may reflect alignment of project owners with the ambition of reform. Of note: in Romania, only regionalised operators are eligible for public funding for capital expenditure.

Financial incentive might be supplemented by preferred treatment for investment projects or expenditure programmes from well-performing consolidated water companies. Such preferred treatment could take the form of less cumbersome authorisation programmes, renewal of licence to operate or other administrative measures that can facilitate the operation of water companies.

Licensing for water operators is another tool that Estonian authorities may wish to mobilise to incentivise local governments and water companies to agglomerate. The renewal of licenses could be faster for efficient water companies. And utilities failing to meet performance targets could lose their licence. This would provide opportunities for more efficient operators to expand their service area. Transition to the incentive-based regulation of water tariffs can play a role of economic incentive to enhance efficiency of water operators.

3.2.4. Tariff policy and methodology

The methodology to set tariff is a foundational driver for change and condition for reform. There are issues with the current methodology, in particular as regards its capacity to reflect investment needs and to drive the performance of water companies.

Tariff methodology and its application

The tariff methodology is a key part of economic regulation. In simple terms, independent economic regulation of WSS aims to ensure that customers receive the appropriate water service for the right price. Appropriate here refers to the combination of various objectives: economic (robust allocation of water and discouraging wastage), environmental (conservation of the resource), social (addressing affordability concerns) and financial (ensuring utilities' capacity to finance the operation of the service, now and in the future).

The tariff methodology developed by Estonian Competition Authority (ECA) is based on its mandate under Public Water Supply and Sewerage Act (Water Law) in Estonia. According to the law, water tariffs must be cost based – including a reasonable rate of profit - and approved by the regulator[1]. According to the legislation in Estonia, the WSS tariffs:

- cover justified operating expenses
- reflect the need for additional investments in order to ensure the sustainability of the existing public water supply and sewerage systems – according to the public water supply and sewerage development plans approved by local governments (development plan)
- ensure justified profitability (Weighted Average Cost of Capital - WACC) of the capital invested by the water company
- support the development of the public water supply and sewerage (incl. storm water) system in specific development areas where over 50% of residential buildings, for which building permits were issued before 22 March 1999, are connected to the system (in accordance with development plan).

Box 3.1. Definitions in economic regulations of WSS

Affordability: Affordability is the capacity of a particular household group to cover all WSS-related expenses (including VAT, taxes and any additional charges). It is often expressed as a percentage of household income or expenditure.

Eligible costs: Those parts of overall costs incurred by an operator that the regulator deems needed to provide the regulated service.

RAB: The Regulatory Asset Base is set by those assets of the operator deemed necessary for providing the regulated service. A higher amount of RAB assets provides for a higher eligible depreciation expense, higher regulated return on assets and thus higher eligible costs.

RIA: The (ex ante) Regulatory Impact Assessment is a systematic process of identification and quantification of important benefits and costs likely to flow from the adoption of a proposed regulation under consideration.

WACC: The Weighted Average Cost of Capital is a calculation of the operator's cost of capital in which each category of capital is proportionately weighted. All long-term capital associated with the regulated service is included. A higher regulated WACC implies a higher cost of capital (of the RAB) and therefore a higher tariff.

Source: OECD (2015), "Regulatory Impact Analysis", in Government at a Glance 2015, OECD Publishing, Paris

The regulation assumes a single volumetric tariff that is the same for households and legal entities. Generally, this is in agreement with the Polluter Pays and Beneficiary Pays principles, as set in the Recommendation of the OECD Council on Water (source: http://www.oecd.org/water/recommendation/#d.en.431326).

Other tariff formula could be considered, to better address the tensions between the various policy objectives. For instance, a two-part tariff structure is applied in Germany and the Netherlands. It would have a sizeable fixed component plus a single volumetric component. The two-part tariff structure does bring the revenue structure more in line with the cost structure of utilities, which have large fixed costs. However, in the absence of targeted social measures, this structure can have socially regressive effects. Some regulators allow limited fixed elements in the tariff structure, namely those related to customer services such as metering, billing and meter maintenance.

Social aspects

Tariffs need adjustment if the affordability of service for segments of the population is at stake. An affordability check is not a part of the tariff setting procedure in Estonia. Here, the issue of affordability of the water tariff is solved at the level of the local government (e.g. income support etc.) by granting social support to specific people.

In practice, the water tariff is less than 2.5% of the income of a household member, which is why affordability is not considered as an issue yet[2]. However, it may have to be considered in the future, when the proper operation, maintenance and upgrade of the infrastructure has to be properly financed.

Ownership and depreciation

Regulatory issues related to tariff formula are most influential. The current tariff regulation system in Estonia is characterised by the following:

- Reinvestment component is not part of the tariff formula for most water companies. The cost of replacing decaying assets is not properly reflected in the tariff-setting process, as assets built with EU fund (the vast majority of recent assets) are not included in the regulated asset base. Therefore, most utilities are unable to generate the revenues to renew and upgrade (where appropriate) existing infrastructures.
- Linear calculation of capital expenses according to the acquisition cost for fixed assets 30-40 or more years. The tariff setting method does not provide options to consider the indexed value of fixed assets instead of the replacement value.
- Despite the inclusion of depreciation costs, it is not possible to reflect in today's water tariff the depreciation costs of assets acquired by EU funds.

The main issue with the exclusion of granted assets from the base over which the return on assets and eligible depreciation expenses is calculated is that the method does not properly reflect the cost of maintaining and renewing existing assets. Accordingly, it prevents water tariffs from generating the revenues water companies need to finance a sustainable provision of water services, now and in the future. In the absence of subsidies, this financing model cannot be sustained, after the rapid extension of water infrastructures in Estonia.

One solution to this dilemma may be to allow for *infrastructure renewal charges*, such as in England and Wales, Scotland or Kosovo. Such charges consider as eligible expense the actual costs to maintain the asset base rather than the depreciation charge.

3.2.5. Independent economic regulation for water companies

Independent economic regulation covers a range of functions as regards water supply and sanitation services. The previous section discussed issues related to tariff setting. This section focuses on two relates sets of issues:

- Driving the performance of water companies
- Reviewing the opportunity of development plan and investment programmes. A related issue is driving the efficiency of expenditure programmes.

Note that independent economic regulation can be delivered via a range of institutional or organisational arrangements. The OECD has reviewed options in place several countries. That review will support tailored discussion on appropriate options to deliver the functions in Estonia.

Figure 3.1. The functions of economic regulation for WSS

Source: Authors elaboration

Driving water companies' performance

Incentives to enhance the performance of water companies can be a key driver for change. Clear performance targets, supported by robust monitoring, adequate rewards (or sanctions) can drive performance, signal deficiencies and urge water companies to take action.

The tariff regulation demonstrates insufficient consideration for the performance of water companies. For instance, staff adjustment, and the reduction of non-revenue water to acceptable levels take several years. This is why in most countries, water companies' business plans are set for multiple years (5 years in England and Wales), in alignment with tariff revision periods and management contracts.

Two interrelated sets of issues deserve attention. The first one relates to the reference to be considered to set tariffs and define eligible costs. Currently, ECA considers local development plans (in practice, drafted by utilities and endorsed by municipalities) as reference documents for setting tariffs. In principle, the key document for the regulator is the operator's business plan, supplemented by its investment plan. The business plan must show and justify the performance improvement that can realistically be achieved, and the (capital and operational) costs associated with that level of performance.

The second set of issue relates to setting, monitoring, and rewarding performance. Estonia has limited experience with benchmarking the performance of water companies. Two distinct institutions monitor compliance: ECA, as the economic regulator (on water resources management and waste), the Health Board (on standards for drinking water). The Water Works Association set up features of a benchmarking programme, with limited results (it compiles partial, often outdated information, which accuracy remains unclear). A tailored set of criteria, aligned with policy objectives, and a systematic review of performance is the foundation of an incentive regime that can only enhance value for money and potentially drive change towards more effective and cost-efficient water industry in Estonia.

Investment planning

In Estonia, economic regulation is based on costs, but it is not clear which institution – if any - checks whether the investment or expenditure programmes are opportune, or incentivises enhanced efficiency. In this situation, each local government has an implicit incentive to draft development plans in isolation, a missed opportunity to look for economies of scope or scale, for instance. This is an issue, in particular as water and sanitation services are capital intensive: risks of duplication are costly, in particular in the long term, when the need to maintain and renew existing assets is factored. The demographic trends mentioned can only increase such unnecessary costs.

Several options can be considered, to address this issue. A National Water Strategy, backed by a thorough and realistic financing strategy could be envisaged, to set the overall level of ambition and provide a reference to assess the opportunity of investment needs, and possibly encourage local governments to join forces. The objective of the proposed strategy would be, for each municipality, to:

- Identify long-term needs (based on population and economic development forecast) and source of water supply
- Identify investment needs for rehabilitation, replacement or extension of the water and sewerage facilities and their costs.
- Explore options for mutual investment and joint action with neighbouring communities. The proposed options could be prioritised when they align with the national water strategy and financial strategy.

This work would help to update and review the needs defined in local development plans, and conduct a proper consolidation of investment needs at the national level in cooperation with the ECA and Ministry of Finance.

3.3. SWOT-analysis for the WSS sector of Estonia

One of the objectives of the Issues paper was to provide an assessment of the centralised WSS in Estonia. The assessment is focused on topics, which form a basis for the consolidation reform; namely, effective legal and regulatory framework, state's role in policy formation and implementation.

The results of the SWOT-analysis are presented in the table below.

Table 3.1. SWOT-analysis for the WSS sector of Estonia

Internal factors		External factors	
Strengths	Weaknesses	opportunities	Threats
Implemented a massive investment programme over the past two decades High level of compliance with the Drinking Water Directive (DWD) Until now, only slight rise in financial pressure on consumers even in case of significant tariff increase Experience of WSS companies to work with EC and IFIs funding requirements Proper public engagement to decision-making process, active sectoral Association	No incentive for operational efficiency Issues with the accountability of municipalities and water companies Lack of reinvestment component in tariff formula. Capital is not amortized adequately Lack of own funds and external financing for retrofits Low salary rates in water companies, high employee turnover rate, low motivation of the personnel (particularly in smaller municipalities) Lack of qualified human resources (including brain drain due to low salaries and migration of population) Insufficient deployment of energy efficiency equipment and technologies High rate of extra water used and lost in the networks Loss-making activity, unsatisfactory financial state of enterprises, poor liquidity Insufficient public information and outreach. This contributes to a negative image of the sectoral enterprises and the consolidation reform	Opportunities to reap the benefits of economies of scale and scope Further compliance with the EU water Directives Access to the EU funds to facilitate new investments Improvement of the legal and regulatory framework (incl. secondary legislation) Improved efficiency of the state regulation over the WSS companies' operation Improved state policy in WSS and relevant state regulation system Available potential to increase the role of domestic finance and IFIs' interest in financing WSS projects Introduction of new water and waste water treatment technologies Transition to the incentive-based regulation of water tariffs Introduction and operation of a sectoral Information and analytical system (incl. benchmarking and monitoring systems)	Lack support of the reform among sector stakeholders Unpredictable revenues, caused by COVID-19 Need for strengthening the strategic vision of sector's development Risk of inefficiency of national sectoral development programmes due to disconnect with local development plans Lack of capacity of local authorities to develop sectoral programmes (e.g. as a result they are developed by utilities) Efficiency of state regulation needs strengthening Limited willingness to pay higher tariffs by the population

Annex 3.A. Benefits of regionalisation of WSS services: selected cases

Chile – Benchmarking the performance of water utilities

Chile is well regarded both for its water sector performance and its well-designed social services. Water sector reform started in the 1970s, leading to regionalisation and gradual tariff increases.

A highlight of this process was establishment of an independent economic regulator *Superintendencia de Servicios Sanitarioss* (SSIS). In addition, four principles of tariff setting were set: non-discrimination, cost recovery, economic efficiency and encouraging conservation. The small SSIS developed a model company against which the 14 utilities operating in Chile could be compared. When setting the tariffs, the future efficiency improvement measures of the utilities were factored in. Under SSIS, leakage levels and cost recovery improved. Still, investment remained too small. SSIS initially failed to have leverage on some of the larger inefficient utilities.

These issues were resolved by:

- granting SSIS more power and independence, including funding through a levy on water utilities
- attracting finance for infrastructure through equity sales, concession contracts and involving the private sector, raising USD 1 bln that was subsequently wholly invested in infrastructure.

Among its main activities, SSIS monitors performance of both the sector and concession contracts.

Chile has a lot to share as regards options to cope with lack of affordability of water tariffs. From a social perspective, having no access to water is more costly than access at cost recovery tariff levels. Social measures have concentrated on funding extension or financing the costs of increased access, half of which went to the poor.

All consumers are billed the same full rate for the metered amount of water consumed. Means- tested poor customers, however, can bring bills to the municipality. The municipality pays part of the bill, provided the beneficiary pays the other part. In this way, municipalities cover on average 6% of turnover of water utilities.

There can be little debate about the success of Chile in water sector reform. It is not clear, however, to what extent others can achieve the same results. Chile has a long tradition of effective administration and an acceptance of a contractual approach in public sector management. As a result, it has been able to provide targeted support to the poor and raise capital, mostly for wastewater treatment investment. The case of Chile illustrates that economic regulation needs periodic recalibration with policy targets, which is a task for the government at large.

Flanders – on social water tariffs

The Flanders region of Belgium has a most advanced system of setting (social) water tariffs. First, there is only a small fixed fee for costs related to customers such as metering and billing. Overall, it is less than 10% of the bill. The volumetric part of the bill is charged either as "normal" or as "social". The normal tariff structure is a straightforward Increasing Block Tariff (IBT), but based on the household size rather than on fixed brackets (blocks). In this way, larger households pay a similar price per cubic metre as small households, provided they are in the same tariff group and have a similar per capita consumption.

The social tariff is zero for the first 15 m³ per person per year or 41 lcd (litre per person per day). Above that threshold, the social tariff is lower than the normal tariff. Figures below illustrate the concept. The built-in cross subsidy between smaller and larger units of consumption ensures the marginal price of water is the most expensive for rich and poor alike. In this way, there is an incentive to reduce consumption.

Annex Figure 3.A.1. Composition of annual water costs for various household sizes and consumption levels, 2017

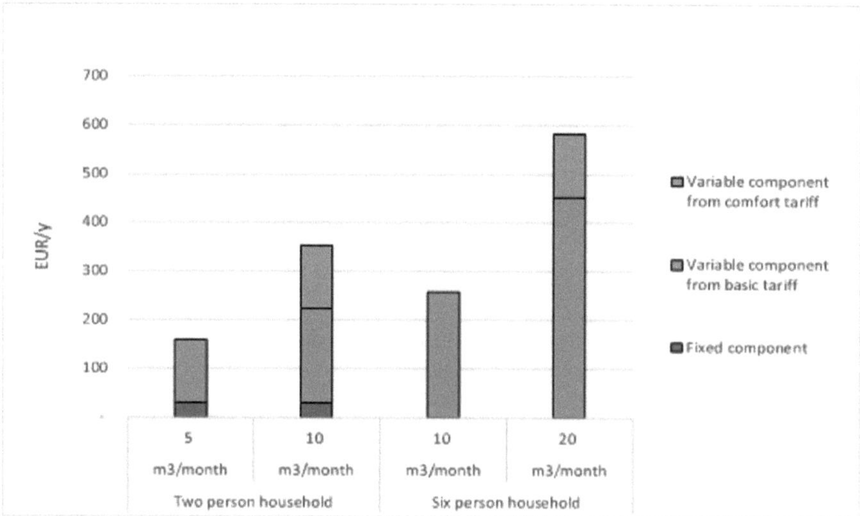

Source: https://www.farys.be/nl/watertarieven

Annex Figure 3.A.2. City of Ghent:2018 total household bill equivalent costs per m3 for different household sizes

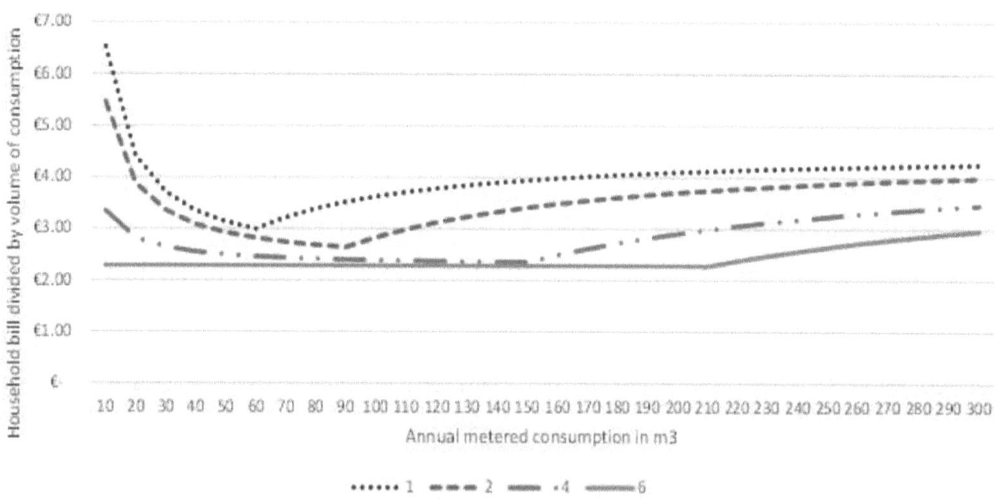

Source: https://www.farys.be/nl/watertarieven

The concept is appealing. It combines social, environmental and financial benefits.

Flanders illustrates an advanced social system carried out through the tariff. The regulator exercises a strong influence on social policy, stipulating the thresholds for the IBT and the relative tariff differential. There are two blocs (below and above 30 m³ per household member per year). The tariff in the first bloc shall be half that of the second one. The regulator also stipulates the size and conditions of the social tariffs, presently at one-fifth of the normal fixed and variable tariff elements.

The dual block tariff, however, puts an administrative burden on the utilities. To charge appropriately, utilities have to maintain records on inhabitants per household. Expenditure for WSS is in the order of 1-2% of household income i.e. quite affordable by international standards. It is difficult to assess how well the system maintains affordability for the poor. The per capita delineation of the tariff blocs addresses the most pressing argument against IBTs. But little is known on how well the blocs and tariffs perform in maintaining affordability in relation to, for instance, single volumetric tariffs. Brackets are not adjusted in light of updated, more recent poverty statistics.

This type of redistribution can only take place within the service area. Small consumers and social cases are subsidised by other customers within the service area. Three factors are necessary for this type of social measure to function optimally:

- The average tariffs should be similar among the service areas in the region
- The distribution of income within the service areas should be similar.
- Per capita income across the service areas should be similar.

Deviations on these conditions bring regional distortions to distribution of benefits that are difficult to quantify. Assuming the conditions have been sufficiently met in Flanders, one can still ask whether the social benefit of increased affordability of services outweighs the costs of the increased administrative burden for utilities.

The Netherlands – achieving economies of scale and scope

In the mid-1970s, the Netherlands considered that its municipal water works lacked *economies of scale and scope* to deliver efficient services in the future. The 1975 Water Law kicked-started a regionalisation process that resulted in the ten current suppliers of drinking water. They are incorporated public entities that are 100% owned by municipalities and provinces.

Wastewater collection has remained a municipal responsibility. It is financed through a special municipal tax. Responsibility for wastewater treatment and water management rests with the democratically elected water boards. Water boards are legal entities, the first one of which was established in 1255. The 23 water boards operate on a regional scale.

Historically, the rationale behind regionalisation has been the need for efficient operations. Regionalisation, however, has supported affordability for the less densely populated areas

If all agglomerations up to 1 000 population equivalent (PE) charged based on cost recovery, then tariff rates in rural areas would need to be three times higher than those in large urban conglomerations. Income of rural households is typically smaller. Regionalisation of operations and harmonisation of tariffs across each expanded service helped share this burden. High-income/low WSS unit cost consumers cross-subsidise the lower-income/high WSS costs rural population through the harmonised tariff.

Municipalities collect the following:

- The wastewater collection charge to cover municipal sewerage costs. The charge can be based on drinking water consumed, property value or the number of inhabitants.
- The wastewater treatment charges and pollution charges on behalf of the water boards. The charge is not based on metered water consumption, but on three categories: single person households, two person households and households with three or more persons.

- The water system charges on buildings and land, also on behalf of the water boards, for water resource management. It is charged on the main occupant of the house or apartment (or land), as a fraction of property value (or as fee per habitant).

These charges mostly provide a fixed component to the WSS- related expenditure and may be seen as regressive.

Municipalities in the Netherlands provide for a WSS-related social measure through a partial or full exemption of (exclusively) their poorer citizens. Exemption of only fixed elements of the WSS-related bills leaves intact the incentives to save drinking water.

The Dutch system of WSS provision is complex and appears fragmented. Because of the long tradition and a strong culture of co-ordination among authorities, it does provide for a high level of service and reliability. The regionalisation of services has enabled an automatic cross-subsidy mechanism that would otherwise have been impossible to set up. In addition, a decentralised targeted WSS-related social assistance is in place through the exemption of fixed charges on poor citizens.

Notes

[1] Note that tariffs for services below 2,000 pe are set by local governments.

[2] A threshold of 3-4% is internationally used as a reference, although its source is unclear and it comes with a number of caveats.

4 Concept note on consolidation options

While the Estonian government is finalising a piece of legislation to set the direction for the future of water supply and sanitation services, the concept note conveys the main messages that derive from the on-going policy dialogue. The emphasis is on the broad options for consolidation (moving away from merger as the only way forward) and the incentives to support a voluntary process.

4.1. Background

The Ministry of the Environment of Estonia jointly with other governmental authorities (the Ministry of Finance, the Minister of Public Administration), the European Commission – DG Reform, and the OECD are partnering to enhance the sustainability of water supply and sanitation services in Estonia. The Project will support the preparation of a roadmap for the consolidation of the water utility sector, a requisite for a sustainable and socially acceptable financing strategy and a broader water sector reform in Estonia.

This chapter provides a concept note that considers potential options for the consolidation of WSS services in Estonia, and sets out a number of key features of a proposed overall approach. More detailed and technical issues concerning potential changes to the legal framework, and to tariff setting and the further use of performance incentives, are considered in Chapter 5.

The development of the approach set out below – which proposes that consolidation be viewed and promoted as a process that could take a range of different forms that can evolve over time – was informed in important respects by an international workshop, which featured a wide range of relevant international participation and experience. Among other things, this experience highlighted the extent to which there are a range of different ways in which benefits from coordination can be achieved, and that different forms of consolidation can coexist within a country in ways that can reflect marked differences in the nature of the challenges that are faced (given, for example, differences in the density of the population that WSS services are intended to serve in different areas). This is identified below as highly relevant to the development of an approach to consolidation, given in particular the range of different circumstances faced within Estonia, and the policy focus on achieving consolidation on a voluntary basis.

The first section makes the case for consolidation, with the scope it offers for enhancing potential gains, both in terms operational efficiency and efficiency in development and investment plans. It also explains why now is the right time to accelerate progress towards consolidation. The second section presents incentives for consolidation, which can support a bottom-up, voluntary process in Estonia. The section explores implications for practical policy approaches to consolidation in an Estonian context.

4.2. Conceptual framework for the reform of consolidation

This section begins by recapping on the case for WSS reform, highlighting in particular some of the different ways in which consolidation matters in terms of meeting the efficiency and associated affordability challenges that lie ahead. The distinction is then drawn between focusing on a specific model of consolidation based on geographical agglomeration – where well-functioning companies gradually absorb smaller, more fragile ones over time – and the adoption of a broader and more open perspective that could incorporate a range of different models and forms of consolidation that would include the geographical merging of companies, but could also include different forms of joint operation that do not require a merger, and may be linked to the shared provision of a set of specific functions. In principle, consolidation benefits could be achieved through either of these routes, and international experience shows that a range of different structures can be used.

This section ends by highlighting that when considering the trajectory that is likely to be best suited to – and most feasible in – the Estonian WSS sector, the commitment to consolidation on a voluntary basis is a key factor. In particular, this implies that careful attention should be given to the extent to which different trajectories can be expected to be compatible with the incentives that different companies and their municipality owners may face. The next section goes on to consider these incentive issues in more detail and to highlight the extent to which incentive effects might frustrate the effectiveness of a voluntary approach that is focused only on a regional agglomeration model. This confirms that a flexible approach that encompasses different modes of consolidation might a pragmatic and effective way forward.

4.2.1. The case for reform and scope for benefits from consolidation

As was noted in Chapter 2, there is a significant level of agreement among stakeholders that the current arrangements for WSS provision in Estonia are not sustainable. There has been substantial investment in WSS infrastructure in Estonia since its accession to the European Union, with this providing a wide range of benefits in terms of service quality and environmental protection. However, the delivery of these improvements has relied heavily on EU funding, which has accounted for around half of Estonia's WSS total expenditure - and around 85% of capital expenditure - in recent years.[1] The European Commission has indicated that financial support for the sector will be gradually phased out, and the Estonian Ministry of Finance has confirmed that domestic public finance will not provide a substitute source of funding. Given this, it will be necessary for a financially sustainable and socially acceptable financing model to be developed, based on prevailing – and expectations of future - WSS tariff revenues.

Substantial further investment will be required over time both to maintain (and where relevant replace) existing assets (including those assets that were funded using EU grants), and to enhance treatment processes where needed in order to meet current and future compliance obligations. This highlights the potential for significant tensions to arise over time related to the affordability and acceptability of associated WSS bill increases. Also, while the implications of the Covid pandemic on demographic changes remains unclear, pre-pandemic forecasts identified trends that would exacerbate the financial challenges to be faced, particularly in those areas of Estonia where a substantial population decline had been forecast.

The likely scale and nature of future investment requirements raises major concerns over the financial and technical capacity of the WSS sector – in its current form – to develop and deliver appropriate programmes of work in efficient ways. These concerns have underpinned the emphasis that has been put on the benefits that could be achieved through greater consolidation within the sector. The economic characteristics of the sector (in particular, the scope for achieving economies of scale and density in the undertaking of relevant activities), and the fact that the WSS sector in Estonia is still highly fragmented (in 2018, there were 177 water companies operating in Estonia), strongly suggests that there may be scope to deliver substantial benefits through consolidation. This can be important for both:

- The efficient delivery of services and planned investments; and,
- The efficient identification and planning of future service and investment requirements.

The efficient delivery of services and planned investments

There are a range of ways in which consolidation may provide opportunities to improve the efficiency with which services and planned investments are delivered, including potentially through:

- More efficient labour resourcing for, and scheduling and financing of, planned work such as enhancement projects (for example, the provision of new treatment technologies), asset refurbishments/replacements, and routine monitoring, repair and maintenance activities. Consolidation may allow for the smoothing over time of (through the use of a more coordinated approach across areas), and enhanced technical capabilities in relation to, what might otherwise by 'lumpier' requirements that are more difficult to finance and manage.
- More efficient approaches to managing unplanned/reactive work, such as may be required to address pipe bursts, sewer collapses, and other relevant incidents. The efficiency of these types of activities can have a significant bearing on a number of dimensions of performance, such as leakage, for example, by improving response times and capabilities.
- More efficient procurement of, and management of the cost risks associated with, inputs such as energy and chemicals.
- More efficient provision of customer-facing, administrative and support activities, where scale can offer considerable opportunities for both cost savings (e.g. through reduced duplication) and

quality improvements (e.g. through the introduction of improved information provision processes).

The efficient identification and planning of future service and investment requirements

The above can be understood as largely taking service provision requirements and investment plans as given, and focuses attention on some potential ways in which the efficiency of delivering those requirements might be enhanced through consolidation. However, the likely scale and nature of the future WSS investment requirements in Estonia makes it critical also to consider efficiency in relation to the identification and planning of future requirements. Importantly, there are likely to be different ways in which policy objectives associated with environmental requirements and service quality/access targets could potentially be tackled, and the decisions over which approaches are selected can be expected to have long-term implications for the cost, quality, and/or environmental consequences of service provision.

Determining the appropriate approach to the development and use of tertiary treatment processes – such as those used to reduce phosphorus concentrations in wastewater discharges – may be particularly challenging. Tertiary treatment can be very costly to introduce, and the 'cost per population equivalent' of introducing such processes can increase steeply as the scale of treatment plant falls and the stringency of discharge consent requirements is tightened.[2] Given this, decisions related to the introduction of such processes can have a particularly marked bearing on costs in areas which are less densely populated. Also, the adoption of a given approach may have the effect of 'locking-in' a service provision model – and the funding implications associated with it - for many years, including, for example, because of the ongoing chemicals procurement costs that will be associated with some treatment approaches.

Consolidation (of one form or another) may provide opportunities for significant efficiency benefits in relation to the identification and planning of appropriate responses to environmental requirements, including because:

- There may be significant benefits associated with the assessment of options in more coordinated ways across broader geographic areas.
- The effectiveness of the options identification and appraisal process may be heavily dependent on the availability of appropriate technical expertise, and this can be much more difficult to provide for at smaller scale (that is, there can be significant economies of scale in the provision of relevant technical expertise).

These factors could have a substantial bearing on the efficiency of the approaches adopted in multiple ways. For example, beneficial opportunities to increase scale may be identified, in a context where (as was noted above) unit costs can fall steeply as plant size increases (such that tertiary treatment may be introduced at one larger plant, rather than separately at two or more other plants, following appropriate network development). Alternative treatment approaches – such as those which use 'natural capital' solutions - may be identified as preferred given estimates of 'whole-life' costs and other sustainability considerations. In principle, there may be opportunities to explore whether the introduction of costly 'end-of-pipe' treatment options can be avoided (particularly at smaller sites) by delivering equivalent environmental outcomes in other ways. We note that it is common, in a range of jurisdiction, for WSS companies to seek to contract with farmers in order to get them to adopt practices which result in reduced concentrations of potentially harmful substances in water courses.[3] This kind of catchment management approach can, in some circumstances, provide substantially less costly way of improving environmental outcomes than the introduction of complex tertiary treatment processes.[4] We understand that, in relation to existing HELCOM requirements, there would not be scope to adopt this type of approach, and indeed that the types of tertiary treatment that have had to be introduced in order to meet those existing have not thus far given rise to disproportionate cost implications for smaller treatment facilities. We note, though, that the exploration of (and the flexibility to pursue) alternative approaches is likely to merit careful attention in the event that the introduction of more stringent tertiary treatment requirements that could apply to smaller facilities comes under consideration.

There may also be significant benefits from adopting a broader (more consolidated) geographic perspective when other policy objectives are being considered. For example, the costs of increasing access to public WSS systems can be expected to differ markedly between areas, including - importantly - because of population density considerations. This may also point to there being particular benefit in effective options identification and development processes being undertaken when efforts are being made to achieve relevant policy objectives in areas with relatively low population density. That is, 'traditional' approaches (such a network extension) may prove very high cost on a per customer basis, and thus alternative approaches – including 'non-physical' network approaches – may merit careful attention. This could include focusing attention in relation to wastewater services in some sparsely populated areas on the effectiveness of the collection and treatment processes associated with Home Sewage Treatment Systems.[5]

Affordability, acceptability and deferral risks

As was highlighted above, the bill impacts associated with appropriately addressing future capital maintenance and enhancement requirements may be considerable. The scale of these likely bill impacts will affect the affordability and acceptability challenges that could be expected to be faced if seeking to proceed with such plans. Given this, there is a material risk that appropriate investments may be deferred if the bill impacts are viewed as 'too great'. This kind of deferral of investment might follow an explicit decision, based on an assessment of impacts, and consideration of relevant priorities. Deferral, though, could also emerge more passively, through understandable localised efforts to avoid, or at least limit the size of, bill increases (which may involve giving relatively limited attention to plans that could – if acted on – result in significant upward pressure).

The broader point here is that future tensions associated with bill affordability and acceptability will have to be addressed one way or another. If it becomes viewed as not feasible to increase charges sufficiently to fund investments that have otherwise been identified as necessary/appropriate, and if external sources of funding (such as EU or central government grants) are no longer available, then some scaling down of investment costs will be required. Addressing the efficiency issues highlighted in the above sections can be critical in this context, as it can help reduce investment costs through efficiency improvements (i.e. doing more 'now' for a given bill impact). The alternative in such circumstances is to scale back investment costs by cutting back on scope through deferral (i.e. doing less 'now' and leaving more for 'later').

There is typically some flexibility available in terms of the scheduling of capital maintenance over time and (subject to legal requirements to which they may relate) the timetable for delivering enhancements. This can provide some degree of 'slack' such that a strategy of deferral may have little impact on efficiency considerations for a period. Also, given the extent of recent asset installations in Estonia under the EU funding arrangements, a period of slack is in any case to be expected ahead of some growth in the need for more significant capital maintenance. However, extended periods of deferral can themselves potentially generate additional problems and efficiency challenges.

In some circumstances, this may manifest itself through increased incidents of asset failure, which may then be costly to address. However, because of the long-lived nature of many WSS assets, there can be a significant time lag between significant asset degradation occurring and failure incidents arising. While this time lag can provide significant benefits in terms of the continuity of service provision in the short to medium term, it can also mean that potentially significant asset degradation can have occurred in a way that may be relatively non-visible.

These considerations may raise only limited concerns when maintenance is viewed on an asset-by-asset basis. However, broader concerns typically relate to the potential for such deferral decisions to result in a capital maintenance 'backlog' that it is then not feasible or economic to address in a timely manner. A deferral approach can therefore result in significant problems being stored up for future years in inefficient ways, as instead of adopting a relatively 'smoothed' approach to the management and delivery of maintenance requirements over time (and across the relevant asset portfolio), it may result in clusters of lumpy requirements that may then be significantly more difficult to address, both in terms of cost and availability of resources and capabilities. Given this, addressing efficiency issues of the kind highlighted in the above sections can be viewed as likely to be critical both in order to try to help address bill affordability and acceptability issues, and – in doing so – to help limit the extent to which deferral tendencies might generate additional problems to be addressed in future years.

A related point is that it would be inappropriate to delay efforts to enhance efficiency in planning future investments and delivery of services until more problems occur. The time lag between deferred decisions (non-action today) and more serious decay of infrastructures and services quality is the time when reform should take place. It provides some room for manoeuvre to design and implement a strategically planned and consulted approach.

4.2.2. Consolidation options and their relevance for Estonian WSS provision

When considering the potential consolidation trajectories that the Estonian WSS sector could take, it seems helpful to distinguish between the following two perspectives:

- A trajectory focused on a particular model of consolidation: the agglomeration of companies on a geographical basis, where well-functioning companies gradually absorb smaller, more fragile ones; and,
- A broader, more open trajectory that could include some consolidation through regional agglomeration, but that could also include a range of different forms of joint operation that do not require a merger, and may be linked to the shared provision of a set of specific functions.

In principle, consolidation benefits could be achieved through either of these routes, but international experience shows that a range of different structures can be used to seek to secure consolidation benefits and thus supports the adoption of the second, broader and more open trajectory. For instance, as mentioned in Chapter 2, not all functions need to be operated at the same scale: water supply could be operated at a different scale than sanitation; investment planning and procurement could be managed at a different scale than consumer relations and billing. Some competences could be available in regional centres, to support smaller utilities. Specific trajectories could be considered for rural areas, which differ from urban ones. As regards managing localised services (including individual sanitation), several options could be considered, from merging, to coordinating local service provision through a public service; such a public service can cover a wide and diverse territory, and could in some circumstances focus on localised sanitation only (as is the case, for example, in France where local SPANC operate and service septic tanks in rural areas).[6] These varied options (and more) deserve attention, as for their relevance and feasibility in the Estonian context.

A key feature of the WSS reform process in Estonia, however, is the commitment to consolidation on a voluntary basis. This implies that careful attention should be given to the extent to which different trajectories can be expected to be compatible with the incentives that different companies and their municipality owners may face. The section below considers these incentive issues in more detail and highlights the extent to which incentive effects might frustrate the achievement of a trajectory focused on the agglomeration of companies on a geographical basis (i.e. the first option identified above), given the commitment consolidation occurring on a voluntary basis. More generally, the consideration of potential incentives – and importantly, disincentives – to consolidation, suggests that there may be significant benefit in designing the policy framework with a broader, more open consolidation trajectory in mind (i.e. in line with the second option identified above). Some international examples that look to provide particularly relevant and helpful reference points are highlighted.

4.3. Incentives for consolidation

Incentives for consolidation are particularly important to consider in the Estonian WSS context given the focus on seeking to achieve desirable consolidation benefits through voluntary processes. Some more specific questions concerning how the tariff setting arrangements, and other aspects of the regulatory framework, can affect incentives to seek to achieve efficiency benefits through consolidation are considered in Chapter 5. However, it is helpful here to give some more high-level consideration to the question of why consolidation may not be considered desirable by individual companies and/or by their local government owners, as this can help inform thinking on the extent to which different consolidation models might be feasible and/or likely to emerge. In doing so, a distinction can be drawn between the following situations:

1. Where companies and/or their local government owners are unaware or unconvinced of the scope for efficiency benefits to be achieved through different forms of consolidation.
2. Where companies and/or their local government owners consider that there would be likely to be material efficiency benefits that could be achieved through some forms of consolidation, but have concerns over what the effects of seeking to achieve such benefits might be.

4.3.1. Awareness and acceptance of the scope for efficiency benefits

This can be viewed as having a number of different dimensions, including awareness and acceptance of:

- Current performance levels (in terms costs, service quality and environmental outcomes), and how they compare to others and to what might be achievable.
- Emerging performance challenges, including capital maintenance and enhancement requirements of the kind discussed above, and the cost and bill pressures that may be associated with meeting them.
- The scope for delivering improvements through different consolidation options.

There is likely to be significant benefit in seeking to improve awareness and acceptance in relation to each of these dimensions, particularly given the circumstances faced in Estonia, which include that:

- The availability of information on the performance of different WSS companies remains relatively limited, as does the use and publication of comparative assessments. As discussed further in Chapter 6, transparency measures – including the use of "traffic light" style summary tables focused on a relatively narrow set of key WSS KPIs that provide a publicly accessible reference point on relative and company performance - have often been used in other jurisdictions to highlight where performance is poor, and in doing so to motivate company (and owner) recognition of, and response to, this. As discussed further in Chapter 6, while there is an existing broader traffic light type system in Estonia that provides for public access to some WSS information that can be compared across municipalities,[7] there looks to be scope to provide much sharper reputational incentives through the use of more focused WSS KPI comparisons. This could include the assessment of performance both within and across different clusters of companies that recognised some of the key differences between the circumstances in which companies operate.[8] A process for developing such an approach is set out in Chapter 5, by reference to a Portuguese example.
- Potential future investment challenges may be viewed (explicitly or implicitly) as insufficient to merit particular attention, when considered alongside the range of more immediate challenges that small WSS companies can be expected to face. Also, given the role played by EU funding in previous years, it may be that the consideration of investment pressures has been viewed as something to be addressed and funded - where necessary - by others (in particular, central government and the EU). This raises a question of whether more clarity (and concreteness) could be provided in relation to what the future delivery obligations and associated investment

requirements of different companies can be expected to be, through the development and publication of regional and/or national strategic planning documents (of the kind used in a number of jurisdictions).

- The limited extent of Estonian WSS company consolidation to date means that there is a lack of clear Estonian examples that can be pointed to as providing evidence of, and a guide to, the sorts of gains that might be achievable. The relatively limited use and transparency of comparative performance management – noted above - is unhelpful in this context, as it can mean that there is a lack of a clear and readily accessible way of demonstrating when relative improvements have been achieved through consolidation. The question also arises as to how information on practical consolidation experiences can be best shared within the sector in order to try to assist other WSS companies and their owners when assessing consolidation options.

The above points may be particularly important in contexts where the senior management and owners of WSS companies may have limited available capacity to consider and attend to longer-term, strategic efficiency and consolidation questions of the kind raised above, given the pressing operational and financial issues that may be faced on a more day-to-day basis. As noted above, increasing the extent of the transparent development and provision of performance information, comparative assessments, strategic planning for the sector, and reports on practical consolidation experiences, can help make the case for greater levels of consolidation more compelling to WSS companies and their municipality owners.

4.3.2. Concerns over the potential for consolidation to have other unwanted effects

In principle, if the consolidation of two companies is expected to result in material efficiency benefits, then one might expect both of those companies to have an incentive to proceed with the consolidation, provided they both expect to be able to secure a reasonable portion of the overall benefit. However, a range of different factors can affect expectations with respect to the securing of future benefits, and thus incentives to proceed with beneficial consolidations.

The following factors look particularly important to consider in the Estonian WSS context:

- Ratchet effects.
- Cross-subsidy and related equity issues.
- The treatment of differences between the WSS charges that are applied by different companies.

Ratchet effects

Ratchet effects can arise because the regulatory conditions that a company faces are likely to be affected by new information that comes available. This can mean that there is a risk that – for a given company - the result of it engaging in successful efforts to deliver efficiency improvements may be a tougher operating environment than it would otherwise have faced. That is, having shown it can operate at lower cost, the extent to which it is allowed to recover costs through charges may be 'ratcheted down' by the regulator such that the company is no better off. It is widely recognised that this kind of ratcheting approach can undermine improvement incentives. The underlying issue here concerns the extent to which companies that take steps to deliver efficiency benefits should be allowed to share in those benefits (in order to give them an incentive to identify and deliver them in the first place).

A standard way of addressing this issue is through the use of some form of 'regulatory lag', such that charges are only fully adjusted to reflect efficiency savings periodically, with the company able to benefit to some extent from lower costs ahead of that adjustment point. A common approach is for costs to be re-assessed, and prices re-determined, at defined intervals (often every five years), with this providing scope for companies to benefit from savings they are able to make in the period between re-determinations.[9] The case for adopting this kind of approach is considered further in Chapter 6.

Cross-subsidy and related equity issues

The above effectively assumed that the motivation for consolidation would be the achievement of efficiency benefits. However, the circumstances in some municipalities raise the question of whether the relevant WSS utility would be financially sustainable - on the basis of the charges paid by customers – even with the sorts of efficiency improvements that might be achievable through consolidation. Also, future demographic changes and changes to environmental requirements can be expected to exacerbate these kind of financial sustainability difficulties.

This raises the prospect of larger, more financially secure utilities being deterred from consolidating with smaller utilities that face serious financial sustainability pressures, because such consolidation may end up with them having to cross-subsidise the smaller companies. There may be some circumstances where that does not raise a material barrier to consolidation. In particular:

- If the financial sustainability issues are relatively modest, then the scope for efficiency benefits may be sufficient to offset them.
- There may be other social, reputational and strategic factors that influence the appetite that larger utilities have for consolidation. For example, a company may be willing to bear some degree of cross-subsidy as part of the development of its regional coverage and reputation.

More generally, however, concerns over the sustainability of the funding model of some smaller companies would be expected to act as a material deterrent to at least some forms of consolidation (e.g. the development of integrated regional companies that take on responsibility for serving the smaller company's area). That is, affordability concerns may be sufficiently acute as to undermine the scope for customer bills to fund investment requirements over time (alongside operating expenditure requirements), and this may make the current funding model unsustainable for the company that currently provides WSS services. In such circumstances, it may be necessary to consider social policy tools to support the affordability of water charges, and there may be little prospect of consolidation with other companies being viewed as a feasible option in the absence of commitments related to such support.

Customer charges and the funding of wider environmental benefits

A common tension that arises in the consideration of WSS costs relates to the difference between:

1. The cost of providing the water and wastewater services to the relevant set of customers; and,
2. The costs the relevant water company faces in order to meet applicable environmental requirements.

The equity issues related to (1) can be viewed as relatively straightforward. The long-lived nature of relevant investments can inevitably raise some questions related to intergenerational equity (i.e. how should costs be shared between current and future customers). Beyond this, though, the WSS customers that receive services from a given company can be readily identified (for the most part), and are typically expected to bear the associated service provision costs (subject to acute affordability issues of the kind discussed below).

Equity issues can become more complicated, though, when the costs of meeting environmental requirements are being considered. A common approach is to simply treat any costs associated with meeting environmental requirements as though they are WSS service provision costs, and therefore should straightforwardly be viewed as to be borne by the relevant set of WSS customers. In some circumstances, however, this may not result in a close alignment between those being asked to pay the costs of meeting the relevant environmental requirements, and those who benefit from the requirements being met. That is, there may be significant positive externality effects.

The extent of geographic consolidation can be highly relevant in this context, as it can affect how closely aligned the group that fund specific environmental improvements is with the group that benefits from them. For example, wastewater treatment plants can face stringent and very costly phosphorus removal requirements that relate to concerns over nutrient levels in receiving waters. It could be viewed that these requirements have widespread benefits across the population, including benefits associated with the meeting of Estonian government commitments in relation to the Baltic Sea. If there was a small number of large regional WSS companies in Estonia, then it may be that there would be little practical difference between who bears the costs of, and who benefits from, phosphorus removal (relevant costs would be shared across a broad range of customers from more urban and more rural localities). However, the fragmented nature of WSS service provision in Estonia may mean that there is a risk of material disparities emerging between the set of customers who bear the costs of, and those who benefit from, some environmental protection measures provided by WSS companies.

The use of EU funds to support environmental improvements in recent years means that this potential source of tension will have been of limited relevance, as – to a large extent – the costs of meeting environmental requirements were not funded by the customers of the particular WSS companies to which those requirements applied. However, as those EU funded assets need to be maintained and replaced, and as other environmental requirements stand to be addressed, this source of tension can be expected to become more important over time.

In practice, the customers of a given company can be expected to both fund some environmental improvements that benefit others, and benefit from some environmental improvements that are funded by other customers (for example, as those other improvements may contribute to the achievement of national commitments, and in doing so confer widely dispersed benefits). The question arises as to whether the fragmented nature of the sector leaves some customers particularly exposed to funding wider benefits, and if that materially affects the financial sustainability of the relevant company.

In terms of consolidation incentives, the key point here is that which was made above: there may be a significant disincentive to agglomerating with a company that is not financially sustainable because doing so may tend to increase the costs to existing customers in order to provide for some degree of cross-subsidy. While such a cross-subsidy may be viewed a reasonable and appropriate from a policy perspective, the question here concerns whether companies (and their municipality owners) would voluntarily seek to cross-subsidise others through an agglomeration process. As is discussed further below, this looks to make it particularly important that a broad perspective is adopted when considering possible consolidation options, because there are a range of approaches that fall short of regional agglomeration through merger in which consolidation benefits can be achieved without requiring this kind of cross-subsidy issue – and the disincentive effects it can bring – to arise.

4.4. Implications for policy approaches to consolidation

The above discussion considered some different reasons why some WSS utilities might be viewed as not financially sustainable (on a forward-looking basis), and described why this may act as a significant deterrent to some forms of consolidation, and in particular to the voluntary formation of broader regional companies. In principle, efforts could be made to address the different factors underpinning the weak financial position that some WSS companies will face. This could include, for example, social policy efforts to support customers that would face acute affordability issues, and/or efforts to provide an external injection of additional funding to address circumstances where customers of a given WSS company have been identified as particularly exposed to funding wider environmental benefits.

Such approaches (if successfully applied) could potentially do much to lessen disincentives to the voluntary formation of broader regional companies that might otherwise apply. However, this would be likely to require considerable policy effort being expended in relation to what may be a relatively large number of small WSS company areas, and the case for prioritising the development of such approaches looks questionable. In particular, one might see the undertaking of the types of detailed assessments and reconfigurations referred to above, as being something that forms part of, and should result from, the consolidation process, rather than something to be undertaken separately and ahead of that process as a preparatory step.

It is important to emphasise that the incentive challenges highlighted above can be expected to have particularly marked implications for voluntary incentives to develop integrated regional companies. Given this, the above points tend to strongly support the view that it would be appropriate to adopt a policy approach aimed at encouraging a broader range of consolidation models, which includes – but is not limited to - the creation of regional companies. The following two examples of French companies look particularly relevant to consider, in particular to bring benefits of consolidation to smaller municipalities:

- **SDEA**: provides an example of how local control over tariff decisions can be retained, while a broad spectrum of WSS activities could be effectively contracted out through a partnership arrangement to secure benefits associated with available economies of scale. Forms of consolidation within this broad approach can differ in a range of ways, including in terms of the scope and depth of service provision activities that are covered: e.g. joint provision of various operational activities vs the pooling of investment planning, the awarding of works contracts, and of financial capacities.[10]
- **SPANC**: a public service company with responsibilities related to equipment, maintenance and functioning of non-connected wastewater treatment systems: sanitation facilities ensuring the collection, transport, treatment and disposal of all domestic wastewater (except rainwater) from buildings not connected to a public wastewater collection network. SPANC provides an example of how the development of a non-fixed network of responsibilities and collection arrangements can provide an effective alternative to costly wastewater network provision in relatively sparsely populated areas, while providing for appropriate environmental protection.[11]

Under any scenario, the points raised above apply: awareness raising via information sharing and nudging can go a long way in making the case for change. It can take the form of strategic planning for the sector (a role for the Ministry of Environment), reporting on practical consolidation experience (this could be arranged by the association of water utilities), and sharing information on individual and relative performance of service providers.

Notes

[1] Based on data for 2011-15. See Figure 2.10 in OECD (2020), *Financing Water Supply, Sanitation and Flood Protection: Challenges in EU Member States and Policy Options*, OECD Studies on Water, OECD Publishing, Paris, https://doi.org/10.1787/6893cdac-en

[2] For an illustration of this, see Figure 15 (p70) in: https://assets.publishing.service.gov.uk/media/5eda1e5ee90e071b734d2ca7/Northumbrian_Water_Reply_to_Ofwat_response_27.05.2020_NON-CONFIDENTIAL.pdf

[3] OECD (2015), *Water and Cities: Ensuring Sustainable Futures*, OECD Studies on Water, OECD Publishing, Paris, https://doi.org/10.1787/9789264230149-en.

[4] Ibid. See also OECD (2020), *Nature-based solutions for adapting to water-related climate risks*, OECD Environment Policy Papers, No. 21, OECD Publishing, Paris, https://doi.org/10.1787/2257873d-en.

[5] See the comments below on the French public service SPANC.

[6] SPANC is discussed further in a later section.

[7] Kohalikud omavalitsused | Ministry of Finance

[8] Such that, for example, the performance of companies that operate at a similar scale and density could be ranked against each other.

[9] More sophisticated 'rolling' incentive mechanisms have also been used to try address concerns over the dampening of incentives for efficiency improvements as the next re-determination point approaches.

[10] See, for example: https://www.slideshare.net/OECD_ENV/joint-workshop-on-enhancing-efficiency-and-sustainability-of-water-supply-and-sanitation-presentation-joseph-hermal-249807561

[11] See, for example: https://www.slideshare.net/OECD_ENV/joint-workshop-on-enhancing-efficiency-and-sustainability-of-water-supply-and-sanitation-presentation-benot-fribourgblanc

5 Report on how to adjust current legal provisions and the regulatory framework

This Chapter provides a legal assessment and opinion of adjustments to the Estonian legal framework in Estonia, which might be required to foster consolidation of water utilities. It was prepared to analyse and give an overview of regulatory provisions to support cooperation between municipalities in the WSS sector of Estonia.

5.1. Background

The Ministry of the Environment of Estonia jointly with other governmental authorities (the Ministry of Finance, the Minister of Public Administration), the European Commission – DG Reform, and the OECD are partnering to enhance the sustainability of water supply and sanitation services in Estonia. The Project will support the preparation of a roadmap for the consolidation of the water utility sector, a requisite for a sustainable and socially acceptable financing strategy and a broader water sector reform in Estonia.

This Chapter provides a legal assessment and opinion of adjustments to the Estonian legal framework in Estonia, which might be required to foster consolidation of water utilities. It was prepared to analyse and give an overview of regulatory provisions to support cooperation between municipalities in the WSS sector of Estonia.

In case of using associations as cooperation vehicles, the following is considered:

- Governance arrangements: how voting rights are allocated among municipalities;
- Conditions required for joining and withdrawing from the association;
- Regime of assets: ownership of assets created under the association and liquidation of an association.

In case of delegation of WSS services provision to a regional service provider the following issues will be described:

- Influence over investment planning and finance;
- How are tariffs set and adjusted across municipalities;
- Monitoring of the performance of the regional service provider;
- Consequences of termination of services by the regional service provider.

As regards the overview of legal and regulatory adjustments to amend licensing of water operators in Estonia, the analysis is divided into three parts:

- Part A: Co-operation between municipalities and/or water undertakings;
- Part B: Delegation to regional service providers;
- Part C: Regulatory questions.

The Chapter was developed by Ain Kalme, Attorney-at-Law.

5.2. Conclusions

For provision of WSS services and investing into WSS assets an Estonian commercial association is to be preferred as the legal form of consolidation vehicle. Any municipality or water company may become a member of a commercial association created for the purpose of facilitating co-operation in the WSS sector. In the general meeting of commercial association each member has one vote. Upon withdrawal from such association, the return of the assets to the original holder (leaving member) may be carried through as prescribed in the articles of association or in the members' agreement.

As a way of consolidation, the municipalities and/or the water companies may share functions, or outsource a part of or whole provision of WSS services to a regional service provider. To facilitate the outsourcing, two main alternatives of asset regime shall be considered: (i) ownership of WSS assets remain with the municipality/water company commissioning the services, or (ii) ownership of WSS assets are transferred to the service provider (see below in chapter 7 for details).

Supervision over water undertakings on compliance with the requirements provided by the Public Water Supply and Sewerage Act and legislation established on the basis thereof is fragmented and is being exercised, pursuant to their competence, by the local municipality governments, the Competition Authority and the Environmental Board (see below chapter 8 for details).

Licencing requirement for water undertakings may be a feasible measure to ensure technological, financial and managerial capacities of water undertakings. Depending on the licencing conditions - such requirements may encourage consolidation within the WSS sector, where service providers with incompetent organization and weak economy are gradually directed to merge or otherwise consolidate their business with regional and/or otherwise sustainable water undertakings.

5.3. General Background

5.3.1. WSS services providers

In Estonia, the areas where population density and the related pollution load and groundwater protection require that wastewater is collected and treated in order to obtain environmental objectives, are designated as agglomerations (wastewater collection areas). In 2019, the number of agglomerations of more than 2,000 PE (population equivalent) in Estonia was 57, and the number of agglomerations of less than 2,000 PE was 463. According to an analysis commissioned by the Estonian Waterworks Association in 2018 (the "EWA Study"), the vast majority (88%) of the residents live in agglomerations of more than 2,000 PE and only 12% live in agglomerations of less than 2,000 PE.

Provision of WSS services is mainly regulated by Public Water Supply and Sewerage Act ("PWSSA"). As main operating model regulated under to the PWSSA, the WSS services is to be provided by a water undertaking (appointed by local government) who is a legal person, e.g., a limited liability company, a commercial association. The provision of WSS services by a water undertaking is subject to compulsory regulations in the PWSSA (and other legal acts), including approval of the water tariff by the Competition Authority.

If a public water supply and sewerage system is in the ownership of a private legal person, it may make a proposal to the local government to appoint the legal person as a water undertaking. If a public water supply and sewerage system is in the ownership or possession of a local government, the local government shall, independently or in cooperation with other local governments, organise a public procurement procedure for entry into a concession contract for provision of WSS services.

Approximately 80% of the total number of the providers of WSS services in agglomerations are legal persons. Most of the providers of WSS services operating in agglomerations of more than 2,000 PE are water companies owned by the local governments. Besides the water companies, WSS services in Estonia are also provided by the local municipality governments (municipal authority, utilities authority, rural or town/city office).

From the perspective of economic efficiency and sustainability, the current arrangements for WSS provision in Estonia are not sustainable. One of the measures to overcome such situation is further consolidation of water companies/WSS provision.

5.3.2. Voluntary consolidation

According to EWA Study, the representatives of larger, economically more well-off water companies do agree that a regional business would provide a solution for the Estonian WSS sector as a whole, but at the same time, no one has a direct interest in acquiring the small water companies who have facilities in poor condition and depreciated pipes in sparsely populated areas, since the parent company itself would not directly benefit from this. Rather, it is recognized that in this case the smaller rural area would be subsidised by the more densely populated area.

5.3.3. Tariffs

A water undertaking shall prepare an application to set prices for WSS services and submit it for approval to the Competition Authority before establishing the tariff to be charged from the clients.

According to PWSSA, the recommended principles for calculation of prices for WSS services shall be prepared and disclosed on Competition Authority's website. Under the mentioned principles and current practice of the Competition Authority, the regulated assets do not include assets purchased or constructed using state funds or European Union funds (aid).

The draft of new PWSSA (currently sent to the parliament to go through the legislative process to be passed) explicitly excludes such assets from the regulated assets, i.e. no depreciation costs (amortization) of such assets are allowed to be included in the tariff. There is an exception – some part of depreciation costs of such assets and reasonable return on capital may be included in the tariff, but only to allow a water undertaking to meet its obligations under loans taken for reinvestments (future maintenance) of such WSS infrastructure (to be evaluated by the Competition Authority in each tariff application procedure if needed).

5.4. Co-operation Between Municipalities and/or Water Undertakings

5.4.1. Association as a Vehicle for Co-Operation

As an option for facilitating co-operation in the WSS sector in Estonia, the OECD Secretariat wishes to explore the use of associations as cooperation vehicles. We hereby analyse and give an overview of regulatory provisions connected to associations.

There are two types of associations regulated in Estonia: (i) commercial associations and (ii) non-profit associations. The respective type of association is regulated by Commercial Associations Act ("CAA") and by Non-profit Associations Act.

Pursuant to the CAA a commercial association is a company the purpose of which is to support and promote the economic interests of its members through joint economic activity in which the members participate:

1. as consumers or users of other benefits;
2. as suppliers;
3. through work contribution;
4. through the using of services;
5. in any other similar manner.

A non-profit association is a voluntary association of persons the objective or main activity of which shall not be the earning of income from economic activity. The income of a non-profit association may be used only to achieve the objectives specified in its articles of association. A non-profit association shall not distribute profits among its members.

As the management and decision-making of both types of association are quite similar, there is an important difference with regard to transfer of membership: (i) in a commercial association a member may transfer the membership to another person who becomes a member of the association; (ii) in a non-profit association membership or right to exercise of voting rights of a member cannot be transferred.

Considering the possible activities of consolidation vehicle (provision of WSS services, investing into WSS assets, etc.) a commercial association is to be preferred as the legal form of an association.

Therefore, we focus on description of governance regulations and other rules applicable to a commercial association.

5.4.2. Commercial Association - Commercial Law and Governance Matters

In the below table please find an overview of the main legal aspects of a commercial association regulated by CAA.

Table 5.1. Selected legal aspects of commercial associations

Nr.	Issue	Regulation
1	Foundation	An association may be founded by at least two persons. A founder may be a natural person or a legal person. The association shall be entered into the Commercial Register.
2	Articles of association	The articles of association shall set out (not an exhaustive list): 1) the business name and registered office of the association; 2) the purpose of the association; 3) the size and procedure for payment of the contribution; 4) an amount which a member may pay to the association in addition to the contribution, or the procedure for determination of such amount; 5) the procedure for assigning additional duties to members; 6) the control bodies of the association, their competence and term of authority; 7) the beginning and end of the financial year of the association; 8) the procedure for the covering of loss; 9) the procedure for the distribution of assets upon dissolution of the association.
3	Membership	A legal person may become a member of an association.
4	Acceptance into membership	Acceptance of a new member is decided by the Management Board. Upon acceptance into the membership of an association, a member shall pay in contribution (a given amount in EUR, similar to a shareholding). A member may hold more than one contribution. The articles of association may prescribe that the contributions or other payments may be made by non-monetary payment (i.e. transfer of assets).
5	Transfer of membership	Membership may be transferred to another person.
6	Highest management body	General meeting of the members of an association.
7	Management board	Legal representative and day-to-day management body of an association is the management board (consisting of one or several persons).
8	Supervisory Board	An association shall have a supervisory board if the association has more than 200 members or the share capital is greater than 25,000 euros or if so prescribed by the articles of association. The provisions of the Commercial Code concerning the supervisory board of a public limited company correspondingly apply to the competence and activity of the supervisory board unless otherwise provided by law.
9	Dividends	As a main rule, the net profit of an association shall be transferred to the reserves which are not subject to distribution between the members of the association. The articles of association may prescribe that dividends may be paid to the members from net profit or from profit of the previous financial year from which uncovered losses of previous years have been deducted.
10	Liquidation	An association may be dissolved e.g. by a resolution of the general meeting. Upon liquidation, after satisfying or guaranteeing all the creditors' claims and the necessary deposit, the contributions paid by members shall be refunded to the members. The assets remaining after the refund of contributions shall be distributed among the members in proportion to the amount of their contributions pursuant to the asset distribution plan prepared by the liquidators, unless the articles of association prescribe otherwise.

Voting rights

Pursuant to the CAA, in the general meeting each member of an association has one vote. It means that the number of votes is not connected to a stakeholder's contribution in the association. If "one member – one vote" arrangement proves to be a significant reason preventing larger municipalities to join the association, a regular limited liability company may be considered as cooperation vehicle. In that case larger municipalities (i.e. municipalities contributing more assets to the company and/or with higher number of clients) could own proportionately larger number of shares and respective voting rights in the company. It should be mentioned that limited liability companies are used as legal bodies for several regional water companies (companies where the shareholders are several local municipalities) already today.

However, the articles of association of some Estonian commercial associations stipulate that the number of votes of a member is in proportion to the nominal value of its contribution, where every 1 (one) euro constitutes one vote. It should be mentioned that such regulation in the articles (as being contrary to the CAA) is not valid and legally applicable in case of a dispute.

Joining and withdrawing from the association

A natural person or a legal person may become a member of an association. The articles of association may prescribe conditions which the members must comply with. Upon acceptance into the membership of an association, the contribution shall be paid unless the articles of association prescribe otherwise. The articles of association may prescribe that the contributions or other payments may be made as non-monetary payment (i.e. transfer of assets).

In general, any municipality or water company may become a member of a commercial association created for the purpose of facilitating co-operation in the WSS sector.

Specific obligations may be imposed on members only pursuant to the procedure provided for in the articles of association.

The management board of an association shall maintain a list of members of the association (similar to a shareholder's list in a company) which shall set out:

1. the residence or registered office and personal identification code or registry code of a member and, if a person does not have Estonian personal identification code, the date, month and year of birth of the person;
2. the amount of the contribution of the member;
3. the size and time of payment of the contributions paid;
4. information on refund of contributions and transfer of membership;
5. the date of acceptance into the membership of the association, leaving or exclusion of members from the association.

A member of an association has the right to withdraw from the association by submitting a written application to the management board. The application shall be submitted at least three months before withdrawal. Upon termination of membership, a member has the right to the refund of the paid contribution.

The right to withdraw may be barred by the articles of association or a contract for up to five (5) years as of acceptance into the membership of the association. The right to leave shall not be completely precluded or made unreasonably complicated.

The articles of association may prescribe that:

- upon termination of membership the contribution is not refunded, but the member shall be paid as compensation the share of the assets which the member would receive if the association were dissolved on the date of the termination of the membership;
- a member of an association shall pay reasonable compensation to the association upon leaving the association if, according to the circumstances, the leaving of the person causes significant damage to the association or may bring about a potential risk to the continuation of the activities of the association.

The association and the members of the association may enter into member's agreement (similar to a shareholder's agreement in a company). It may be prescribed in the articles that upon termination of membership, the member has the right to refund of the paid contribution and compensation as agreed in detail in the members' agreement.

Regime of Assets of an Association

An association is a legal person. Any assets built and/or acquired by the association is the property of the association and in association's ownership (unless leased or otherwise possessed under any other arrangement).

The potential members of the association may transfer WSS assets to the association as non-monetary payments for their contributions (shares) in the association or under contractual arrangements where the ownership passes to the association.

Upon withdrawal from the association, return of the assets to the original holder (leaving member) should be carried through as prescribed in the articles of association or in the members' agreement. A clear set of rules concerning return of assets in case of withdrawal will establish clarity for a member of the association upon use of right to withdraw from the association. A solution upon withdrawal from the association may be as follows:

- The member may (re)acquire any WSS assets it has transferred to the association and/or any assets created by the association that are located in the territory of the member municipality (or in the previous service area of a water undertaking);
- As a general rule, the leaving member may (re)acquire such assets free of charge (except as set out below);
- If the association has outstanding loan obligations connected to the creation of such assets, the leaving member shall compensate the association any such outstanding amounts;
- If such WSS asset is used to provide services to several members, the leaving member shall compensate the association the potential loss or damage resulting from such asset being removed from the possession of the association;
- Any other reasonable technical or financial conditions upon (re)acquiring the assets (e.g. if the assets are created using financial aid, the conditions of the financier must be met).

Upon dissolution of the association, return of the assets to a member may be carried through as prescribed in the articles of association (and/or in the members' agreement). Under the CAA, after satisfying or guaranteeing all the creditors' claims and the necessary deposit, the contributions paid by members shall be refunded to the members. The assets remaining after the refund of contributions shall be distributed among the members in proportion to the amount of their contributions pursuant to the asset distribution plan prepared by the liquidators, unless the articles of association prescribe otherwise.

5.4.3. Delegation to Regional Service Providers

As a way of consolidation, the municipalities and/or the water companies may outsource a part of or whole provision of WSS services to a regional service provider. In such case several questions arise how the WSS assets and services are managed, maintained and financed.

Overview of the main aspects of an outsourcing arrangement

Table 5.2. Selected legal aspects of outsourcing arrangements

Nr.	Issue	Assets to remain in the ownership of the municipality/water company commissioning the services	Assets to be transferred to the ownership of regional service provider (operator)
1	Underlying legal relationship	Operating (lease) agreement /concession agreement[1]	Ownership through shareholding in the regional service provider and/or operating agreement
2	Maintenance: Financed by:	By operator Operator using tariff revenues	By operator Operator using tariff funds
3	Investments: Financed by:	By operator By municipality / by operator	By operator By operator (or by municipality under a contractual arrangement)
4	Investment planning	Agreement / public water supply and sewerage development plan	Agreement /shareholder's decision / public water supply and sewerage development plan
5	Appointed water undertaking	Operator	Operator
6	Tariffs	To be paid by the client to operator (alternative: to the owner, if the owner is appointed water undertaking)	To be paid by the client to operator
7	Environmental liability	Operator (may be divided with the owner)	Operator

1.Pursuant to PWSSA, if a public water supply and sewerage system is in the ownership of a private legal person, it may make a proposal to the local government to appoint the legal person as a water undertaking. If a public water supply and sewerage system is in the ownership or possession of a local government, the local government shall, independently or in cooperation with other local governments, organise a public procurement procedure for entry into a concession agreement for provision of WSS services.

Investment planning and financing

To facilitate the outsourcing, two main alternatives of asset regime shall be considered: (i) ownership of WSS assets remain with the municipality/water company commissioning the services ("Alternative A"), or (ii) ownership of WSS assets are transferred to the service provider ("Alternative B").

Alternative A financing and decisions

In case of a regional service provider (operator) is commissioned to provide WSS services, simultaneously the financing model must be agreed. If the owner of the infrastructure is a company, an operating or lease agreement should be entered into between the owner and the operator. If the owner of the infrastructure is a municipality, a concession agreement shall be entered into between the owner and the operator. The daily maintenance should be carried out and financed by the operator.

As a part of the operating agreement, an investment plan or regulation for adopting an investment plan should be agreed upon. Such investment plan should follow as much as possible the relevant public water supply and sewerage development plan adopted by the local municipality. The investment plan should identify the sources of financing, e.g. the owner of the infrastructure shall cover a part of or all investments exceeding certain threshold.

As the only influence of the owner on the investment decisions is exercised through a contractual relationship, the owner shall have the right to participate in the renewal of the investment plan.

As a sub-alternative to Alternative A, only a part of the WSS services may be provided by a third-party service provider (while the owner of the infrastructure remains as the appointed water undertaking). In such case the contractual relationship between the operator and the owner shall include regulation of the maintenance/financing issues.

Alternative B financing and decisions

In Alternative B the owner of the infrastructure either:

- becomes a shareholder in the operator (if the current shareholders of the operator agree to issue shares to the owner of the infrastructure);
- does not become a shareholder in the operator - the operating and financing of the infrastructure is based on a contractual relationship.

A shareholders' or operating agreement should be entered into between the (previous) owner of the infrastructure and the operator. The daily maintenance should be carried out and financed by the operator.

Similarly, as in Alternative A, an operating or shareholders' agreement shall contain the investment plan (or regulation for adopting an investment plan) which should follow as much as possible the relevant public water supply and sewerage development plan. The investment plan should identify the sources of financing, e.g. the previous owner of the infrastructure/local municipality shall cover part of or all investments exceeding certain threshold.

Depending on whether (the previous) owner of the infrastructure becomes a shareholder in the operator or not, influence of the (previous) owner on the investment decisions is exercised through a contractual relationship and/or through participating in adoption of shareholders' decisions.

5.5. Regulatory Questions

5.5.1. Monitoring the Performance of the Regional Service Provider

Under the PWSSA Section 15-4 supervision over a water undertaking on compliance with the requirements provided by the PWSSA and legislation established on the basis thereof shall be exercised, pursuant to their competence, by the local municipality governments, the Competition Authority and the Environmental Board.

The supervisory duties between different authorities are divided as follows:

- Competition Authority: Supervision over (i) compliance of the prices for water services and the connection charges with the legislation and compliance with the requirements for establishment thereof as well as compliance of the methodology for calculation of connection charges; (ii) compliance by a water undertaking with the requirements related to accounting and price regulation for water services;
- Environmental Board: Supervision over compliance of the activities of a water undertaking and of a client of a water undertaking with the requirements for handling hazardous substances;
- Local government: Supervision over compliance of the activities of a water undertaking with PWSSA and the legislation of the local government, including (i) local government rules for connection to the public water supply and sewerage system; (ii) local government rules on use of the public water supply and sewerage systems; (iii) local government public water supply and sewerage development plan[1]; and (iv) conditions of services agreements between the clients and water undertaking;
- The Competition Authority shall exercise supplementary supervision on its own initiative, and inspection on the basis of a reasoned request of a local government authority, the Ministry of the Environment or the Environmental Board, over the connection charges and prices for water services.

As an example, local government rules on use of the public water supply and sewerage systems shall be approved by the local government council and it shall include:

1. the procedure for measuring the water to be abstracted and for calculating the waste water:
2. the limit values for pollutants in the waste water and rain water discharged to the public sewerage system such that the waste water discharged from the public sewerage system conforms to the requirements established on the basis of the Water Act and the waste water discharged to the public sewerage system does not damage the functioning of the public sewerage system;
3. the procedure for checking the pollutant content;
4. the procedure for payment for the service of supply of water and sewerage;
5. the definition of water abstracted without authorisation and of waste water, rain water, drainage water and other soil and surface water discharged without authorisation and the procedure for determining the volume and cost thereof;
6. the procedure for interruption and restoration of the supply of water and the reception of waste water and rain water;
7. the procedure for restriction or suspension of supplying water and leading off waste water in the case of damage to or an accident in the public water supply and sewerage system;
8. the minimum permitted limit value of water pressure at the point of connection to the public water supply system depending on the overall height of buildings;
9. the maximum permitted limit value of headwater level at the point of connection to the public sewerage system.

The draft of new PWSSA will confer to the municipalities rights to introduce additional rules for water undertakings on the qualifications of the staff and quality of services.

Another example of the authority of local government is a situation, where the public water supply and sewerage system is in the ownership or possession of a local government. Then the local government shall organise a public procurement procedure for entry into a concession contract for provision of WSS services.

In such case the municipality has the authority to determine the conditions of the tender process. According to PWSSA Section 7 (31) the following information shall be included in the source documents of the public procurement organised for finding a water undertaking:

1. the extent of the licensed territory of the water undertaking and technical description thereof;
2. information concerning the public water supply and sewerage development plan;
3. information concerning the rules for connection to and use of the public water supply and sewerage system;
4. the obligations of the water undertaking;
5. requirements for competence of the water undertaking in order to ensure proper functioning of the public water supply and sewerage system;
6. the terms of provision of the public water supply and sewerage service;
7. the term of the public contract;
8. the investment obligations of the water undertaking in terms of years;
9. the draft public contract to be entered with the water undertaking.

However, as the majority of the public water supply and sewerage systems are in the ownership of a private legal persons (usually owned by the municipalities), the water undertakings will be appointed based on a proposal from the system owner and no tender will be organised.

5.5.2. Potential conflict of interests and possible measures to avoid it

A vast majority of water undertakings are in the ownership of local municipalities. There are municipalities, where the system is owned by the municipality but operated by a legal person belonging to the same municipality. Such conditions may raise questions whether local governments, in using their power to regulate provision of WSS services, use their authority to favour companies in their ownership and whether such regulative power should shift to state entities.

Currently we do not possess direct evidence that such conflict or discrimination exists. Without such direct proof, no recommendation is hereby put forward with regard to potential conflict of interests. At a later stage, should the Estonian government consider a system of licencing water utilities, due diligence on potential conflicts of interest could be considered prior to awarding a licence to operate.

5.5.3. Consequences of termination of services by the regional service provider

In case a water undertaking loses its rights as a water undertaking under PWSSA or wishes to terminate its activities the following will apply[2].

Pursuant to PWSSA Section 7 (7) termination or suspension of activities of a water undertaking is permitted only if the performance of the obligations of the water undertaking arising from the PWSSA and the contracts entered into with the local government is ensured by another water undertaking appointed by the local government council or if the performance of the obligations of the water undertaking is ensured in another manner and the Competition Authority approves it.

Pursuant to PWSSA Section 7 (6) a water undertaking shall, at least twelve months before suspending or terminating the offering of water services, notify the local government and the Competition Authority in writing of the time schedule for suspension or termination and submit an overview of measures ensuring the performance of the requirements arising from the PWSSA and the contracts entered into with the local government. Similar regulation is proposed to be inserted into the draft of new PWSSA; however the notice of termination is to be filed only with the local government.

The main infrastructure assets of such water undertaking cannot be removed and used in other activities. As organising the provision of WSS services is the obligation of municipalities, then the continuance of the WSS services is to be resolved by the affected municipality. Most likely a water undertaking which is terminating the provision of WSS services will be reorganised an/or its WSS assets be transferred to a (new) service provider.

Pursuant to PWSSA Section 12, in order to use structures necessary for ensuring trouble-free functioning and development of the public water supply and sewerage system, local governments have the right to establish compulsory possession or to acquire, including expropriate, the structure pursuant to the procedure provided in the Acquisition of Immovables in Public Interest Act.

5.6. Expanding the Role of the Competition Authority

The OECD has delivered its Analyses and Action Plan towards Sustainable Water Services in Estonia, which aim is to support the preparation of a roadmap for the consolidation of the water utility sector in Estonia. Chapter 6 reviews aspects of the framework for the economic regulation of WSS services in Estonia, and proposed ways in which that framework could be further developed to assist in the achievement of strategic objectives, including by encouraging efficiency improvements through consolidation in WSS sector.

We hereby analyse and describe which regulatory changes and/or amendments must be carried through in order to implement some of the proposed measures in the subsequent chapters.

5.6.1. Price reviews by the Competition Authority and enhancing the incentive arrangements

In Chapter 6, the OECD makes the following recommendations:

- **Recommendation 1:** The Competition Authority ("CA") maintains its approach to applying the tariff formula, which allows for companies to raise financeability concerns. It is recommended that the CA provides guidance on the conditions that the CA might expect to be met in order for accelerated depreciation to be allowed for;
- **Recommendation 2:** The CA introduces a periodic approach to price reviews and develops principles which limit the extent to which existing price controls would be 're-opened' as a result of consolidation activity. The use of periodic price reviews could be undertaken in clusters (e.g. regional clusters), and focused on larger companies initially, in order to help manage resource implications;
- **Recommendation 3:** The CA develops a Service Performance Incentive framework (The CA develops, makes publicly available and publicises a KPI framework that provides concise, credible and easy to understand comparisons between companies, using the Portuguese ERSAR approach as a guide);
- **Recommendation 4:** The CA develops incentives that focus on company plans, and planning processes, i.e., the CA develops guidance (i) setting out how it will enable companies that present credible, efficiency-enhancing consolidation plans to share in the benefits they result in, through the treatment of consolidation costs, and commitments concerning how rapidly future efficiency savings will be reflected in allowed prices.; and (ii) setting CA's expectations with respect to companies being able to demonstrate that robust options appraisal processes have been undertaken in the development of capex plans, and how capex applications will be treated where a company is unable to adequately demonstrate that.

5.6.2. Regulatory adjustments needed to broaden role of the Competition Authority

In order for the Competition Authority to play such scrutiny role within an Estonian context, there would clearly need to be some further development of its competences and capabilities in relation to the tariff approval process, assessment of performance and whether adequate options appraisal process has been undertaken (including possible efficiency-enhancing consolidation plans) ("Assessment Procedure"). To be effective and equal to all parties, it should be clearly regulated how the Assessment Procedure is carried through and what is to be expected from a water undertaking ("Assessment Rules").

The competence and activities of the Competition Authority are regulated in several legal acts and regulations. Mainly the statute of the Competition Authority and several laws regulating WSS, electricity, heating, gas supply, aviation, railways and competition.

The possible solutions to establish the Assessment Rules are to amend and/or adjust the following legal acts and/or regulations:

- PWSSA: The main underlying rules of water tariff and its approval by the Competition Authority are regulated in the PWSSA. Also, according to the PWSSA, the recommended principles ("Tariff Principles") for calculation of prices for WSS services shall be prepared and disclosed on Competition Authority's website. The Competition Authority has disclosed the Tariff Principles.
- In the draft of the new PWSSA the main underlying rules of water tariff are regulated in some greater detail, but the Tariff Principles are continuously to be prepared and disclosed by the Competition Authority.
- If Assessment Procedure and Assessment Rules are to be introduced in Estonia, the most suitable regulation, where to set out the main rationale of Assessment Procedure, is the PWSSA

itself. A priori, it would seem to make sense to set the more technical mechanisms in the regulatory framework to allow some capacity to adjust over time.

- Tariff Principles. As pointed out in Chapter 6, an assessment of a specific tariff request by a water company is a complex and challenging task, which must be regulated in reasonable detail to enable water companies to understand and comply with it. Therefore, the detailed Assessment Rules should be prepared by the Competition Authority (undoubtfully having the best expertise in that area) and incorporated into the Tariff Principles, i.e. the Tariff Principles are to be preferred for incorporation of the Assessment Rules.

The following table indicates the most suitable legal act or regulation to be amended in order to incorporate the specific proposals set out in Chapter 6.

Table 5.3. Suitable acts or regulations to be amended to reflect selected recommendations

Recommendation No.	Issue	Most suitable legal act or regulation
1	Tariff formula	Tariff Principles
2	Periodic approach to price reviews Principles which limit the extent to which existing price controls would be re-opened and/or formula which provides for prices to be adjusted automatically	PWSSA Tariff Principles
3	Service Performance Incentive framework (KPI framework)	Tariff Principles
4	CA's guidance: (i) on consolidation plans (ii) on assessment of options appraisal processes have been undertaken in the development of capex plans	Tariff Principles

National water strategy (plan)

As pointed out above, the EWA Study concluded that at least regional WSS business arrangement would provide a somehow sustainable solution for the Estonian WSS sector as a whole.

For the Competition Authority to verify that in a tariff application adequate options appraisal process has been undertaken, it would be highly recommendable that each application could be verified against a national water strategy (or development plan) setting out the desirable principles of consolidation and/or or cost efficiency measures in WSS sector.

Such national strategy can be established through several means. The most suitable form for such strategy document would be a national WSS consolidation plan adopted by the Estonian Government or by the Ministry of Environment. Reference to <u>a</u> national strategy could be made in the legislative framework, even if the strategy itself could be considered a secondary piece legislation. This would allow some flexibility to adjust the strategy to shifting conditions without shattering the legislative framework.

5.6.3. Overview of Possible Legal and Regulatory Adjustments for Licensing of Water Operators in Estonia

In order to enhance monitoring of water undertakings' performance and/or facilitate the consolidation of WSS sector, an obligation to apply for licence (authorization) may be introduced.

Currently, in Estonia no specific licence requirement apply for water undertakings (except for environmental licences to use water resources). Under current regulations of the PWSSA, a water undertaking who is allowed to provide water services within a specific service area will be appointed by the respective local government.

As mentioned above, supervision over compliance with the requirements provided by the PWSSA and legislation established on the basis thereof shall be exercised, by local governments, the Competition Authority and the Environmental Board.

However, in areas of electricity network services, distribution of natural gas and distribution of heating services licencing requirements apply. Applications for licence (authorisation) are processed by the Competition Authority. Supervision of the service provider in the electricity, natural gas and heating sectors is performed by the Competition Authority as well.

As an example, the authorization for the provision of electricity network services through a distribution network is issued to the undertaking if that undertaking fulfils among others the following requirements:

- the organization of the undertaking is suitable considering the extent and nature of the activity applied for;
- the undertaking employs a sufficient number of staff with the necessary qualifications, including persons qualified to perform electrical work and to supervise electrical installations;
- the undertaking possesses commercial prerequisites for operating in the area of activity applied for;
- the undertaking possesses other prerequisites necessary for operating in the corresponding area of activity in accordance with this act and the legislation enacted under it;
- the actions of the undertaking do not jeopardize the security of supply;
- A distribution network operator must have at its disposal the technical, physical, financial and human resources requisite for the preservation and development of the assets required for the provision of network service.

Similarly, a licence requirement could be introduced to water undertakings that provide public water supply and sewerage services and which are appointed as water undertakings by the local government. The responsible authority could be the Competition Authority, which has previous experience of licencing procedures of utilities. The purpose of the licencing requirement may be to ensure that a water undertaking has the technological, financial and managerial capacity to supply water services in accordance with the requirements of legal acts and in compliance with the special conditions of the licensed activity.

As an alternative solution, the PWSSA should set out (i) which requirements a water undertaking must fulfil (broadly in line with requirements applicable to the energy sector); and (ii) that only companies fulfilling such requirements can be appointed as water undertakings (the draft of new PWSSA will confer to the municipalities rights to introduce additional rules for water undertakings on the qualifications of the staff and quality of services).

To allow water undertakings to adapt to such measures and conditions, a transition period of 3-5 years may be reasonable.

The application to obtain licence shall be submitted by the water undertaking. General particulars and documents required for a licence application is regulated by Estonian General Part of the Code of Economic Activities Act. An economic administrative authority (the Competition Authority) adjudicates applications for activity licences by grant of or refusal to grant an activity licence within 30 days after submission of the application. The time limit for adjudication of applications commences from the submission of all the required information.

Revocation (termination) of the licence shall be carried out in accordance with section 37 (Revocation of activity licence) of the Estonian General Part of the Code of Economic Activities Act.

Licensing of water undertakings will create inevitably more procedural burden on the authority to be responsible for issuing the licences (e.g., the Competition Authority). As already mentioned, the draft of new PWSSA will confer to the municipalities rights to introduce specific rules for water undertakings on the qualifications of the staff and quality of services (i.e., if such conditions are not met, municipality can refuse to appoint the specific company as a water undertaking). The new draft law indicates that the legislator intends to leave the supervisory duties to the municipalities. To introduce an (additional) licencing requirement to be managed by a state authority needs significant reasons.

In conclusion - licencing requirement or additional rules for water undertakings on the qualifications of the staff and quality of services set out in the PWSSA may be a feasible measure to ensure technological, financial and managerial capacities of water undertakings. Depending on the conditions - such requirements may encourage consolidation within the WSS sector, where service providers with incompetent organization and weak economy are gradually directed to merge or otherwise consolidate their business with regional and/or otherwise sustainable water undertakings.

Notes

[1] As recommended in subsequent Chapters, significant benefits would derive from endowing the Competition Authority with the capacity to challenge development plans, to benchmark their level of ambition and how thoroughly they explore options to enhance efficiency (including through some form of consolidation); see in particular Chapter 6 and the discussion on benchmarking development plans.

[2] These provisions are specified in the draft PWSSA.

6 Report on tariff regulatory framework

Tariff policy and related regulatory framework have a major role among the modalities and incentives towards aggregation of water services in Estonia. While the framework in place is robust and essentially in line with the needs and policy priorities, some adjustments could be considered – in particular to the depreciation method for granted assets - to provide stronger incentives for utilities and municipalities to consider aggregation as a practical way forward. Other dimensions include benchmarking and information sharing on the performance and ambition of utilities.

6.1. Background and objectives

The Ministry of the Environment of Estonia jointly with other governmental authorities (the Ministry of Finance, the Minister of Public Administration), the European Commission – DG Reform, and the OECD are partnering to enhance the sustainability of water supply and sanitation services in Estonia. The Project will support the preparation of a roadmap for the consolidation of the water utility sector, a requisite for a sustainable and socially acceptable financing strategy and a broader water sector reform in Estonia. See the Detailed Project Description, for more information on background, scope and process.

The specific objectives of this Project are:

- to support the initiatives of national authorities to design their reforms according to their priorities, taking into account initial conditions and expected socio-economic impacts
- to support the efforts of national authorities to define and implement appropriate processes and methodologies by taking into account good practices of and lessons learned by other countries in addressing similar situations
- to assist the national authorities and water utilities in enhancing the efficiency and effectiveness of human-resource management, inter alia, by strengthening professional knowledge and skills and setting out clear responsibilities.

This report is focused on the tariff regulatory framework, and in line with this it considers the methodology and process used for tariff setting purposes. It is common, however, for economic regulators – as part of their assessment of the appropriateness of potential tariff setting decisions – to consider what utilities plan to, and have been, delivering while charging the relevant tariff level. This is of considerable significance because the approach to tariff setting can have a material bearing on decisions that may affect future performance, both in terms of the cost efficiency with which services are provided and the quality of those services. Given this, in addition to addressing a number of tariff methodology issues, this report highlights and recommends a number of ways in which broader incentive considerations can be incorporated into the regulatory framework, and treated as an integral feature of the tariff setting process.

The current arrangements, and potential options for further development, are considered and assessed below in the light of relevant international experience. The relevance of considering international experience is enhanced by the fact that the overall economic regulatory framework for WSS in Estonia shares a range of common features with those which apply in many other jurisdictions (for example, in terms of some of the responsibilities given to an economic regulator, and the broad ('building blocks') approach the regulator applies to tariff regulation).[1] Also, the broad question of how to meet WSS-related environmental challenges in financially sustainable and socially acceptable ways can be understood as one that all jurisdictions have had to, and will continue to face to some extent.

At the same time, the feasibility and appropriateness of adopting different potential approaches will be heavily dependent on the specific circumstances that currently apply to WSS provision in Estonia, and on how those circumstances have emerged over time. Given this, the report does not seek to provide a broad overview of international experience, as there would be a significant risk of such an overview being unhelpfully generic and of limited value. Rather, the approach adopted below is to focus attention on circumstances that apply, and the current and emerging challenges faced, in WSS provision in Estonia, with international experience then drawn upon more selectively either to help highlight closely related experiences, or to illustrate potential options that look to merit particular attention.

The first section situates the prevailing approach for depreciation used by the CA to set WS tariffs vis-à-vis other options. It concludes the prevailing approach is suitable in the Estonian context, but could be more effective if the conditions to allow accelerated depreciation were clearly stated. Affordability and performance incentives are used as main criteria in the discussion.

The focus then shifts to the basis upon which price reviews are triggered, and potential adverse incentive effects associated with the current (voluntary) arrangements are highlighted. The potential for using periodic reviews, and regulatory commitments with respect to the scope of price reviews, to address these incentive issues is highlighted.

Another section presents different methods that can be used in Estonia to incentivise consolidation by using more systematic comparison of utilities performance and by challenging the level of ambition of development and investment plans. References are made to international experience, in particular Australia, England & Wales and Portugal. A final section captures the recommendations that derive from the analyses.

6.2. The tariff formula and how it is applied

The Competition Authority (CA) was established as the economic regulator of WSS companies in Estonia in November 2010, with responsibility for approving prices for WSS services[2] in relation to wastewater collection areas with a population equivalent (PE) of 2000 or more. Before that time, all WSS prices were set by local governments, and local governments had continued to approve prices in relation to wastewater collection areas with less than 2000 PE up until the end of 2021. From the beginning of 2022 the CA has had responsibility for approving all public WSS charges (i.e. including those in relation to areas with less than 2000 PE).

The CA adopts a form 'building block' approach to determining allowed price levels that has been widely used internationally over many years. In particular, it approves prices based on its assessment of allowed revenues, which are made up of its assessment of a reasonable allowance for:

1. Operating expenditure (opex) requirements;
2. Depreciation; and,
3. A return on capital.

Based on the duties and powers it has under the Public Water Supply and Sewerage Act, the CA has issued:

- The methodology it uses for calculating cost-based tariffs.
- Two questionnaires (one more detailed, the other simplified) for companies to complete as part of the price approval process.
- Guidelines to water companies on submitting price applications (i.e. how to fill out the questionnaires and what additional documents should be provided).
- The CA's view of the weighted average cost of capital (WACC) that should be used when determining a reasonable allowance for a return on capital.

The broad 'building block' approach that the CA uses is well established, and provides a flexible framework that is well suited to addressing the range of issues it may face, with the application of this broad approach in different international contexts having included and been supplemented with a range of other regulatory initiatives (including in terms of the approaches that have been developed for cost assessment and recovery, and for incentivising aspects of service delivery).

The remainder of this section focuses on two issues related to the tariff formula and how it is applied that look to merit particularly careful attention:

- The approach taken to cost assessment.
- The approach to determining the allowances for depreciation/capital maintenance to be included in the tariff formula.

6.2.1. Cost assessment

The use of cost assessment approaches in the determination of allowed prices is central to the economic regulation of utilities. The use of these approaches can be highly relevant to consolidation incentives in Estonia because they can provide a basis for the CA to constrain the funds that companies are allowed to recover from their customers over time. The application of such constraints has the potential to incentivise companies to find ways of achieving efficiency improvements, including through consolidation approaches, in order to improve the financial position they face, and can expect to face in future years.

In its cost assessment work, the CA applies three broad approaches that have been widely used internationally:

1. The review of how cost levels have evolved (and are forecast to evolve) over time, including by reference to relevant available price indices (the CA considers movements relative to the Consumer Price Index).
2. Benchmarking approaches that involve the comparisons being made with relevant cost measured for other companies.
3. Detailed assessments of particular cost areas, and of the justification presented for the appropriateness of the associated actual and forecast cost levels.

Each of these approaches can be applied in a range of different ways at different levels of aggregation, and potentially serve a range of different purposes within the price review process given the specific circumstances under consideration. It is notable with respect to (1) above, that a focus on the relationship between the evolution of total (and/or average) costs and relevant price indices can be viewed as concentrating attention on the overall implications of cost levels for consumers (in line with the initial development of the RPI-X approach). At the same time, regulators typically also look at cost dynamics at a range of more disaggregated levels, with this potentially providing a basis upon which more detailed assessment work can be prioritised (e.g. with close attention paid to areas where costs are forecast to materially increase).

Regulators also often apply benchmarking approaches at different levels of aggregation that can include:

- Totex benchmarking: i.e. the benchmarking of total opex + capex requirements.
- The benchmarking of 'base' totex (or 'Botex'): i.e. the benchmarking of total opex + capex, excluding expenditure on enhancements, such as the achievement of water quality improvements.
- Opex benchmarking.
- Totex, Botex or Opex benchmarking focused on particular business units/activities: e.g. water treatment, treated water distribution, wastewater collection, wastewater treatment.
- The benchmarking of the costs associated with more narrowly defined activities: e.g. pipe replacement costs, billing and customer support costs, etc.

The CA looks to have adopted a pragmatic approach to its use of benchmarking to date, including through the grouping of companies for comparison purposes depending on their ratio of sales volume to length of pipe. International experience has highlighted some of the complexities that can be faced when seeking to develop reasonably robust benchmarking models, particularly when the implications of significant differences in density/sparsity conditions need to be taken into account, as is the case with Estonian WSS services.

A specific assessment concern that has been highlighted in the Estonian context is that some of the reference data that is available for benchmarking is too old, such that it does not provide an accurate and up-to-date reflection of relevant costs. Where cost conditions are relatively stable over time, older data may continue to provide a valuable input into benchmarking assessments in a relatively straightforward way. However, where cost conditions are subject to material changes, more careful consideration typically needs to be given to whether, and if so how, it is appropriate to use older cost data. In practice, much will depend on how straightforward it is to isolate what driven changes in conditions over time, and on the availability of adequate techniques for taking these drivers into account. For example, it may be possible to reflect some differences in cost conditions by references to available indices, either when considering costs are a relatively aggregated level (which broad measures of price movements, such as a consumer price index, may be helpful), or considering more specific areas such as labour or energy costs. Another underlying driver may be changes to the types and levels of activity that companies are undertaking over time, with this flowing through to material differences in the cost pressures that are faced (as may be the case, for example, where costs are higher because of the need to meet more stringent environmental requirements). Where there are considerable changes to cost conditions over time, and where it is not feasible to take them into account adequately through seeking to identify the effects of workload changes and broader cost pressures, then it may simply be that older cost data comes to be viewed as relatively uninformative, and it may be appropriate for benchmarking to focus primarily on the use of data that been gathered relatively recently.

The most appropriate way to develop the specific benchmarking practices that are to be applied will depend on a range of detailed and context specific matters that go well beyond the scope of this assessment. Also, importantly, the quality and sophistication of benchmarking (and of the information collection arrangements on which it is based) is typically something that evolves gradually over time, as potential detailed options are identified and tested, and experience with existing methods grows. A key broader consideration therefore concerns how effective this process through which benchmarking evolves over time is likely to be. Transparency and effective stakeholder engagement are typically key factors in this context. In particular, transparency in relation to relevant cost and cost driver information can help improve both the usefulness of, and the confidence that companies and other stakeholders have in, benchmarking models by allowing more open consultation and challenge processes to inform what is inevitably a difficult and approximate process. Further comments on transparency issues are provided in a later section in relation to performance incentives.

6.2.2. The determination of appropriate allowances for depreciation/capital maintenance

Under Estonian water law,[3] the allowances for capital costs (the depreciation and return on capital allowances) that are included in the tariff formula should not cover:

- Assets funded by connection charges paid by consumers; or
- Assets financed by EU funds, by state or local governments or by other institutions to the extent of the value of financial assistance.

The exclusion of assets funded by connection charges from the Regulatory Asset Base (RAB), which companies receive a depreciation and return on capital allowance on the basis of, is a standard approach across many countries, and reflects the different basis upon which connection assets are typically funded. However, the treatment of assets funded from financial assistance raises some broader questions concerning the basis upon which it is appropriate to make provisions for depreciation, and associated questions concerning the funding of future capital maintenance requirements.

Allowances for depreciation/capital maintenance can be viewed as having both a backward and a forward-looking role:

- The backward-looking role can be understood as concerned with the recovery of capital expenditure that was incurred in previous years.[4] Under the standard building block approach (which, as noted above, the Estonian tariff formula broadly follows), capital expenditure is added to the Regulatory Asset Base (RAB) and recovered over time through depreciation of the RAB. Depreciation under this approach is sometimes referred to as the return <u>of</u> capital, as it can be understood as providing for the return of part of the stock of past capital expenditure that has yet to be recovered by investors (with a return on capital also provided for by applying the Weighted Average Cost of Capital (WACC) to the residual (as yet unrecovered) RAB in each given year).

- The forward-looking role can be understood as more directly concerned with the financeability of future capital maintenance requirements. In particular, the depreciation allowance results in an additional cash income that can be earned from charges, and that additional cash income may affect the extent to which a company will be able to fund future capital maintenance requirements through revenues from customers, and its ability to (and terms upon which it can) raise external funds, typically through borrowing.

The approach adopted in Estonia of excluding the value of assets provided by EU funding when calculating a reasonable depreciation provision, can be viewed as clearly consistent with the backward-looking role referred to above. That is, the grant-based nature of the assistance means that this funding has not resulted in WSS companies facing outstanding accumulated amounts of past investment that stand to be recovered from consumers. Given this, one key question with respect to the regulatory treatment of this past funding looks to concern its implications for the financeabilty of future capital maintenance requirements (i.e. the forward-looking role referred to above).

We understand the approach adopted by the CA to this future capital maintenance financeabilty issue to be broadly as follows:

1. Future capital maintenance is treated in the same way as any other new capital expenditure: it is added to the RAB, and allowed for over time in the tariff formula through the allowances made for depreciation of the RAB, and for a return on the outstanding level of the RAB.
2. A company can identify financeability difficulties it may have under this approach as part of its price review application process, and the CA may be willing to allow for a more accelerated depreciation assumption to apply (than it would otherwise expect to use), where a compelling case has been made that such a change would be appropriate.

We consider that, in broad terms, this existing CA approach is likely to provide an appropriate basis upon which to determine the allowances provided for depreciation/capital maintenance within the tariff formula, because it can provide a pragmatic and flexible way of allowing financeability issues to be addressed where they have been shown to be material, while also guarding against the risk of WSS customers facing unduly high charges. We explain further why we consider this to be the case below, including by highlighting some of the limitations that may be associated with adopting potential alternative approaches. We also highlight some ways in which it might be desirable to develop the broad approach that we understand the CA to be currently applying.

Three further key factors that underpin our assessment of this issue are as follows:

- Affordability considerations;
- Efficiency incentives;
- Intergenerational equity considerations.

These factors are highly relevant when one assesses the desirability of potential alternative approaches that could be adopted to the determination of allowances for depreciation/capital maintenance. Two alternative approaches that are used in a range of jurisdictions are: (a) a form of current cost depreciation (CCD) approach applied in relation to all relevant assets; and, (b) an infrastructure accounting approach that effectively treats capital maintenance as though it were opex (and so involves funding expected capital maintenance requirements directly through prevailing charge levels).

Limitations of a CCD based approach

Adopting a form of CCD approach would involve including a depreciation provision in relation to EU funded assets. The case for adopting such an approach can be viewed as relying heavily on the anticipated long-run average relationship between appropriately calculated depreciation requirements on the one hand, and future capital maintenance requirements on the other. Put differently, it relies on a depreciation approach being viewed as a 'good enough' estimate of likely long-run average capital maintenance requirements and – given this - of the contribution to (current or future) capital maintenance requirements that it is considered appropriate for the current cohort of consumers to make.

In practice, however, this kind of CCD approach looks to suffer from major limitations in relation to both affordability considerations and efficiency incentives. Affordability considerations are important as adopting the approach would result in a substantial increase in allowed WSS charges, other things equal. In principle, one could seek to dampen this effect through the use of some form of glidepath, such that there was a transition to this kind of CCD approach over time that took some account of affordability concerns. However, it is important to recognise the potential cash implications for utilities of adopting such an approach. There looks to be a significant risk that such an approach could provide a considerable over-estimate of likely capital maintenance requirements over at least the next few years, particularly given that many of the EU assets were installed relatively recently. Given this, the approach would likely result in companies effectively being funded for capital maintenance some years ahead of when spend requirements would actually arise

This could have the effect of materially relaxing the financial pressures that utilities might otherwise face, as the higher depreciation allowances would (in the absence of other regulatory protections) effectively provide additional financial headroom when costs are being managed. While - in principle - this financial headroom could be used to build up a financial provision for when higher capital maintenance levels are required, there may be a material risk that the headroom instead is effectively used to insulate the utility to some extent from the pressures for efficiency improvement that it may otherwise face. That is, there is a risk that the better financial position utilities would be in as a result of applying this kind of CCD approach would tend to allow a greater degree of deferral in relation to the achievement of efficiency improvements, because it effectively softens the efficiency improvement constraints that the regulator would otherwise be putting on the utility.

While it is sensible to take stock of how these points fit with intergenerational equity considerations, it is not obvious that such considerations should be viewed as particularly supportive of applying a CCD approach to EU funded assets. The application of the current tariff methodology would – without any change of treatment in relation to EU assets – tend towards the full application of a form of CCD approach over time (albeit perhaps quite a long time, given relevant asset lives), as EU assets are refurbished/replaced. The key intergenerational equity consideration therefore can be understood as concerned with how the benefits of EU funding should be shared between different cohorts of customers over time. The EU funding provides for significant flexibility in terms of what the profile of movement towards some kind of full CCD approach could look like. While different choices in relation to that profile will have different intergenerational implications, it seems important that decisions concerned with that choice of profile should be guided to a significant degree by efficiency and affordability considerations in the short- to medium-term, given in the central importance of efficiency improvements to the achievement of more affordable outcomes in the medium and longer-term.

Limitations of an infrastructure accounting-based approach

The infrastructure accounting approach that has been used for many years in England and Wales (and in different ways in a number of other jurisdictions and contexts) for a large category of long-lived assets (typically underground assets: pipes, sewers, etc.), provides a notable alternative to the use of a depreciation approach. Under this approach, the cost of infrastructure renewals is effectively expensed each year (i.e. treated as though it were opex) rather than added to the RAB. In line with this, it can be regarded as a form of 'pay as you go' approach to funding capital maintenance of a given set of assets. As such, the approach assumes that these capital maintenance requirements are funded directly from customer charges, and thus do not result in additional financeability challenges.

This approach would not be expected to have the same extent of adverse effect on efficiency incentives highlighted above as potentially arising under a CCD approach. Under the CCD approach, that incentive problem arises because funding decisions are effectively decoupled from specific future identified capital maintenance requirements, and are instead determined by reference to the value of past investments that were funded by external sources (and hence do not themselves give rise to ongoing financing costs). Under an infrastructure accounting based approach this decoupling issue does not arise, as attention is focused instead on estimating, and then fully funding, likely capital maintenance requirements in the next period. That said, the efficiency of the proposed approach to capital maintenance may itself be an important matter for the regulator to seek to test, and so the basis upon which funding for capital maintenance through charges can be secured may be important in terms of seeking to generate desirable efficiency incentives (discussed further below).

Beyond this, the limitations of adopting a 'pay as you go' approach can be expected to relate largely to affordability and bill volatility considerations. Affordability concerns can arise because under this approach, all relevant capital maintenance would be recovered through charges in (roughly) the same time period in which the costs are to be incurred, such that this approach may imply a steep upward movement in prices in the relatively short-term in order to fund capital maintenance requirements. Bill volatility concerns arise from the often lumpy nature of WSS capital maintenance requirements. The adoption of a depreciation-based approach can be understood as addressing this lumpiness through temporal smoothing, with customer charges including a provision for future capital maintenance requirements to be paid each year irrespective of actual capital maintenance requirements. The 'pay as you go' approach does not include this kind of explicit temporal smoothing, but where it is applied to relatively large regional water companies – as for example in England and Wales - considerable temporal smoothing is provided for indirectly, given the mixed age and condition profiles of the portfolios of assets across those companies. Applying a 'pay as you go' approach to a smaller company could imply considerable tariff instability, as overall capital maintenance requirements may be highly sensitive to lumpy requirements associated with a relatively small number of assets, with that then raising questions over its feasibility as an approach.

Allowing some scope for accelerated depreciation as a hybrid option

The CA's current broad approach gives it scope to consider allowing some accelerated depreciation on a case-by-case basis. It is notable that, in principle, the use of accelerated deprecation could (in the extreme) deliver a pay as you go approach: that is, depreciation could be accelerated such that all of the relevant capital maintenance costs are allowed to be recovered in the year they are incurred. The CA's approach can, therefore, be viewed as a form of hybrid option that allows movement towards a pay as you go approach, but only when – and to the extent that – a number of regulatory conditions are satisfied. There may be significant benefit in seeking to further formalise and articulate this regulatory approach – for example, through publishing guidance – so that there is greater clarity over the scope for utilities to seek accelerated depreciation provisions to help address financeability constraints they may face, or expect to face, and over the conditions that are likely to need to be satisfied in order for that accelerated depreciation to be allowed.

Those conditions could be developed in ways that take explicit account of the risk that providing more funding through charges may tend to dampen the efficiency incentives that might otherwise apply. In line with this, regulatory decisions on the extent to which accelerated depreciation should be allowed could take account of the utilities performance (including evidence on the efficiency of its operations), with this providing a means of guarding against the risk that the allowing of accelerated depreciation could act to 'soften' the budget constraints that utilities would otherwise be expected to face, and dampen efficiency improvement incentives. The CA could underpin this approach by identifying relevant cost and service performance criteria that it would expect companies to satisfy in order to qualify for potential access to accelerated depreciation provisions.

The approach could also be linked directly to the extent to which different forms of consolidation plans were being pursued, with greater scope for the acceleration of depreciation provided to utilities that develop such plans in a robust and credible manner.[5] Some forms of consolidation may greatly enhance the scope for managing bill profiles over time as significant levels of capital maintenance come to be required in relation to what were EU funded assets. In particular, as well as potentially increasing the borrowing capacity of companies (and therefore their ability to fund future capital maintenance requirements without seeking additional revenues from customer charges through accelerated depreciation), consolidation can also allow for future capital maintenance and funding requirements to be managed across a larger and more diverse portfolio of assets, and thus allow for greater smoothing of associated work requirements and bill impacts.

6.3. The basis upon which price reviews are triggered

This section focuses on the specific issue of what triggers price reviews, and highlights some potential incentive issues associated with the current approach. It is proposed that consideration be given to the use of defined periodic review criteria such that companies can expect to face a price review every few years.

6.3.1. Potential incentive issues under the current arrangements

Under the current WSS arrangements in Estonia, price reviews are triggered by an application from the relevant water company. Once determined by the regulator, approved prices apply until the regulator determines a new price following a subsequent review triggered by a further application from the company.

These arrangements have the potential to result in a self-selecting asymmetry with respect to when companies apply for, and thus are subject to price reviews. That is, companies may face relatively strong incentives to apply for a price review when their current tariff levels are viewed as insufficient to cover their actual and/or forecast costs. By contrast, the incentive to apply for a price review might be expected to be relatively weak for companies that are able to cover their actual and/or forecast costs based on current tariff levels.

Given this, the current basis upon which price reviews are triggered could have a number of potential incentive implications for companies that are operating relatively successfully under their existing price control. For example, it is possible that:

- If that company had managed to reduce its costs such that it could be viewed as earning a financial surplus at the current allowed tariff levels, then it would be unlikely to want to apply for a price review, as that review might be expected to result in a reduction in the allowed tariff levels (other things equal), and removal of the surplus (with the benefit of the cost savings it had made passed on to its customers).
- Success in opex reduction might be associated with a tendency to seek to avoid other changes that may be expected to trigger a price review, and potentially result in a tougher control. This could potentially affect broader attitudes and decision making in a range of different ways including that:
  - The company may tend to prefer delaying investments that would require a price review to be triggered (i.e. the decision to undertake the investments may result in a requirement for additional funds from customer charges and thus a request for a tariff review)

- The company may tend to prefer to avoid other changes - including potentially consolidation – that might be expected to trigger a price review, and remove financial headroom that the company might otherwise have: by providing 'successful' companies with a means of choosing to defer when its tariffs are subject to regulatory review, the current arrangements may tend to disincentivise companies from engaging in consolidation activities that may trigger a review at an earlier date.

The above points are presented in a relatively speculative manner, because they are based on identified possibilities under the current arrangements rather than on evidence that these possibilities have eventuated and resulted in harmful effects. However, it is important that consideration is given to the sorts of tendencies that might arise when regulatory frameworks are being developed and reviewed. The identification of the above possibilities is not intended to imply that any 'wrongdoing' is likely, or to suggest that avoiding the triggering of price reviews is likely to be a prominent motivation when investment and consolidation options are being contemplated. But at the same time it would be perfectly understandable if companies did give some weight – implicitly or otherwise – to the prospect of avoiding or deferring a price review, and there may be many good reasons for doing so, including that the review may generate unwanted distractions from and disturbances to ongoing service provision plans. As a matter of regulatory design, it is important to try to avoid the emergence of such tensions, as they can result in undesirable diversions of effort and attention, and to shift focus away from the kinds of improvements that are likely to be important for the future development of the WSS sector in Estonia.

It is also notable that the issues described above can be understood as forms of a broader type of regulatory incentive problem that can arise and that relates to what can be described as 'ratchet effects'. Ratchet effects can arise because the regulatory conditions that a company faces are likely to be affected by new information that comes available. This can mean that there is a risk that – for a given company - the result of it engaging in successful efforts to deliver efficiency improvements may be a tougher operating environment than it would otherwise have faced. That is, having shown it can operate at lower cost, the extent to which it is allowed to recover costs through charges may be 'ratcheted down' by the regulator such that it is no better off. It is widely recognised that this kind of ratcheting approach can undermine improvement incentives. The underlying issue here concerns the extent to which companies that take steps to deliver efficiency benefits should be allowed to share in those benefits, in order to give them an incentive to identify and deliver them in the first place. Considering the underlying concerns noted above in relation to this broader regulatory issue of ratchet effects can help with the identification of potential policy responses which is considered below.

6.3.2. The use of periodic reviews and regulatory commitments

Two approaches that could help guard against problematic tendencies of the kind noted above arising are:

- The use of periodic reviews; and,
- The development of some relevant regulatory commitments/policy positions.

These are considered in turn below.

The use of periodic reviews

A standard way of seeking to address ratchet effect concerns is through the use of some form of 'regulatory lag', such that charges are only fully adjusted to reflect efficiency savings periodically. This can allow the company to benefit to some extent from lower costs ahead of that adjustment point. A common approach is for costs to be re-assessed, and prices re-determined, at regular defined intervals, with this providing scope for companies to benefit from savings they are able to make in the period between re-determinations.[6] The use of pre-defined price review points would remove the scope for a relevant company to seek (implicitly or otherwise) to influence when a review would take place through its decision making. That is, it would remove the scope for a self-selection bias to arise in relation to when the relevant company is reviewed.

Using defined price review periods can, however, result in other potentially undesirable effects. Perhaps most notably, they can result in material divergences between allowed charges and underlying costs enduring for a significant amount of time ahead of the next review. The forecasts upon which a price control was set may end up significantly out of line with prevailing conditions, and this can itself become a material source of tension, including because the ongoing financeability of a company may be undermined because of divergences between regulatory forecasts and outturn conditions.

One important issue this raises is the extent to which it may be feasible and desirable to provide for prices to be adjusted automatically in between regulatory reviews by reference to movements in defined indices. In particular, where feasible it may be desirable for some input price risks (including potentially those associated with movements in energy prices – a source of significant current concern) to be managed through the use of some form of indexation, such that prices can better reflect prevailing conditions without the need for further regulatory review. The extent to which such approaches (which effectively involve allocating some relevant input price risks to water customers rather that to companies) are desirable is likely to depend on the degree to which companies may be better placed to manage the relevant risks (given the options they have available to them, including in terms of potential hedging strategies). Where input price movements are largely outside of the control of WSS providers, allowing for some automatic adjustments to prices between regulatory price reviews can provide an effective means of ensuring that water tariffs do not get too far out of line with relevant costs when circumstances change. This can help provide for a more robust price control arrangements, as it can avoid material changes in circumstances resulting in pressures for the price control to be 're-opened' and another regulatory review to be initiated.

These forecasting issues also raise important questions over what duration it is likely to be appropriate to set a price control for. The use of longer defined price control periods is typically viewed as potentially providing for more high-powered incentives during the control period. However, where there is material uncertainty over the evolution of relevant variables, and where there are material limitations in the extent to which it is credible for companies to bear the risks associated with longer price control periods, there may be a strong case adopting a relatively modest defined price control period. While the use of 5-year controls is common in the water sector, if - and to the extent that - periodic reviews were to be used, a shorter time period - such as 3 years - may be more appropriate for consideration in Estonia while understanding of the risks that may associated with setting longer control periods is further considered and better understood.

The scope for using such a periodic review approach, though, is likely to be heavily affected by the context which the regulator currently faces in Estonia. Perhaps most importantly (and as was noted earlier), the CA now has responsibility for approving all WSS tariffs, and – given the fragmented nature of, and the number companies currently operating in, the WSS sector – the prospect of implementing periodic reviews of charges for across all companies may raise major practical and logistical challenges.

This raises an important question of prioritisation, and associated risk management considerations. Relevant factors here include the following:

- There may be a strong proportionality-based case for focusing on larger companies, at least initially.
- The 'ratchet effect' concern highlighted above was related, to a significant degree, to companies that may be relatively successful and in a position to contemplate consolidation with one or more currently less successful other companies. This may provide a further, policy-targeting based rationale for focusing on larger companies, at least in the first instance.

A further important consideration concerns the scope for coordination benefits. This may suggest some benefits from seeking to review companies – to some extent at least – in clusters. The development of clusters could take explicit account of the likely scope for efficiency benefits being secured through different forms of consolidation, such that – for example – WSS utilities in defined geographic regions could be reviewed together, with this providing an opportunity for companies to submit evidence and be challenged on their assessment of the scope for consolidation benefits to be achieved. Price control determinations in specific regions could be adapted to and reflect the consolidation plans that have been developed and presented, and in particular, assessments of the scale and timing of relevant consolidation costs and benefits.

In principle, this issue of the clustering of reviews could be treated as distinct from, and could be approached separately to, decisions over the extent to which defined, periodic reviews are to be used. For example, the adoption of a cluster-based approach might imply that, when reviewing a given 'large' company, it would be desirable to also undertake some form of price review for other smaller companies in the same broad geographic location. But this need not imply that that the same review approach be used, or that the same duration of price control be imposed. Rather, clustering could be used more selectively and separately, where identified as potentially beneficial. The broader point here is simply that there may be some benefit from reviewing tariffs in clusters, and so giving some consideration to the potential options for and benefits of adopting clustering approaches may be desirable when price reviews are being initiated.

The development of regulatory commitments

The above focuses attention largely on constraints over <u>when</u> price reviews take place (i.e. such that they may only be expected to take place at defined intervals). A different, and potentially complementary, approach would be to consider trying to identify constraints on <u>how</u> future price reviews would take place. In particular, if consolidation activity would be likely to generate a price review, then there may be significant benefit from seeking to define some principles that would be expected to guide how that price review was undertaken. For example, it may be that the scope of the price review that would be triggered by consolidation activity could be explicitly defined in a relatively narrow way, such that it was focused on determining what the forward-looking approach should be to the sharing of the benefits (and risks) associated with the proposed consolidation activity. This could involve identifying a principle that the price review process should not be seeking to re-open the price controls that had been set for the companies individually.

The approach taken to the assessment of water mergers in England provides an example of one form that this kind of assessment could take. That is, the merger assessment can be viewed as taking the prevailing price control arrangements as given, and as the starting point, and focusing on the question of whether any adjustments to those existing arrangements would be justified as a result of the scope for the merger to have other adverse effects. In the water sector in England, the key consideration is typically whether the merger can be expected to hinder the ability of the regulator to set appropriate controls given the loss of a comparator company that could otherwise be used in benchmarking assessments. However, this comparator loss issue looks highly unlikely to throw up significant concerns for some time in the Estonian WSS sector, given the extent of fragmentation at present. The broader relevance of this example, though, is that it illustrates the scope for limiting the assessment of pricing associated with consolidation proposals to a narrow set of issues, in order to try to avoid the act of consolidation triggering a more general pricing 'reset' (given that – as was above - that could potentially act as a deterrent to otherwise desirable behaviour).

6.4. Options for enhancing the incentive arrangements

The tariff formula currently provides a way of applying some incentives related to the management of cost levels. In particular, it provides a framework that can be used to underpin price reviews over time, and that can allow regulatory challenges and adjustments to charge level proposals to be identified and applied through a widely recognised structured approach (i.e. the assessment of the building blocks discussed above). This section focuses on three potential ways in which the existing incentive arrangements could be enhanced that look to be well suited the current Estonian context. In particular, the following options are considered:

- Scope for greater use to be made of KPIs to generate desirable reputational incentives and transparency benefits; and,
- The development of more targeted incentives to encourage the development of efficiency-enhancing consolidation plans.
- Incentives that seek to guard against unduly limited considerations of potential consolidation options.

6.4.1. KPIs, reputational incentives and transparency benefits

Attention so far has been focused on performance in relation to costs. While this is central to economic regulation, regulators typically also put considerable effort into providing for broader performance assessments, and associated incentives. One reason for this is simply that there are a broader range of measurable aspects of performance that can be expected to have significant relevance for the overall outcomes that are delivered for customers and the environment. The monopoly nature of WSS services can mean that unduly limited attention would be given to these factors in the absence of some form of regulatory pressure, and that customers have limited access to information that can help them identify and compare the cost and quality of the services they are required to pay for. Where bill increase are required, this kind of lack of transparency and accountability can underpin significant customer acceptability problems, and make it more difficult to articulate – in credible ways – why bill increases should be viewed as justified, and as delivering demonstrable improvements.

An important additional consideration here concerns the risks of focusing incentive regulation on costs in a relatively narrow way. A standard concern in incentive regulation is that cost pressures may be resolved (deliberately or otherwise) through some form of 'under-delivery'. That is, one way in which a company may be able to out-perform a price control settlement (or lessen the extent of financial underperformance that might otherwise result), is to simply deliver less. This could manifest itself is through cost savings being made in ways that tend to undermine some aspects of service quality, and the risk of this has tended to be an important factor in the attention regulators in wide range of jurisdictions and sectors have given to the identification of service quality measures that can then be monitored alongside (or as part of the mechanics of) price control arrangements.

The transparency of performance information is a key consideration here, and the approaches that are adopted to providing for transparency – and, more broadly, for stakeholder engagement – provide an important part of the way that regulators typically seek to encourage performance improvements and guard against the deterioration of performance. The following first sets out some of the different ways in which transparency can help generate better outcomes from regulatory processes, before describing a particular example – the approach used by ERSAR in Portugal – that looks well suited as a relevant reference point against which potential developments to the transparency arrangements in Estonia could be considered.

Recognising the scope of potential transparency benefits

Transparency requirements have been used as an important tool by many regulators internationally, and can help promote improvements in a wide range of ways, including by:

1. Improving company, and company owner, awareness of how performance compares with that of others in terms of those measures that are made available, and of what 'good' might look like.[7] This may, in and of itself, help to motivate desirable change by 'shining a light' on relevant

disparities in relation to features of performance that may otherwise be receiving relatively limited attention (given other prevailing company and company owner priorities).

2. Improving customer, and other stakeholder awareness of the comparisons that are made available. This can increase the scope for customers and other stakeholders to challenge companies, and local governments, on their performance in ways that may create desirable pressures for improvement.
3. Increasing the quality and sophistication of performance comparisons that can be made (which can in turn magnify the impact of (1) and (2)). Important underlying issues here typically include improvements to the development of standardised ways in which information must be compiled and made available. This can have a range of different dimensions, including because:
   - With more comparative information being made available, and/or information being shared in more accessible and prominent ways, companies can face strong incentives to seek to ensure that comparisons are made on a reasonable basis, in a context where observed performance differences for some measures may relate closely to differences in relevant underlying circumstances (such as the density of the population that different companies serve). That is, a context where there may be greater scope for undesirable inferences to be drawn from available comparative information can result in greater effort being put into refining the basis upon which it is viewed as reasonable to make such comparisons, which can provide a more robust basis for subsequent regulatory assessments. Importantly, it is to be expected that there will be significant divergences of interest between companies in terms of how comparisons are made, because a change in approach that improves the relative performance of one company can be expected to imply worse performance for some others. This can create for a tension between companies that a regulator can seek to use (by providing a forum in which evidence in relation to different approaches can be presented) to try to identify and test which comparison approaches may indeed be most appropriate.
   - Transparency arrangements typically raise important questions over how potentially complex and extensive information on different aspects of company performance can be communicated in more accessible ways. In line with this, regulators often put considerable effort into the development of standardised and streamlined performance reports that can provide a relatively simple means for customers and other stakeholders to get a high-level view of WSS company performance across some key areas of interest (further comments on how this might be done are included below in the discussion of the Portuguese ERSAR example).
4. Extending the ways and enhancing the effectiveness with which the regulator can seek to use comparative information in its price review determinations, and its associated development of incentive arrangements.
5. Improving customer and other stakeholder awareness and understanding of the trade-offs faced in relation to the sector, and improving the credibility of company and other communications related to those trade-offs (because those communications sit within a broader framework of information provision and challenge). This can provide a basis for better informed and more credible engagement with water customers in ways that can improve the likely acceptability of bill increases where that can be shown to be necessary for the delivery of valued improvements.

It is important to note that the information under discussion here concerns different aspects of the performance of monopoly public service providers. While there is likely to be some relevant performance information that it is appropriate to treat as confidential (for example, for security reasons), experience from other countries clearly shows that substantial levels of performance information can be made available while at the same time taking appropriate account of relevant confidentiality concerns. This is the case even where companies are privately owned (as in England), notwithstanding the potential for this to raise additional types of commercial confidentiality concerns.

Given the public service nature of WSS companies, and the broad range of benefits that can be associated with transparency requirements, there looks to be a strong case for adopting a presumption that the regulator is able to introduce transparency requirements, other than where companies are able to provide compelling reasons as to why that would not be appropriate.

In line with the above comments, there may be significant benefits associated with enhancing the transparency of – and the accessibility of, and prominence given to – WSS company performance information. There is currently a form of 'traffic light' approach used in Estonia that provides for public access to some WSS information that can be compared across municipalities.[8] However, there looks to be scope to provide for much more effective communication of relative company performance, and – as a result – much sharper reputational incentives, through the development and prominent use of a dedicated set of WSS KPI 'traffic light' comparisons. As is discussed further below, a key issue here is the extent to which performance comparisons can be viewed as concise, credible and easy to understand from the perspective of customers and other stakeholders, with these features underpinning the force that this form of information provision can have. The current WSS 'traffic light' information that is provided sits within a much broader set of municipality information, and while it provides some relevant information that can be compared across municipalities, it does little to inform the relevance of the information that is provided, or to provide confidence that consideration of the WSS information that is provided could be expected to provide reliable basis upon which to draw comparative inferences.

In large part these limitations stem from the inherent difficulties associated with developing benchmarking arrangements in a context where company circumstances can differ materially in a range of ways relevant to service provision. The current information that is provided can be viewed as a useful first step, but much more could be done to seek to improve and refine the set of KPIs that are presented, to develop ways of providing more meaningful benchmarking of performance between companies (including through comparisons within and between different clusters of companies that may share broadly similar operating conditions, at least in some important respects), and to communicate that information in more prominent and easier to understand ways. The intention here is not to say that there is an alternative and readily available better set of KPIs and benchmarking approaches that should be applied and more extensively communicated in place of the current approach, but rather to emphasise the potential benefits of putting policy effort into a developing a process that can be expected to improve the measurement, use and public awareness of relevant KPIs over time. ERSAR provides a useful example of what that kind of process for the enhancement of transparency might look like, and its performance benchmarking arrangements are summarised below.

ERSAR as a helpful reference point

The approach to WSS quality of service regulation that has been developed and applied by ERSAR, the Water and Waste Services Regulation Authority in Portugal, looks to be particularly well suited as guide for considering ways in which it may be desirable for the Estonian service performance arrangements to be developed. It is notable, that the ERSAR quality of service arrangements are applied in a context where there are currently 263 water supply utilities, and 266 wastewater management utilities, all state or municipality owned.[9] ERSAR has described the goals of its quality of service regulation as being to:

- Protect the interests of users regarding the quality of service provided.
- Compare results between entities through benchmarking.[10]
- Guide entities towards efficiency and effectiveness; and,
- Consolidate a culture of providing information that is: concise, credible and easy to understand.[11]

These goals look to fit well with the circumstances faced in Estonia, and the approach to quality of service regulation that ERSAR applies – which relies on the development of 'soft', reputation-based incentive –

could provide a valuable complement to the CA's current approach to regulating tariff levels, or to a refined version of that included some of the other framework refinement options referred to in this report. While it is notable that regulators in some other jurisdictions (including in England and Wales, and Scotland) have applied financial incentives to service performance metrics, the use of such approaches can generate further risks of unwanted effects arising, and the relatively limited regulatory use that has been made of such metrics to date in Estonia strongly suggests that the consideration of such approaches would be premature at present. In any event, experience strongly suggests reputation-based approaches, focused on the provision of concise, credible and easy to understand comparative information, can have powerful incentive effects.[12]

ERSAR operates an annual process that involves utilities submitting the required data, that data being validated and treated to provide for benchmarking, and utilities then getting a right of reply before the finalised data is then published and publicised (including through an App). The approach focuses on providing information on around 15 Key Performance Indicators for each service (i.e. water and wastewater), with indicators designed to reflect performance in relation to the protection of user interests, service provision sustainability and environmental sustainability.[13] The specific KPIs to be used could, of course, be adapted to the Estonian context where appropriate, and it is notable that data related to many of the broad areas covered by ERSAR KPIs is already collected in Estonia.[14]

Also, it is notable that many of the KPIs used by ERSAR appear routinely in service performance assessments that are produced in a number of other jurisdictions, including, for example:

- Service interruptions (water supply).
- Mains failures (water supply).
- Water losses (water supply).
- Flooding incidents (wastewater).
- Sewer collapses (wastewater).
- Compliance with discharge permits (wastewater).
- A customer complaints metric (water and wastewater).
- An affordability metric (water and wastewater).

The notable features of the ERSAR approach, therefore, are less to do with the specific indicators that it provides for collection of (because, as above, it is common for similar types of indicators to be collected in other jurisdictions, including Estonia), and more to do with the processes and approach through which that performance information is presented and communicated in clear, concise and accessible ways. For each performance indicator, companies are ranked and compared with their peers through the use of clusters, based on the different regions in which they operate, and the characteristics of the area (e.g. rural vs urban).[15] As can be seen in diagrams below, this is used to provide an easy to understand 'traffic light' based presentation of comparisons that allow for straightforward identification of those operators that are best performing, above and below average, and so on. The annual reports allow for comparison between expected and actual performance, and for performance levels to be monitored over time, with this assisting with the prioritisation of improvement opportunities.

Figure 6.1. Extracts from ERSAR service performance information

Centro e Lisboa

(densidade de ramais igual ou superior a 20/km de rede)

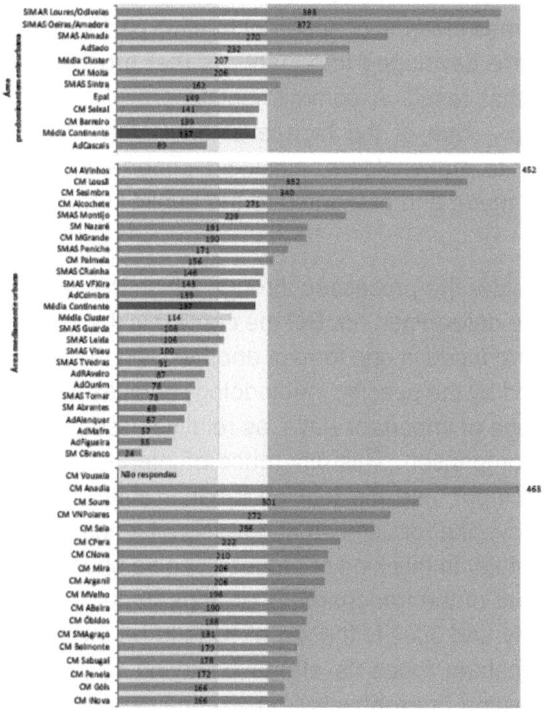

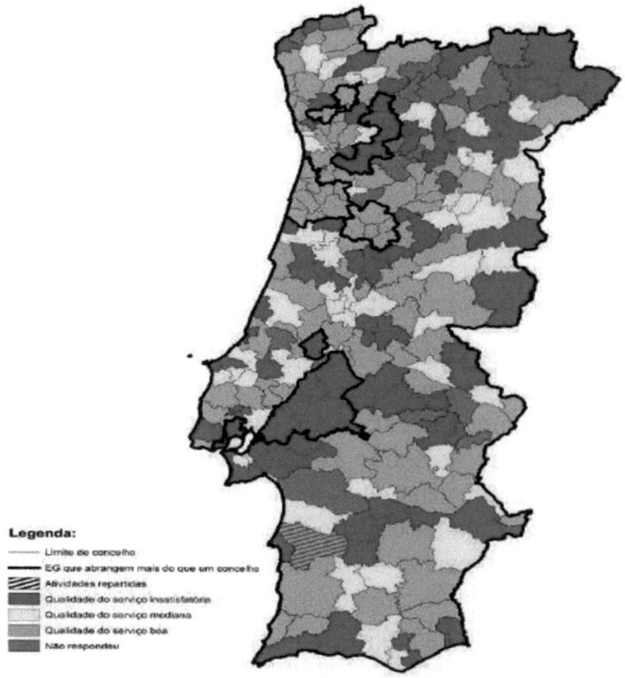

Figura 67. Distribuição geográfica da avaliação do indicador AA12 para o serviço em baixa

In line with the comments above, the purpose of highlighting the ERSAR approach here is not to present the specific methodologies that are used for to calculate and compare performance indicators as ones that should be considered for usage in Estonia. Rather, the ERSAR example is intended to provide a useful reference point when considering how WSS performance data can be communicated in ways that can enhance the scope for comparative, reputational pressures to highlight better and worse performing areas, and in doing so to help make more visible where improvements may be both possible and appropriate. The adoption of this kind of approach could be tailored to reflect the relevant circumstances in Estonia (including, for example, in terms of likely data quality), with a range of underlying choices being required in relation to matters including:

- The specific KPIs that should be use
- How data should be audited
- How KPI information should be clustered and otherwise organised and adjusted when benchmarking results are being presented.

In line with the comments on cost assessment above, the most appropriate way to develop the specific performance benchmarking approaches that are to be applied will depend on a range of detailed and context specific matters that go well beyond the scope of this assessment, and is best viewed as something that would be expected to evolve over time. The ERSAR approach looks to provide a helpful reference point when considering the framework and processes within which benchmarking arrangements could be developed and applied. In particular, it focuses attention on trying to make available, and communicate, clear and easy to understand information on comparative performance. With this treated as an appropriate objective, attention can then be turned to the detailed and ongoing work that is likely to be needed to deliver on that. This is not a question of simply seeking to identify what the 'right' set of measures and underlying methodologies (e.g. for clustering municipalities) are as a stand-alone exercise. Rather, it is more a question of seeking to develop processes that can be expected to help provide ways of building and refining more appropriate approaches over time, recognising that this is challenging to do.

The challenges arise because there are different dimensions of performance that could be measured and compared in different ways, and decisions in relation to those dimensions and measurement and comparison techniques may imply materially different outcomes in terms of apparent relative performance. This tends to make the process through which methods are developed important, as that process can potentially help give legitimacy to the overall outcomes that result. A commitment to providing clear, concise and easy to understand performance information – one of the high-level goals that ERSAR identifies – is important here, because it makes it clear to stakeholders, including importantly WSS companies, that performance comparisons are going to be made and presented to the public in relatively simplified formats of the kind illustrated above.

Having made such a commitment, it then important to consider the processes through which the specific performance measurement and comparison methods will be determined on. But the context is then one in which all companies know that this kind information will be produced in one form or another, and they know that how they are shown as performing is likely to be affected by the specific methodology choices that are made. Company interests, though, will clearly differ in a range of important ways, as relative assessments will show some as performing well and others poorly by comparison. This difference of interests across companies provides a valuable source of information and input, and the tension it can create between companies can be used by the regulator to try to help improve the robustness and reasonableness of the measures being generated. Importantly, the role of the regulator in this kind of process can be understood as effectively 'chairing' a forum/process for the development of the transparency arrangements. That is, the regulator would not be expected to itself seek to identify and specify the set of KPIs to be used, and bases upon which they would be compared, but could instead focus its efforts on trying to promote improvements through encouraging the submission and testing of proposals from companies and other stakeholders. Again, the commitment to producing and publicising the comparative information is key as it can allow attention to focused on more productive questions concerning how that information should be developed, rather than on the question of whether it should be developed, where company interests may be more aligned, in that there may be a general preference for limiting the extent to which there is broader emphasis put on company performance levels.

6.4.2. Incentives to encourage the development of efficiency-enhancing consolidation plans

A number of regulators internationally – including the Essential Services Commission (ESC) in Australia,[16] and Ofwat in England and Wales[17] - have introduced forms of business plan incentives, typically to try to address concerns that companies may otherwise have an incentive to be unduly conservative in their planning, and to do too little to address the future challenges that are faced. Such approaches can be understood as effectively rewarding early movers for the information they provide in terms of the improvements that their plan presents as achievable. Where the company delivers on that more challenging plan, the outcomes can then form part of future benchmarking efforts that can increase the pressure on other companies to improve, while also providing a practical example of how that improvement may be achievable.

The PREMO framework

The approach developed by the ESC (the economic regulator of the Victoria water sector in Australia) is referred to as the PREMO[18] framework, and provides a useful reference point. Under the PREMO framework, instead of applying a uniform weighted average cost of capital (WACC) across companies, the allowed return on equity is varied depending on the level of 'ambition' shown in the relevant company's price submission. The diagram below illustrates how a higher return on equity is when setting allowed charges where the ESC identifies a plan as more efficient, with four different categories having been identified:

- Basic: where the submission is identified as reflecting stagnating or declining performance the allowed return on equity would be set at a level commensurate with the benchmark real cost of debt.
- Standard: where a slightly higher return on equity allowance is provided for to reflect that the submission is viewed as a good value proposition for customers but that represents a continuation of existing outcomes and cost efficiency targets.
- Advanced: a more ambitious submission that will generally commit to improved outcomes in terms of services, prices or both, and would receive a higher equity return allowance.
- Leading: where the proposals place the company as a sector leader on key aspects of performance.

Figure 6.2. Illustration of (real) return on equity allowances under the ESC's PREMO approach

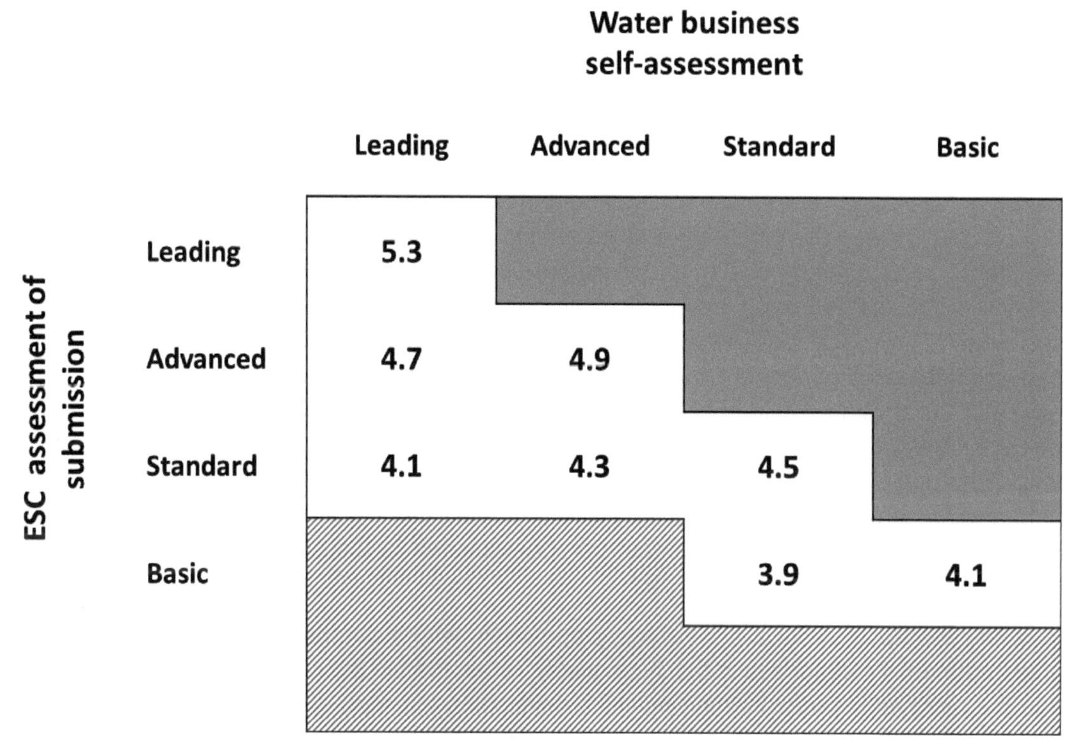

Source: Figure 2.1 in: https://www.esc.vic.gov.au/sites/default/files/documents/Water-Pricing-Framework-and-Approach-Final-Paper-Oct-2016.pdf

As can be seen in the diagram, the allowed return on equity is also made dependent on the company's own assessment of the level of ambition of its plan, with this intended to encourage company's to put forward their 'best offer'. In particular, it is notable that - under the approach – a company gets a lower allowed return on equity if ESC judges it as having a lower level of ambition than had been presented in the company's self-assessment. The ESC identifies the red shaded area as indicating where it reserves the discretion to adopt a different approach, such as setting a shorter control and/or requiring resubmission.

Some core features of business plan quality incentives

The PREMO approach provides an interesting example in part because of the clear and explicit way in which adjusts the return equity allowance depending on assessments of level of ambition. At the same time, it includes levels of complexity (including the use made of company self-assessments) that seem unlikely to be necessary or well suited in the current Estonian context. In practice, this kind of business plan quality incentive approach can be viewed as comprising of three core features:

1. Scope for identifying company business plans as falling into more than one quality category.
2. Identification of the criteria that would be used to determine which quality category a business plan should be identified as in.
3. Explicit and credible up-front identification of how companies will be treated differently when identified as falling in one quality category rather than another.

The following considers how each of these features might be applied in an Estonian WSS context.

Identifying categories of business plan quality

The PREMO approach involves the regulator having to determine which of four 'quality' categories a price submission falls into: basic, standard, advanced, leading. Ofwat (the economic regulator in England and Wales) also used four categories – significant scrutiny, slow-track, fast-track, exceptional – in its review of price controls for the 2020-25 period, although in practice only allocated companies to three of those categories (with no business plans categorised as 'exceptional'). It is notable that in an earlier development of this kind of approach, the British energy regulator Ofgem applied a simpler categorisation that distinguished only between whether companies should treated as 'fast-track' - because their proposals had been identified as of 'high' quality and therefore appropriate to implement quickly - or 'slow-track' – because their proposals had been identified as of relatively lower quality and as requiring further, more detailed scrutiny. The use of four (rather than two) categories in the PREMO and Ofwat approaches can be viewed as a simple refinement of Ofgem's approach, that allows a further subcategorization of the 'high' (fast-track) and 'lower' (slow-track) quality categories. It is not obvious, however, that this further refinement would be particularly helpful if such an approach were to be introduced in Estonia, at least in a first iteration. In particular, the use of additional categories increases complexity, and the burden that the regulator (in seeking to specify and apply the categories) and regulated companies (in seeking to understand and determine how to respond to the categories) can be expected to face, but may provide little additional benefit over a simpler two category approach.

Given this, the development of a two-category approach, where companies can explicitly expect more favourable treatment if categorised in the 'high quality' rather than in the lower quality category, looks likely to provide the most appropriate starting point for developing this kind of approach in Estonia. That said, there may be a case for explicitly identifying the possibility of using two separate 'high quality' categories (with only one lower quality category), if there are some sources of additional benefit – for example, additional support from EU funds – that may be available in some circumstances but not others. Where this is the case, access to the additional support could be made conditional on achieving 'high quality' status in the regulator's business plan assessment, but would then involve some further hurdles having to be overcome.

Criteria for assessing which category a plan should be identified as in

For its review of 2020-25 business plans, Ofwat developed (ahead of company submission of business plans) a relatively extensive assessment framework that highlighted both the 'test areas' that were going be explicitly assessed, and what the characteristics of high quality, ambitious and innovative plans would be likely to be in each of those test areas.[19] The test areas included a range of core priority matters such as securing costs efficiently, addressing affordability and vulnerability, and securing long-term resilience, and for each test area, Ofwat identified some questions it would be relevant to consider. For example, in relation to securing long-term resilience, the following questions were identified:

- How well has the company used the best available evidence to objectively assess and prioritise the diverse range of risks and consequences of disruptions to its systems and services, and engaged effectively with customers on its assessment of these risks and consequences?
- How well has the company objectively assessed the full range of mitigation options and selected the solutions that represent the best value for money over the long term, and have support from customers?

For a plan to be viewed as 'high quality', Ofwat identified that (among other things): the company will provide clear evidence that they have objectively considered and assessed the full range of resilience management options. For a plan to be viewed as ambitious and innovative, Ofwat identified that the company would need to present strong evidence that it has used robust, ambitious and innovative approaches to assess and mitigate risks to long-term resilience in the round.

Developing this kind of business plan inventive approach in Estonia would not require the extent of development – in terms of assessment criteria and questions - that Ofwat undertook. However, some up-front specification of what the key test areas would be, and what sorts of questions would be expected to guide the assessment in those areas, is likely to be helpful both because it can give greater clarity to companies on what they can expect, but also because the regulator plan and deliver the subsequent assessments (by making it clear what practical steps that is likely to involve). When seeking to specify how companies should be assessed, it can be helpful to distinguish between the following:

- Hygiene factors: to what extent are there criteria should be viewed as a necessary condition for any company's business plan to even be considered as potentially 'high quality' (such that the meeting of this criteria can be treated as a form of hygiene factor in the assessment process)? This may include reference to current performance levels and financial health.
- Other differentiating factors: given its strategic importance for the Estonian WSS sector, it would be expected that consideration of other differentiating factors would be heavily focused on the extent to which companies are bringing forward new consolidation options, and the extent to which they are able demonstrate, robustly, that those consolidation options can be expected to be efficiency enhancing.

The relevance of different potential forms of consolidation is considered later in this section when some of the potential constraints to consolidation options emerging are considered.

The benefits of a plan being identified as of higher quality

Regulators have typically sought to provide for financial, reputational and procedural incentives to be associated with the identification of a company's business plan as 'high quality' within this kind of assessment framework. In line with this, in Estonia, the development and submission of credible, efficiency enhancing consolidation plans could be encouraged in a number of different ways, including through:

- The use of a higher WACC in the tariff setting methodology than would otherwise have been allowed for (as is explicitly provided for in the PREMO approach).
- The explicit provision of some other form of financial reward: for example, access to grant funding or preferential borrowing opportunities.
- Greater scope for support with respect to financeability using accelerated depreciation (where that can be shown to be consistent with bill affordability and acceptability issues being sufficiently addressed).
- Scope for the price control to be determined for a longer period: in line with the comments earlier, this may be important in providing consolidating parties with an opportunity to share in the benefits

of the plans they bring forward (particularly where there may be some time lag associated with the securing of those benefits).

- Presentation of the outcomes of the assessment in a way that can be expected to provide material reputational benefits for those associated with successful companies: the regulator can actively seek to highlight and publicise its assessments of 'high quality' proposals, and then use the companies actions as a positive case study to promote further change.
- Procedural benefits associated with less extensive review requirements, providing overall performance remains sufficiently 'on-track'.

The importance and implications of credibility

For business plan incentives to encourage companies to put more effort into developing efficiency enhancing consolidation plans than they would otherwise, attention needs to be given to the overall attractiveness of the rewards that are potentially on offer. The scale of financial rewards can be expected to be an important part of this, and to merit careful consideration by reference to the sorts of decision making that companies face (i.e. in terms of the risks they may be taking on if pursuing novel consolidation approaches). Another key factor, however, concerns credibility. Credibility can be enhanced to some extent through the publication of up-front information on available rewards, and the PREMO framework can be viewed as notable in this respect in terms of its clear articulation of the different WACC outcomes that can arise. However, interpretations of the relevance of reward information will be heavily dependent on perceptions of how the arrangements might be applied in practice. This can leave scope a significant dampening of incentives to arise as a result of concerns over the likelihood of a company actually securing a reward even where it seeks to respond in appropriate ways through the development of consolidation plans. For example, a company may envisage a situation where it has developed a challenging and innovative consolidation proposal only for the regulator to classify it as somehow deficient and not meriting the 'high quality' classification, and the associated securing of the identified rewards.

To some extent, this kind of issue is inevitable with the introduction of a novel assessment mechanism, and given uncertainty over what plans might actually be presented to the regulator, it can be very difficult to address this kind of issue up-front, other than through the development and publication of the kind of a assessment criteria discussed above. However, in practice, much can be done to address this matter through the way in which the regulator engages throughout the process. Uncertainty (and the potential dampening of incentives) may be greatest where the regulator adopt a relatively arms-length approach to the process, such that – once its broad intended approach has been outlined – it is viewed as being for companies to interpret and respond to that approach, with the regulator's next key role in the process coming at the business plan evaluation and categorisation stage. Under this kind of arms-length approach companies may expect to be poorly sighted in terms of how well-aligned their plans are with regulatory expectations, and thus may heavily discount the prospect of actually securing the rewards that have been presented as potentially available. There may be a significant risk that the incentive arrangements have little impact, and indeed there may end up being little basis for the regulator to provide any rewards.

A different approach, though, would be for the regulator to be very clear up-front that it recognises this uncertainty (and the effects it could have), and is committed to seeking work with companies to help reduce that uncertainty, and then to allow for rewards under the incentive mechanism providing it is presented with credible consolidation plans. Under this kind of more active approach, the business plan assessment process can be explicitly presented as iterative one, in which the regulator will seek to provide guidance to companies who consider themselves potentially in contention for a reward, in order to try to resolve concerns they may have about misalignment of views. This can provide a situation in which there is limited remaining uncertainty over the final regulatory assessment (i.e. companies should have good sight of how their plans will be assessed) because of commentary the regulator has already provided along the way. In practice, this could be applied by adopting something like the following stages:

1. Clearly identify the hygiene factors (referred to above) that the earning of rewards would be conditional on: the development of these could include some engagement with companies that might be expected to bring forward consolidation plans to ensure the criteria are not unduly restrictive (while at the same time act as an appropriate initial filter).
2. Provide an explicit option for companies to check they have satisfied the hygiene factor requirements: this would not be a requirement, but would be expect to initiate a process of engagement with potentially successful companies.
3. Provide scope for companies to 'check-in' periodically on their developing plans, with the aim of identifying potentially material limitations (and where there are significant misalignments of view) at an early stage.
4. Where common issues are identified through the check-in process (for example, with respect to sufficiency of evidence on likely long-term impacts), the regulator could publish a brief update note in order to improve on the broader transparency of the arrangements.
5. Allow for early submission of draft plans on which formal feedback (with 'points to address') could be provided.

To some extent, the above can be viewed as similar to a form of procurement process in which – after an initial 'pre-qualification' phase – some ongoing negotiation and engagement is often an important part of ensuring that final 'bids' are well suited to the buyer's requirements. Although the context clearly differs here in some key respects, it is notable that there is scope for regulator and company interests to be relatively well-aligned, and the purpose of adopting something like this kind of more active engagement approach is to try to keep the scope for that high-level alignment clearly in mind for all sides, and to reduce the scope of unhelpful surprises to emerge (the prospect of which – in line with the above comments – may be viewed as a significant deterrent to the development of potentially beneficial plans).

6.4.3. Incentives that seek to guard against unduly limited consideration of potential consolidation options

The above has focused on how incentives based on the overall quality of company business plans might be used to encourage the development of beneficial consolidation proposals, in particular by seeking to reward plans that are identified as 'high quality'. However, a different form of incentive that also merits consideration (alongside the use of such approaches), involves providing scope for penalties to be applied as means of encouraging the more extensive and effective use of options appraisal methods.

The extent to which investment plans are based upon sufficient consideration of alternative potential options – including options that involve consolidation – is likely to become an increasingly important factor over time and raises questions over the appropriate scope of the regulator's cost assessment activities. A distinction can be drawn between:

- Identifying how desired outcomes are best met (i.e. the choice of approach); and,
- Identifying the efficient cost of delivering the approach that has been selected.

A narrow cost assessment exercise may focus only on the second bullet point above. However, there may be substantial scope for efficiency improvements associated with the first bullet, particularly where there may be opportunities to deliver services in more coordinated and consolidated ways that enable greater economies of scale benefits. In line with this, there may be some benefit in seeking to directly target the sufficiency of 'how' assessments.

When considering ways of addressing this, it is helpful distinguish – in principle – between the following two types of assessment that a regulator might undertake:

- Providing for detailed, expert reviews of the options appraisals that companies have undertaken.

- Assessing whether companies have undertaken appropriately robust options appraisals processes.

Historically, many regulators have tended to adopt the first 'expert reviewer' role (or have appointed engineering consultants to undertake it on their behalf). However, this can involve the regulator effectively taking on responsibility for demonstrating why a given assessment by the relevant company should be regarded as not sufficiently well founded, by reference to the regulator's own assessment of alternatives. Such an approach can be resource intensive as it will often require considerable detailed work in relation to specific matters where the regulator inevitably has relatively limited information and expertise. This can then put significant limitations on what it is realistic to expect the regulatory review process to achieve (given, in particular, relevant information asymmetries).

The second role noted above seeks to address matters in a different way by taking a step back and focusing regulatory attention on the adequacy of the options appraisal processes that companies have undertaken, rather than on the detailed analysis and findings of the specific appraisals they have produced. From this perspective, it is viewed as for companies to demonstrate to the regulator that they have conducted appropriate options appraisal processes, and if companies are unable to do that sufficiently, then that – in and of itself – could be treated by the regulator as a basis for some form of penalty to be applied (through making a downward adjustment to the cost allowance the company).

Ofwat has adopted this latter kind of approach in England and Wales in some of its stand-alone (i.e. not benchmarked) assessments of proposed investments, where it has applied the following approach:[20]

- If a company provided evidence that a lower cost option was available but gave no reasons as to why it was rejected, Ofwat would use the lower cost option when calculating the allowed costs.
- Where a company has not provided evidence that its selected option is optimal (i.e where there is insufficient evidence that the potential for using alternative, lower cost, options was explored and assessed), Ofwat would apply a 20% reduction to the company's proposed cost estimate, intended to protect customers from the risk that a potentially sub-optimal solution was being adopted.

On the face of it, this kind of approach might be viewed as relatively arbitrary, in that it could result in a substantial gap between the amount a company has identified as needed to deliver on a specific project, and the amount the regulator allows to be recovered through charges, without the regulator having explicitly identified that the lower amount should be viewed as sufficient. However, the regulatory approach can understood as intended to incentivise companies to ensure that high quality options appraisal processes have been undertaken (and that the company can demonstrate this), in a context where the quality of the appraisal processes is viewed as potentially having a substantial impact on costs that may be recovered from customers over many years.[21] The approach can therefore be understood as having risk-based foundations, in that companies that seek to proceed with highly material projects without having undertaken an adequate options appraisal process can be viewed as exposing customers to significant risks of funding inefficient investments.

Ofwat's penalty-based approach is applied in a context where it sits within a broader set of reward and penalty arrangements that private water companies are subject to. The different context in Estonia may mean that such an approach would be unlikely to be feasible or desirable. However, an alternative to applying this kind of downward adjustment to allowed costs would be to effectively not accept the relevant part of the price control submission, and to send it back to the company to address the limitations in its assessment of options. That is, the regulator could be viewed as introducing a form of assessment 'gateway' that companies must successfully pass through in order to secure funding for significant new investment projects. If the company has not shown that relevant options have been appropriately taken into consideration, then that part of the price control application could get stripped out and sent back.

This may provide a more practical and appropriate means of proceeding in Estonia, with the regulator providing some guidance on what is expected in terms of options appraisal including in terms of the consideration of consolidation options. In this way, evidence of having conducted an adequate options evaluation process could be effectively become treated as a condition of a successful application for relatively large-scale requests for the recognition of new investment costs in the tariff formula. The availability of practical evidence of potential consolidation options – including from pilot study activity – can be of considerable importance under such an approach. In particular, such evidence provides a concrete basis upon which a regulator could question the adequacy of a company's consideration of options, as it can look for evidence that the lessons from the pilot study have been recognised, and that the potential relevance of those lessons have been explored and tested. By making pricing assessments in other company areas dependent, to some extent, on the consideration that has been given to pilot study evidence, the regulator can effectively raise the prominence and importance of that evidence, and increase the scope of the likely impact of pilot study activity.

6.5. Summary and recommendations

This Chapter has reviewed aspects of the framework for the economic regulation of WSS services in Estonia, and sought to identify ways in which that framework could be further developed to assist in the achievement of strategic objectives, including by encouraging efficiency improvements through consolidation. It has considered – drawing, where helpful, on examples of international experience – some ways in which the identification and achievement of WSS efficiency gains might be further encouraged. The key points that have been identified are summarised below through the identification of a set of recommendations and suggestions concerning how the current arrangements could be developed so as to help tackle the key WSS challenges that are likely to be faced.

6.5.1. Recommendation 1: The CA maintains but develops its pragmatic approach funding depreciation

The CA maintains its approach to applying the tariff formula, including its current pragmatic approach to funding depreciation, which allows for companies to raise financeability concerns (and for the CA to consider the case for accelerated depreciation) on a case-by-case basis. In practice, this can be understood as providing scope for some allowance for the amortisation of EU funded assets to be provided for in tariff levels, but on a case-by-case basis. It is recommended that the CA provides guidance on the extent to which there may be available scope for this flexibility that identified conditions that the CA might expect to be met in order for accelerated depreciation to be allowed for (with those conditions intended – in particular – to guard against the risk that providing for a higher level of depreciation allowance might dampen incentives for efficiency improvements).

This looks to provide a reasonable and pragmatic approach to adopt while other policies aimed at promoting consolidation are pursued, and could itself form part of an approach that encourages consolidation (e.g. by making access to accelerated depreciation conditional on appropriate consideration of consolidation options). Greater levels of consolidation should allow for the smoothing of capital maintenance requirements between companies and help ease the transition to use of more long-term, sustainable depreciation allowances over time.

6.5.2. Recommendation 2: The CA introduces a periodic approach to price reviews, and develops principles which limit the extent to which existing price controls would be 're-opened' as a result of consolidation activity

The CA replaces the current application-based approach to the triggering of price reviews with an approach that involves companies being subject to price reviews at defined intervals. The use of periodic price reviews could be undertaken in clusters (e.g. regional clusters), and focused on larger companies initially, in order to help manage resource implications.

The current application-based approach has the potential to discourage the bringing forward of consolidation plans, as that may be expected to trigger a price review that may then leave one or more of the potentially consolidating parties worse off.

6.5.3. Recommendation 3: The CA develops a Service Performance Incentive framework

The CA develops, makes publicly available and publicises a KPI framework that provides concise, credible and easy to understand comparisons between companies, using the Portuguese ERSAR approach as a guide.

The development of this kind of framework has the potential to deliver substantial benefits by providing more robust protection of customer interests, and guiding companies toward the use of more efficient and effective approaches, using reputational incentives. A key starting point would be a commitment to the adoption of such an approach so that industry attention could be focused on how that would be best achieved (rather than whether performance comparisons should be made more prominent).

6.5.4. Recommendations 4: The CA develops incentives that focus on company plans, and planning processes

The CA develops guidance setting out how it will enable companies that present credible, efficiency-enhancing consolidation plans to share in the benefits they result in, through the treatment of consolidation costs, and commitments concerning how rapidly future efficiency savings will be reflected in allowed prices. The CA also develops guidance setting its expectations with respect to companies being able to demonstrate that robust options appraisal processes have been undertaken in the development of capex plans, and how capex applications will be treated where a company is unable to adequately demonstrate that.

These proposals directly target key aspects associated with encouraging the bringing forward of efficiency enhancing consolidation plans: the extent to which companies can expect to benefit from bringing forward such plans (given the scope for 'ratchet effects' to otherwise undermine such incentives); and the risk that companies do not adequately explore or consider different ways of addressing outcome requirements when developing their capex plans. Examples from Australia and the UK look to provide a useful reference point.

Notes

[1] The responsibilities of the Estonian economic regulator, and its approach to tariff regulation are considered below.

[2] And approving the methodology for calculating connection fees.

[3] In particular, the Water Act and the Public Water Supply and Sewerage Act.

[4] Although presented as a 'backward-looking' role here, it should be noted that the approach to funding the recovery of capital expenditure incurred in previous years is typically viewed as critical when the credibility of the cost recovery arrangements is being considered, and can therefore have a significant bearing on the ability of companies to raise new finance, and the costs of raising that finance.

[5] A broader framework for applying business plan incentives is discussed in a later section.

[6] More sophisticated 'rolling' incentive mechanisms have also been used to try address concerns over the dampening of incentives for efficiency improvements as the next re-determination point approaches.

[7] The identification of appropriate indicators is discussed further below.

[8] Kohalikud omavalitsused | Ministry of Finance

[9] With direct management, delegation or concession operating models used.

[10] The selection of specific indicators is discussed below.

[11] The extracts from ERSAR reports shown below illustrate how this has been done through the use performance comparison charts and a map-based comparison of performance between utilities using a traffic light system.

[12] Some comments on how this kind of process might be applied in Estonia are provided below.

[13] Some comments are provided below on the implications this may have for the approach adopted in Estonia.

[14] See: https://keskkonnaagentuur.ee/analuusid-ja-indikaatorid/indikaatorid/vesi#heitveega-keskkonda- .

[15] Some brief comments on the development of clustering approaches are provided below.

[16] https://www.esc.vic.gov.au/sites/default/files/documents/Water-Pricing-Framework-and-Approach-Final-Paper-Oct-2016.pdf .

[17] See, for example: https://www.ofwat.gov.uk/regulated-companies/price-review/2019-price-review/initial-assessment-of-plans/ .

[18] The terms PREMO comes from the different identified elements of the assessment process: Performance; Risk; Engagement; Management; Outcomes.

[19] A detailed description of Ofwat's assessment approach is provided in: https://www.ofwat.gov.uk/wp-content/uploads/2017/12/Appendix-13-IAP-FM.pdf .

[20] See p54-55 of: https://www.ofwat.gov.uk/wp-content/uploads/2019/12/PR19-final-determinations-Securing-cost-efficiency-technical-appendix.pdf .

[21] It is notable that, in presenting its approach, Ofwat highlighted that option can range considerably in cost, and pointed to companies as having provided evidence that there could be a 35% difference in cost between reinforcing as opposed to replacing a main.

7 An action-oriented strategy and an action plan to carry out reform

An action-oriented strategy brings the threads together. It recapitulates the case for reform, essentially claiming that business-as-usual is not an option and the time for reform is now. It captures the main elements of a voluntary reform. It is supported by an action plan, which offers a sequence of reforms (from urgent to medium-term action) and allocates responsibilities across stakeholders.

7.1. Background and objectives

The Ministry of the Environment of Estonia jointly with other governmental authorities (the Ministry of Finance, the Minister of Public Administration), the European Commission – DG Reform, and the OECD are partnering to enhance the sustainability of water supply and sanitation services in Estonia. The Project will support the preparation of a roadmap for the consolidation of the water utility sector, a requisite for a sustainable and socially acceptable financing strategy and a broader water sector reform in Estonia. See the Detailed Project Description, for more information on background, scope and process.

The specific objectives of this Project are:

- to support the initiatives of national authorities to design their reforms according to their priorities, taking into account initial conditions and expected socio-economic impacts
- to support the efforts of national authorities to define and implement appropriate processes and methodologies by taking into account good practices of and lessons learned by other countries in addressing similar situations
- to assist the national authorities and water utilities in enhancing the efficiency and effectiveness of human-resource management, inter alia, by strengthening professional knowledge and skills and setting out clear responsibilities.

This action-oriented strategy draws the threads together and offers a structured and sequenced approach to implement the recommendations offered in previous chapters. Some of the key actions to be considered relate to the points:

- Making the case for reform
- Scenarios for the aggregation of water utilities in Estonia
- Incentives to foster consolidation of utilities
- Technical – including legal - issues to be tackled
- Tariff policy and methodology
- Independent economic regulation for WSS.

The strategy is supplemented by an action plan, which devolves responsibilities to specific stakeholders, based on OECD Secretariat's understanding of respective competences and capabilities. The strategy and the action plan benefitted from feedback from stakeholders.

The strategy and the action plan would benefit from increased resources at the Ministry of Environment, the Competition Authority and the Estonian Environmental Investment Centre. Institutional reforms in 2022 suggest that the Competition Authority now has the capacity to generate the resources required to play its role in the suggested strategy. The note suggests options to secure funding for the Centre. The capacities of the Ministry would need to be increased, in particular in terms of staffing: the necessary engagement with stakeholders, the development of much needed guidance and practical support require time. Considering the massive benefits of an action plan designed to set the water supply and sanitation sector on a path towards performance and financial sustainability, this would be public money well spent.

7.2. Make the case for reform

Estonia has achieved a remarkable rate of construction of infrastructures for water and sanitation services, since its accession to the European Union, with multiple benefits for the population. Financing these assets has essentially relied on EU funding. These assets need to be properly operated and maintained. Failure to do so will lead to a rapid decay and a need to rebuild existing assets, putting human health and freshwater ecosystems at risk and adding costs to the community.

To date, the water supply and sanitation industry in Estonia is highly diverse and fragmented. While some services have gained experience in consolidation, 177 water companies were operating in Estonia in 2018; 44 local governments are serviced by more than one water company.

This fragmentation, and the limited size of multiple service providers, hinder the industry's financial capacity to operate, maintain and renew existing assets. Some service providers operate several services (e.g. district heating) and the water service may be subsidised by revenues from other services. In other cases, lack of financial resources leads to postponing investment decisions to renew existing assets, potentially affecting service quality now and in the future, and risking a rapid decay of assets, which then will have to be rebuilt sooner than initially needed, merely increasing needs and creating future liabilities. The current crisis triggered by energy prices illustrates how fragile the industry is in Estonia.

The consequences in terms of quality of service are already visible, as the industry faces issues of compliance with the EU regulation. Five wastewater treatment plants (WWTP) of more than 2,000 population equivalent (pe) fail to comply with the Urban Wastewater Treatment Directive (UWWTD). Several WWTP of less than 2,000 pe – too small to fall within the scope of the UWWTD - release poorly treated wastewater, potentially affecting compliance with national requirements (which are driven by the Baltic Marine Environment Protection Commission – HELCOM).

In the future, demographic trends will further exacerbate financial challenges for water services. While the national population is projected to decline by 2.7% by 2045, population in four counties is projected to decline by 1/3, with negative consequences on water demand and the revenues of water services.

In that context, the prevailing financing model for water and sanitation services in Estonia is obsolete:

- EU funds, which represent 85% of capital expenditures, will gradually be phased out and
- the Estonian Ministry of Finance confirmed that domestic public finance will not be a substitute.

Municipalities and utilities need to acknowledge that they should – rapidly - transition towards a model where they are financially sustainable, for OPEX and CAPEX. This can only result from a combination of 2 lines of action:

- Increase revenues from user tariffs. There is some room for manoeuvre. OECD analyses for DG Environment in 2020 and comparison across 27 EU member states suggest that 90% of the population can afford to pay more for water services. As is often the case, keeping water tariffs low hurts the poor as it deprives water utilities from the revenue they need to operate, maintain and extend services. In a country like Estonia, affordability issues would be much more effectively addressed through targeted social measures than through water bill measures.
- Deliver substantial efficiency gains, at both operational and investment level. Considering the operational costs of water utilities, operational efficiency can result from streamlining labour, enhancing energy efficiency, or increasing the efficiency of networks. It is noteworthy that most of these measures require some initial investment to deliver medium or long-term benefits. Efficiency at investment level requires robust planning and sequencing of investment. While utilities can enhance the relevance and robustness of development plans, there are limits to what can be achieved at utility level: rooms for manoeuvre expand significantly when development plans explore opportunities to do things in common, joining forces and potentially exploiting economies of scale and scope. This is where some form of consolidation is required.

Combining these 2 lines of action is tricky, as they are not necessarily mutually supportive: on the one hand, raising tariffs can relax the pressure to generate efficiency gains – in addition to inflating affordability issues; on the other hand, keeping tariffs too low deprives service providers from the resources they need to achieve efficiency gains. The national strategy sketched here explores the preferred option to combine these two lines of action. Consolidation is key, but it is not the silver bullet and needs to be accompanied by a range of measures.

It would be inappropriate to delay efforts to enhance efficiency in planning future investments and delivery of services until more problems occur. The time lag between deferred decisions (non-action today) and more serious decay of infrastructures and services quality is the time when reform should take place. It provides some room for manoeuver to design and implement a strategically planned and consulted approach.

7.3. Preferred scenario for the aggregation of water utilities in Estonia

Discussions on consolidation of water utilities in Estonia have been dragging on for years, if not decades.

So far, discussions essentially considered one model of agglomeration, on a geographical basis, where well-functioning companies gradually absorb smaller, fragile ones. This model faces push back on two grounds:

- Well-functioning utilities (or the municipalities where they operate) are reluctant to merge, as absorbing less efficient entities would result in tariff increases, affecting their customer base (or dwellers)
- Smaller entities resist merging as they fear their voice will not be heard in the larger entity, and funding and investments will be redirected towards other, initially larger municipalities or utilities. Note that the recent administrative reform has diminished the number of –small - local authorities, making this concern less prominent.

This can explain that over the last 2 decades, experience with aggregation has remained minimal. This further suggests that aggregation will not materialise at scale or in time, should it only result from voluntary arrangements across local authorities.

The government then faces a dilemma: either keep aggregation voluntary, with limited ambitions; or consider an alternative model for aggregation. The first option will not deliver the efficiency gains required to put the sector on a (financially) sustainable path. This national strategy supports an alternative model for aggregation.

The point is not to move away from aggregation, but to provide some flexibility in aggregation patterns. For instance, not all functions may need to be operated at the same scale:

- Water supply could be operated at a different scale than sanitation
- Urban sanitation could be treated at a different scale (municipal) than rural (where a public entity could be created to monitor and service the operation of sceptic tanks
- Sludge management could be operated at yet another scale (regional, building on larger agglomerations)
- Investment planning and procurement could be managed at a different scale than consumer relations and billing
- Some competences could be made available in regional centres, to support smaller utilities
- Specific trajectories could be considered for rural areas, which differ from urban ones. For instance, localised wastewater management systems could serve individual or small groups of properties. They would be coordinated through a public service, able to cover a wide and diverse territory, focusing on localised sanitation only.

The national strategy does not ambition to set a priori – from the top – what the appropriate scale is for each function. It is designed to set up the policy and regulatory framework and incentives to urge municipalities and service providers to explore different scenarios and aggregate as it makes most sense in their particular context. Decisions would still be made by local authorities and utilities, on the basis of multiple criteria, including:

- Opportunities to minimise cost (investment needs in infrastructure; operation and maintenance costs) and enhance financial sustainability of WSS

- Opportunities to mutualise skills (technical skills to operate and maintain assets; commercial skills to interact with users, including through billing)
- Opportunities to optimise performance (quality of service to users), now and in the future (sustainable service provision)
- Opportunities to strengthen monitoring and supervision (assessing development plans and expenditure programmes; monitoring performance of service providers).

A range of actions need to be taken in parallel, such as the adjustment of the tariff setting methodology, setting up capacities to review and assess the opportunity of investments and expenditure programmes (going beyond the assessment of eligible costs), organising benchmarking capacities to set performance objectives and review performance of water companies. Some of these actions relate to strengthening economic regulation. The action plan sequences these measures to ensure a smooth and effective transition towards the agreed-upon vision for a sustainable water industry in Estonia.

7.4. Incentives to foster consolidation of utilities

Considering the state of the water sector in Estonia, incentives have to do with easy or accelerated access to finance. The Estonian Environmental Investment Centre provides access to public finance. The amount of finance available for the water sector in the Centre could be gradually increased, to reflect the state of the sector and its importance for sustainable development in Estonia[1]. With this notable exception, and in a context where EU and public funding will not be available, the primary source of finance now and in the future is expected to be revenues from tariffs.

Other sources of finance can be considered, such as commercial loans or private investments, but they would need to be paid back by a combination of EU funding, public finance or revenues from tariffs. This point confirms that private finance will only be accessible in practice when a number of requisites are met, including robust management of utilities and a stable revenue flow through tariffs.

The proposed option to enhance revenues from tariffs is to offer accelerated depreciation of assets under certain conditions. In essence, the proposed line of action is to keep the tariff setting principles as they are, and to add an option for accelerated depreciation of assets under conditions to be agreed upon by the economic regulator and the Ministry of Environment.

One additional incentive is recommended: to reward utilities that explore ambitious options to enhance the efficacy of development plans. Those utilities that submit more ambitious plans from that perspective could be offered preferred treatment for investment projects, more advantageous conditions to raise tariff, access public finance (possibly through the Estonian Environmental Investment Centre), or smooth economic regulation such less cumbersome authorisation programmes or other administrative measures that can facilitate the operation of water companies.

As it is not practical to define and measure the ambitions of development plans in an abstract way, this could be done through a benchmarking process that would go beyond the comparison of costs and include the comparison of levels of performance and of development plans. Such an extension of performance benchmarking for water supply and sanitation in Estonia would require collaboration between the economic regulator (tasked with the review of development plans) and the Ministry of environment (which sets the level of ambition required for the sector) and local authorities (formally accountable for development plans).

The proposed incentives would deliver most effectively if backed by some pressures or threats. Two kinds of pressures have been evoked in the course of the project:

- Set a timeline to achieve a set level of collective performance[2]. Should that level not be achieved on time, the government would take mandatory action to aggregate utilities according to its preferred pattern. This would strip municipalities from their capacity to decide on the organisation of water services; it would deprive utilities from exploring options that may be more advantageous to them. The risk is that the pattern imposed from the top may not be optimal.

- Revoke licences for utilities that are unable to achieve a certain level of performance or that do not demonstrate the appropriate level of ambition to enhance efficiency. This line of action assumes that water utilities are licenced first. Indeed, licencing requirements for water undertakings may be a feasible measure to ensure technological, financial and managerial capacities of water undertakings. Depending on the licencing conditions, such requirements may encourage consolidation within the WSS sector, where service providers with incompetent organisation and weak economy are gradually directed to merge or otherwise consolidate their business with regional and/or otherwise sustainable water undertakings. A decision is required on who manages services, which licences have been revoked. In Lithuania, where licences are already in place, a guaranteed operator (the largest in the region) has been defined by default and would be mandated to step in.

7.5. Technical – including legal - issues to be tackled

Implementation of the strategy sketched above requires that a range of legal and regulatory issues are tackled. They are listed below.

7.5.1. The legal forms and patterns of inter-municipal co-operation

An Estonian commercial association is to be preferred as the legal form of consolidation vehicle. This provides a status and the needed flexibility to support gradual functional integration - and aggregation, should it occur.

Any municipality or water company may become a member of a commercial association created for the purpose of facilitating co-operation in the WSS sector.

In the general meeting of commercial association, each member has one vote. International experience provides an example of how local control over tariff decisions can be retained, while a broad spectrum of WSS activities could be effectively contracted out through a partnership arrangement to secure benefits associated with available economies of scale. Forms of consolidation within this broad approach can differ in a range of ways, including in terms of the scope and depth of service provision activities that are covered: e.g. joint provision of various operational activities vs the pooling of investment planning, the awarding of works contracts, and of financial capacities.[3]

As a way of consolidation, the municipalities and/or the water companies may share functions, or outsource a part of or whole provision of WSS services to a regional service provider. To facilitate the outsourcing, two main alternatives of asset regime shall be considered: (i) ownership of WSS assets remain with the municipality/water company commissioning the services, or (ii) ownership of WSS assets are transferred to the service provider.

Upon withdrawal from such association, the return of the assets to the original holder (leaving member) may be carried through as prescribed in the articles of association or in the members' agreement.

7.5.2. Support from the Ministry of Environment

While it is not primarily legal in nature, support from the Ministry to local authorities may include the following accompanying measures:

- Strengthen the role of county associations or cooperation between municipalities, to support the creation of larger (regional) utilities, if and when appropriate

- Support to contractual arrangements between such associations (where in place) or municipalities and the larger utilities. In 2006, the Ministry of Environment drafted models of agreements for water companies; they can provide a basis on which to build, although they need to be updated. Performance-based management contracts could be promoted
- Water Operators Partnerships (WOP) consisting of reputable operators. Partnerships with experienced operators are critical to develop and strengthen the newly formed organisations. Adequate incentives can encourage consolidated utilities to support localities that are not yet part of the association.

7.6. Tariff policy and methodology

This section covers both the tariff setting methodology and the tariff setting process.

7.6.1. The tariff setting methodology

In broad terms, the tariff policy and tariff setting methodology are adapted to the Estonian context. However, that can be refined and improved in several ways.

An important feature of the tariff setting process is the depreciation method. The existing CA approach is likely to provide an appropriate basis upon which to determine the allowances provided for depreciation/capital maintenance within the tariff formula. It can provide a pragmatic and flexible way of allowing financial sustainability issues to be addressed where they have been shown to be material, while also guarding against the risk of customers facing unduly high charges.

This approach would benefit from further formalisation and articulation – for example, through publishing guidance – so that there is greater clarity over the scope for utilities to seek accelerated depreciation provisions. Those conditions could be developed in ways that take explicit account of the risk that providing more funding through charges may tend to dampen the efficiency incentives that might otherwise apply. The CA could underpin this approach by identifying relevant cost and service performance criteria that it would expect companies to satisfy in order to qualify for potential access to accelerated depreciation provisions.

The approach could also be linked directly to the extent to which different forms of consolidation plans were being pursued, with greater scope for the acceleration of depreciation provided to utilities that develop such plans in a robust and credible manner (see the following section, on benchmarking).

7.6.2. The tariff setting process

The tariff setting process and formula could provide for prices to be adjusted automatically in between tariff reviews by reference to movements in defined indices. In particular, it may be desirable for some input price risks (including potentially those associated with movements in energy prices, but also, although more complicated, labour or construction costs) to be managed through the use of some form of indexation, such that prices can better reflect prevailing conditions without the need for further regulatory review.

The tariff setting process could benefit from some alignment with international good practices. At the moment, tariffs are reviewed at the demand of utilities, leaving scope for strategic behaviour by utilities to only request a review when they expect to benefit from it. The CA may wish to introduce a periodic approach to price reviews (for instance, every 3 years), and develop principles which limit the extent to which existing price controls would be 're-opened' as a result of consolidation activity. This provides scope for companies to benefit from savings they are able to make in the period between re-determinations. At the same time (or while managing the transition towards periodic price reviews, the CA could review companies – to some extent at least – in clusters. This would ease comparison of data and state of play.

Of note: in cases of aggregation, while it makes sense to converge towards a uniform tariff within the new entity, the convergence process can be phased over several years, to minimise impact on consumers, and let time of the benefits of aggregation to materialise, thereby minimising the need to increase tariff at all.

7.7. Independent economic regulation for WSS

In addition to tariff setting, economic regulation plays a critical part in the aggregation policy. This section covers other functions to be taken on board by the Competition authority in Estonia. The focus is on the organisation of a benchmarking process, which builds upon - but significantly expands - the existing practice and traffic light system.

7.7.1. Develop a Service Performance Incentive framework

In Estonia, economic regulation is based on costs. This can be an issue, as one way in which a company may be able to out-perform a price control settlement is to deliver less. This could manifest itself is through cost savings being made in ways that tend to undermine some aspects of service quality. Therefore, cost-based regulation needs to be supplemented by robust monitoring of service provision and quality.

In Estonia, it is not clear which institution – if any - assesses whether expenditure programmes are opportune and identifies eligible costs (eventually reflected in tariffs). Currently, the CA considers local development plans – often drafted by utilities and endorsed by municipalities - as reference documents. This leaves no room to assess the potential benefits of considering development plans at an aggregate level, thereby generating economies of scale or scope.

In that context and considering the case for reform made above, it would be most appropriate if the CA develops incentives that focus on company plans, and planning processes. In the absence of such development plan incentives, companies may be unduly conservative in their planning, and do too little to address the major efficiency and financial challenges they face. In practice, this kind of development plan quality incentive approach can comprises of three core features:

1. Identify categories of development plan quality
2. Identify criteria to determine which quality category a development plan should be identified as in
3. Identify how companies will be treated differently, depending on the category they fit in. For instance:
    a. The explicit provision of some other form of financial reward: for example, access to grant funding or preferential borrowing opportunities
    b. Greater scope for support with respect to financial sustainability, using accelerated depreciation (taking account of bill affordability and acceptability issues)
    c. Scope for the price control to be determined for a longer period
    d. Presentation of the outcomes of the assessment in a way that can be expected to provide material reputational benefits for those associated with successful companies
    e. Procedural benefits associated with less extensive review requirements, providing overall performance remains sufficiently ‘on-track’.

7.7.2. Harness transparency as a policy tool

The approaches that are adopted to providing for transparency of performance information – and, more broadly, for stakeholder engagement – provide an important part of the way that regulators seek to encourage performance improvements and guard against the deterioration of performance.

The current information that is provided can be viewed as a useful first step, but much more could be done to seek to improve and refine the set of KPIs that are presented, to develop ways of providing more meaningful benchmarking of performance between companies (including through comparisons within and between different clusters of companies that may share broadly similar operating conditions, at least in some important respects), and to communicate that information in more prominent and easier to understand ways.

It is important to note that the information under discussion here concerns different aspects of the performance of monopoly public service providers. While there is likely to be some relevant performance information that it is appropriate to treat as confidential (for example, for security reasons), experience from other countries clearly shows that substantial levels of performance information can be made available while at the same time taking appropriate account of relevant confidentiality concerns.

Moving beyond sharing information on individual and relative performance of service providers, awareness raising via information sharing and nudging can go a long way in making the case for change. It can take the form of strategic planning for the sector (a role for the Ministry of Environment) or reporting on practical consolidation experience (this could be arranged by the association of water utilities).

7.7.3. A role for the Ministry of Environment

A National Water Strategy, backed by a thorough and realistic financing strategy, could be envisaged, to set the overall level of ambition and provide a reference to draft development plans and assess the opportunity of projected investment, and possibly encourage local governments to join forces. The objective of the proposed strategy would be, for each municipality, to:

- Identify long-term needs (based on population and economic development forecast) and source of water supply; impacts of climate change (and risks of flooding or scarcity) could be factored in, as appropriate
- Identify investment needs for rehabilitation, replacement or extension of the water and sewerage facilities (including granted assets, which will need to be renewed even though they were financed without domestic finance) and their costs
- Explore options for mutual investment and joint action with neighbouring communities. The proposed options could be prioritised when they align with the national water strategy and financial strategy.

Table 7.1. Wrapping up

ISSUES	PREFERRED OPTIONS
Overarching strategy	functional aggregation voluntary, performance-bound
Technical – including legal – issues to be tackled	governance arrangements conditions required for joining and withdrawing from associations regime of assets tariffs of the aggregated company (separate but converging)
Incentives to foster consolidation of water companies	financial incentive (accelerated depreciation, preferred access to public and EU funding) preferred treatment (e.g. authorisation programmes, licencing)
Tariff policy and methodology	accelerated depreciation
Independent economic regulation for water companies	benchmarkig costs + performance + development plans rewards/sanctions for performance achievements a national plan

7.8. A tentative action plan to transition towards aggregated water services in Estonia

Table 7.2. A tentative action plan to transition towards aggregated water services in Estonia

Objective	Action	Champion / Partner(s)	Deadline
Set levels of expectations. Provide a reference for service quality, operators' performance, and ambition of development plans	Develop a national strategy for WSS[1], supported by a financing strategy. The national strategy would set performance objectives for utilities (to be considered when setting licensing criteria, performance benchmarking) and / or targets for aggregation	MoE (in consultation with all stakeholders)	Short
Consider setting up licenses for water and sanitation utilities	Engage a consultation with the association of water utilities to set up licenses for WSS services. Criteria would be defined by the CA, in line with the overall ambition set by the MoE	The MoE initiates the discussion. The CA defines the criteria, in line with the MoE's priorities and in consultation with the association of water utilities	Short
Provide guidance for the governance of aggregated entities	Strengthen the role of county associations and regional entities Support contractual arrangements	MoE (in consultation with municipalities and association of utilities)	Medium
Enhance potential financial incentives	Increase public funding available for WSS in the Estonian Environmental Investment Center	MoE (as field ministry) in consultation with MoFinance	Medium
Provide incentives through tariff methodology and process	Clarify criteria to be granted accelerated depreciation, and modalities Define the modalities of periodic reviews and of clustered reviews Include indices in the tariff formula (e.g. on energy, labour, construction costs)	CA (in association with association of utilities)	Short
Provide guidance for performance benchmarking (including development plan benchmarking)	KPIs and a process to interest utilities Set up development plan benchmarking (define number of categories; criteria to assess development plans; special treatment for most ambitious plans)	CA (in coordination with MoE and association of utilities) MoE engages with local authorities	Short Medium
Address affordability issues (in particular in small communities)	Consider other instruments to finance environmental policies that benefit the larger population (beyond water users)	MoE (in consultation with MoFinance and the association of local authorities)	Long
Raising awareness. Nudging	Engage with local authorities to make the case for change Report on successful functional coordination	MoE (in consultation with association of local authorities) Association of municipalities and Association of utilities	Short Short

1. Chapter 5 suggests that, while a reference to a national strategy could feature in the legal framework, the strategy itself could be considered a secondary piece legislation.

Notes

[1] In principle, this could be done in two ways: 1) budget allocation to the Centre are revised in the context of the budgetary process; 2) economic policy instruments that generate (earmarked) revenues to the Centre could be increased. The second is preferable as it is less dependent of the vagaries of budgetary decision making.

[2] During stakeholder consultation, 5 years was suggested as a reasonable – though ambitious – timeline, considering that discussions on consolidation has been going on for decades in Estonia.

[3] See, for example: https://www.slideshare.net/OECD_ENV/joint-workshop-on-enhancing-efficiency-and-sustainability-of-water-supply-and-sanitation-presentation-joseph-hermal-249807561

Annex A. Addendum to the Issue paper. Lessons from six aggregation case studies

Aggregation of water services has been a common endeavour in a number of jurisdictions. This Annex captures the main messages that derive from a review of 6 reforms in Europe (Austria, Croatia, France, Italy, Romania, Scotland). Lessons emerge that can inspire Estonia, in particular as regards the benefits and modalities of a voluntary process for aggregation.

This report proposes an international review of water and sanitation services (WSS) aggregation processes in selected countries. It presents a wide variety of situations and experiences encompassing voluntary (bottom-up) and mandated (top-down) processes incentivised or not; different levels of reform maturity ranging from preliminary phase, to ongoing and completed; different purposes, governance models, scope and scale. Each case study explains the key drivers for the aggregation, its main implementation practicalities, the achievement of the reform and the difficulties faced when implementing the reform.

The following section sets out the key learnings from the six case studies, and further builds upon observations on WSS aggregation trends at international level.

Key drivers for aggregation are investments needs and efficiency gains

Among the six aggregation case studies presented in this report (Austria, Croatia, Romania, France, Italy and Scotland), the key drivers triggering aggregation reforms are investment needs and efficiency gains. Technical and economic efficiency are sought through economies of scale or economies of scope to improve WSS services performance, to implement effective investment strategies, to ensure solidarity across territories and social groups for investment planning.

In Austria, the Wasserwirtschaftsfonds (Water Management Fund, WWF) was created in 1958 with the purpose to support the construction of water supply and sanitation infrastructure in cities and urban areas, and thus boost the urban connection rate to WSS services. Inter-municipal entities were eligible for higher financial support from the WWF than municipalities operating a utility that would only operate on their sole territory. The underlying argument behind this policy was the achievement of cost-efficient solutions and economies of scale through larger water infrastructure and pooled investment. Since 1993, the fund is targeted towards small communities and rural areas.

In France, as stated in the explanatory memorandum of the aggregation law, "the transfer of water and sanitation competences from municipal to inter-municipal authorities [...] make it possible to effectively pool together the necessary technical and financial resources in order to ensure an efficient management of water and sanitation networks." Furthermore, this transfer of competence will also allow inter-municipal entities to have the financial and technical skills to undertake the significant and necessary investments to renew and upgrade WSS infrastructure while implementing a solidarity principle between urban and rural areas.

In Romania and Croatia, huge investment needs were necessary to reach EU water legislation compliance. Aggregation was seen as a cost-effective solution to meet those needs, and was supported by EU funds financial incentives. In addition, in Romania, aggregation helped improve WSS coverage in urban and rural areas.

A majority of mandatory aggregation processes, supported by financial incentives, following administrative boundaries and encompassing all services & functions

A vast majority of countries from the case studies opted for a mandatory process for aggregation, with a top-down approach led by the National level. Austria is the only country among the six case studies that relied on a voluntary process promoting a bottom-up logic driven by local governments. When looking at WSS aggregation trends worldwide, this finding is in line with the international situation. In countries where aggregations happened over the past decades, 60 percent of the aggregation followed a top-down mandated process (World Bank, 2017[1]).

Except for France and Scotland, all other aggregation processes have been supported by financial incentives either through EU funds (Romania, Italy) or through national grants and soft loans (Austria).

In all case studies, aggregations have eventually followed administrative boundaries although in Italy and Romania they were initially deemed to follow river basin territories. Except for Austria, the aggregation process encompasses all services and functions[1] of both water and wastewater services. These findings correspond to the observed aggregation trends at international level, where 56 percent followed administrative boundaries, and only 11 percent sought to match watershed limits[2]. The scope of almost all aggregation processes covers both services and functions (86 percent) (World Bank, 2017[1]).

A complex and difficult process requiring strong stakeholder engagement

In many case studies, the aggregation process proved more difficult and complex than expected. Most difficulties encountered are linked with local governments' reluctance, if not resistance, to aggregate WSS services, and thus lose control and power over local public services. This reluctance can also be encountered when well-performing utilities resist merging with low performing utilities. To some extent, these difficulties can be overcome by providing incentives and financial support for aggregation. Nevertheless, these difficulties commonly led to delays in the reform implementation (France, Italy, Romania) or to a limited number of effective aggregation among utilities (Italy) thus demonstrating inertia strategies from local governments. As a result, most aggregation reform still appear in progress in several case studies (France, Romania, Italy). Both the design and implementation of aggregations take time; in particular, implementation is a continuous process that can spread over decades. Consequently, aggregation benefits also take time to materialize. A gradual strategy can be effective to spread the efforts and changes to be made over time, thus not burdening utilities with having to do too much too quickly.

In Croatia, although the aggregation design was completed, it was delayed and then lost political support following the change of the central government. The reform was largely driven by technocrats within the line ministry, who failed to acknowledge that they lacked the political champion and national government power to impose the reform process over the concerns of local stakeholders. When political leadership changes over time, aggregation can be jeopardized. Due to political cycles, national and local representatives may not be re-elected. As a result, leadership stemming from a single national party or local stakeholder may disappear over time, thus potentially jeopardizing the aggregation design and implementation.

As a result, building ownership and aligning the interests of stakeholders at all levels is essential. When aggregation is mandated and generally designed at the national level, systematic consultations with local stakeholders should be organized early in the process to ensure they can inform the process and to strengthen alignment of interests between the national and local levels. Such an early engagement helps build stakeholder ownership of the reform. It allows implementers to tackle potential problems or resistance, and diffuse their potential impacts, thus improving conditions for success.

Accompanying measures are necessary to promote a successful aggregation

Corporatisation of utilities is a requisite as aggregation involves the creation of a new, separate, organizational entity that is accountable to more than one stakeholder. Corporatization gives financial autonomy to water utilities, as they have their own budget, duly separated from municipal budgets. Moreover, water companies make their own economic and financial decisions thus aiming at financial sustainability and resisting political interference. Corporatization brings efficiency improvements as utility managers and staff behave in a more business-like fashion (Romania).

Setting clear exit and entry clauses that set out the technical and financial conditions under which a service can join or withdraw from the aggregation, encourages joining and ensures orderly withdrawal (Romania, France).

A balanced institutional arrangement in which reaching consensus is embedded as a practice is key to align local interests and ease decision making in aggregated utilities. This alignment is generally done through decision-making arrangements and voting rights allocation.

Thoroughly preparing staff transfer from former municipal structures into the newly aggregated utility is crucial as labour costs often represent the main operational expenditure of WSS utilities. Transaction costs (see Annex) associated with staff transfer can delay or jeopardise potential efficiency gains and expected benefits from economies of scale and scope (Romania, Scotland).

Liabilities for suppliers and financiers can represent important transaction costs for aggregating utilities. As such, they must be covered, either during the aggregation by the aggregated utility or separately from aggregation by the local government budgets (France, Romania).

Defining principles but allowing flexibility in implementation ensures local ownership. National, top-down, mandated aggregation reforms are more likely to be successful when they follow the principle of subsidiarity and allow flexibility for local stakeholders to own the aggregation process and adapt it to their local context. Furthermore, not acknowledging local context when designing an aggregation can lead to failure (Croatia).

Not all aggregations are successful and reforms sometimes show mixed results

While aggregation can enhance the performance of service provision, and the efficiency of expenditure programmes, slow diffusion and risk of sherry picking can affect or delay overall benefits at national level.

In Scotland, as part of the aggregation process, considerable efforts were made to enhance efficiency that successfully led to a reduction of almost 40% in operating costs over a decade. In Austria, the voluntary and incentivised aggregation process proved successful as it allowed boosting water and wastewater coverage in both urban and rural areas through cost-effective investment solutions.

In Romania, the aggregation reform also allowed increasing service coverage and performance in urban and rural areas. However, during the implementation of the process, a risk of cherry-picking practices arose. Service providers naturally prefer to extend services to wealthy populations for cost recovery reasons, and to easy-to-reach areas where infrastructure already exists. By doing so, they select solvent customers for good revenue collection and seek to avoid sunk investment costs and associated OPEX increases. In Italy, the overall outcome of the aggregation reform show very limited benefits in terms of efficiency gains and investments increases.

Voluntary Aggregation Process. Austria

Table A A.1. Key data on aggregation of water utilities in Austria

Number of municipalities	Average population by Municipality	Level responsible for WSS provision	Number of WSS utilities	Average population served by WSS utilities	Aggregation index[1]	Formal policy or legal reform supporting aggregation	Predominant scale of aggregation	Predominant scope of aggregation	Process of aggregation
2,095	4,237	Municipal	5,465	1,624	28%	No	Administrative boundaries	Stages	Voluntary

1. The Aggregation Index measures the degree of fragmentation of service provision of the water sector in a country, using a simple normalized index based on the number of local governments and the number of service providers.

Key drivers for the aggregation process

Overview of water and sanitation services provision

In Austria, the WSS sector is regulated at the national level, and the nine state governments are in charge of implementing and enforcing national regulations via their administrative districts. The responsibility for water supply and sanitation lies within the municipalities and the communities. Thirty large and 1,870 small municipal utilities serve nearly 70% of the population. One hundred and sixty five municipal associations (Box A A.1) and 3,400 cooperatives each provide water to 11% of inhabitants, and the remaining 8% rely on piped self-provision (Figure A A.1.). Twenty-four percent of Austrians are served by water utilities supplying less than 5,000 inhabitants, and 66% are connected to water utilities supplying more than 5,000 inhabitants (ÖVGW, 2015[2]). With an average population of approximately 1,600 inhabitants per utility, the water sector appears quite fragmented.

Figure A A.1. Water services provider types and market shares, Austria

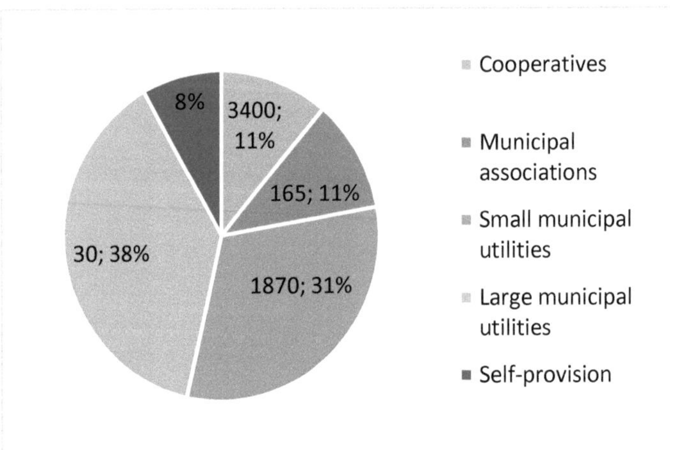

Source: (World Bank, 2017[1])

Box A A.1. Upper Austria Water

Founded in 1946, Upper Austria Water is an autonomous non-profit association of more than 1,700 rural service providers located in the Federal State of Upper Austria (Figure A A.2.). Chaired by a board of seven directors, it is in charge of operations and maintenance of small-scale water supply and sewerage systems in rural areas through technical assistance (emergency supply, mobile technical equipment), pooling programs (for water meter purchase and water analyses, for example), and measurement services (such as leak detection, pipe and valve location, flow rates and pressure, and aquifer tests). It aims to supply sufficient high quality and cost-efficient drinking water through the construction and operation of autonomous installations. It also provides capacity building and staff training, and supports service providers on legal and financial issues. Similar models exist in other states of Austria.

Figure A A.2. Water cooperatives in Upper Austria

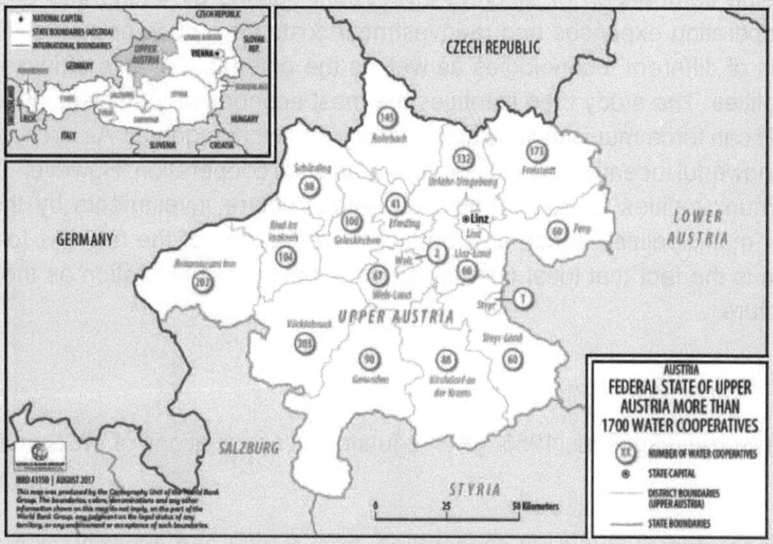

Source: (World Bank, 2017[1])

WSS services are provided predominantly by public utilities (e.g. municipalities or associations of municipalities or public enterprises) or publicly owned companies. In addition, cooperatives play an important role in some parts of Austria, especially in rural areas. The number of private companies providing water or sanitation services is negligible.

Financial incentives to support voluntary aggregation and boost water and wastewater investments

In 1949, the Austrian *Wasserbautenförderungsgesetz* (Hydraulic Engineering Promotion Act, WBFG) replaced former laws and set up regulation for potential financial support from the national government for all kinds of waterworks. In 1958, the WBFG was amended to create the *Wasserwirtschaftsfonds* (Water Management Fund, WWF) within the Ministry of Trade. This fund was used to allocate national grants and soft loans in the water and sanitation sector, with low interest rate (1-3 percent) and long payback periods of up to 50 years. The purpose of this financial scheme was to support the construction of water supply and sanitation infrastructure in cities and urban areas, and thus boost the urban connection rate to WSS services. Inter-municipal entities such as municipal associations were eligible for higher financial support than municipalities operating a utility that would only deliver services on their sole territory. The underlying argument behind this policy was the achievement of cost-efficient solutions and economies of scale through larger water infrastructure.

Revised financial incentive scheme to support rural areas and small communities aggregation and asset development

Following the success of the WBFG for water and wastewater works development in urban areas, it was revised in 1993, and the *Umweltförderungsgesetz* (Environmental Support Act) was passed. The funds were no longer granted in the form of soft loans but in the form of grants, and the main target of the new support scheme shifted towards rural areas and small communities. Furthermore, the 1993 reform transferred the management of the Fund from the Ministry of Trade to a bank specialising in the financial needs of municipalities, the *Kommunalkredit*.

To promote efficient investment solutions an additional lump-sum support scheme was introduced offering the applicant the possibility of getting higher support when aiming at the most economically efficient solution. Municipalities have to submit an economic analysis when requesting financial support from the national government for any investment in the water sector. This analysis, called *Variantenuntersuchung*, includes a cash value comparison of different investment options by taking into account the potential investment costs, operating expenses and re-investment costs for a 50-year period. The various options include the analysis of different technologies as well as the potential benefits of investing in association with other municipalities. The study then identifies the most economically efficient investment option, and the *Kommunalkredit* can force municipalities to join forces and work together. As such, the funding support scheme remains a powerful incentive to push for inter-municipal cooperation. However, despite the existing incentives, some municipalities favour carrying out infrastructure investments by themselves, without grouping with other municipalities. It can only be assumed that one of the reasons for this economically inefficient approach is the fact that local politicians favour having full discretion as the single operator of the water infrastructure.

Some practicalities of aggregation arrangement

The Water Act (*Wasserrechtsgesetz*, 1956, §87) regulates all associations of WSS municipal services.

Constituencies

There is a wide-range of inter-municipal cooperation, both formal and informal, in Austria. Cooperation arrangements include collaboration, mutual assistance, private law contracts, associations and companies under the Austrian Civil Law Code and company law, and inter-municipal associations under public law (as stipulated in the Austrian constitution, *Österreichische Bundesverfassung*).

Associations are special purpose entities based on public-public partnership. They deliver public services to several municipalities with the aim to overcome the challenges of fragmentation and diseconomy of scale. The management and operation tasks, related to the water and sanitation provision in the participating municipalities, are delegated to the association.

A 2011 federal constitutional amendment facilitates cooperation initiatives in Austria. It enables municipalities to participate in inter-municipal associations that go beyond *Länder* borders. However, a formal agreement of the concerned *Länders* for the establishment of a cross-border association is required.

Funding

In general, revenues generated from water tariffs contribute to between 74 and 85 per cent of the total annual revenues of water utilities in Austria (Kommunalkredit Public Consulting, 2009[3]). Municipalities, even when they are part of an association, generally set their own water tariffs. Decision-making over tariff thus remains in the hands of each municipality. Hence, there is no uniform water tariff within an association, and water tariffs of municipalities belonging to the same association can diverge.

Nevertheless tariff setting should comply with the user/polluter pays principle and the cost-recovery principle. Tariffs are based on a revenue cap. Referring to the cost recovery principle, water utilities assess the cost for 1 m³ and set a tariff accordingly under the approval of local municipal governments. According to the law, the tariff can be up to twice the annual financial requirement of the water utility. Any additional demand to raise tariffs must be made with regard to a specific context affecting the water service. Many water utilities also link their tariff to the annual inflation rate (World Bank, 2015[4]).

Achievements of the aggregation arrangement

After the Second World Ward, one of the objectives of the Austrian water policy was to extend water and sanitation systems, thereby increasing the number of inhabitants connected to the public water and sewer system. This was done through a financial support scheme at the national level that acted as the main driving force to pool municipal resources together, and turned out to be rather successful as showed by the development of inter-municipal cooperation in the water and sanitation sector.

According to a study from the *Kommunalkredit*, two thirds of municipalities carry out all stages of water service (water abstraction, production, transportation, and distribution) thus demonstrating a high degree of vertical integration. These municipalities are mainly located in the alpine and rather wet western area of the country. The remaining one third of municipalities outsource at least one of the above-mentioned water service stages to associations or other municipalities. Cooperation between municipalities can primarily be found in water extraction and transport stages. These municipalities are mainly located in the dry and flat east and southeast parts of Austria.

For wastewater services, the situation is quite different as more than half of the Austrian municipalities are part of an association throughout the country. In such cases, municipalities still operate sewer networks while associations are generally in charge of wastewater transport and treatment.

The current organisational structure of the Austria WSS sector has been largely shaped by the WBFG that acted as a powerful financial incentive to support voluntary aggregation through pooled investment for water and wastewater Infrastructure. This incentivised WSS investment policy resulted in the creation of an important number of municipal associations from 1958 to 1993. Nevertheless, this scheme did not lead to a decrease in the number of WSS utilities but rather in the pooling of resources to jointly build and manage WSS asset among several municipalities. As such, municipalities were encouraged to cooperate rather than consolidate.

Mandatory Aggregation Reform at Preparatory Phase. Croatia

Table A A.2. Key data on aggregation of water utilities in Croatia

Number of municipalities	Average population by Municipality	Level responsible for WSS provision	Number of WSS utilities	Average population served by WSS utilities	Aggregation index[1]	Formal policy or legal reform supporting aggregation	Predominant scale of aggregation	Predominant scope of aggregation	Process of aggregation
556	7,316	Municipal	156	26,074	78%	Yes (still pending)	Administrative boundaries	Services & functions	Mandated

1.The Aggregation Index measures the degree of fragmentation of service provision of the water sector in a country, using a simple normalized index based on the number of local governments and the number of service providers.

Key drivers of the aggregation reform

Overview of water and sanitation services provision

In Croatia, local governments are responsible for water and sanitation services and provide them through 156 public utility companies (140 for water and sanitation service and only 16 for sanitation service). With an average population served of 24,962, the market is dominated by Zagreb Waterworks, servicing about 17% of the population, with a further 84 larger multicity companies servicing 59% of the population. The remaining 24% of the population is either served by 55 small municipal providers (5%) or uses self-provision (19%) or individual water resources (Figure A A.3.). Most utility companies provide both water and sewerage services, although in larger cities, separate utility companies exist (World Bank, 2015[5]).

Figure A A.3. Water services provider types and market shares, Croatia

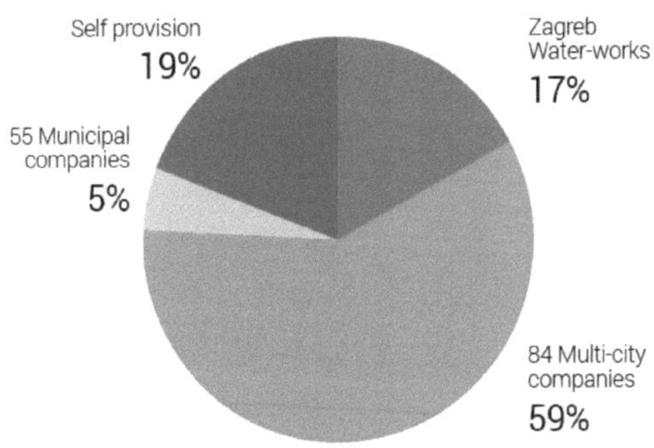

Source: (World Bank, 2015[5])

Access to publicly provided services reaches 81% for public water supply and 44% for sewerage. Access to wastewater treatment is much lower but is expected to increase dramatically based on Croatia's commitment to implement the EU Urban Wastewater Treatment Directive.

Purpose of aggregation

Following the accession of Croatia to the European Union, huge investments are needed to comply with the requirements of the Water Framework Directive (2000/60/EC), the Drinking Water Directive (98/83/EC) and the Urban Waste Water Treatment Directive many (91/271/EEC). Approximately EUR 4.5 billion should be invested in the water sector from 2010 to 2023, (Revised implementation plan for water utility directives, Zagreb, 2010), and water supply and mainly wastewater infrastructure (secondary and tertiary waste water treatment plants) needs to be vastly expanded (Table A A.3.).

Table A A.3. Strategic goals for water and wastewater services provision

Service	Strategic goal 2023	Increase compared to current situation
Water supply connections	85-90%	+15% to +20%
Sewerage connections	60%	+17%
Wastewater treatment	Depending on the size of the agglomeration	+0% to +100%

Source: Revised implementation plan for water utility directives, Zagreb, 2010

In order to facilitate the achievements of the 2023 Strategic Goals, the Ministry of Agriculture (which is in charge of water and wastewater policy) has contemplated a sectoral institutional reform aiming at aggregation of utilities. Such developments, which have been discussed for several years, were already mentioned in the 2009 Croatia Water Strategy:

"It is necessary to carry out a reform rationalization of the utility sector in the direction of institutional merging of utility systems at technically, technologically and economic sustainable level" (Croatian Water Strategy, *Hrvatske Vode*, 2009).

The 2010 Water Act (and a separate Water Financing Act) was passed as part of the country's harmonization with the European Water Framework Directive and daughter directives. It also created a legal basis for a significant aggregation process, which should turn the more than 150 local utility companies into around 20 regional providers, generally along county borders. Water services areas have been established within which the government will recognize only one service provider (Croatian Parliament 2009, 2013). The change was expected to allow more effective European Funds absorption, create cross-subsidies between smaller and larger cities, and further professionalize service providers. The process was also seen as an important opportunity for the sector to improve the efficiency of service providers.

From the optimal size to the aggregation model

About 70 % of Croatian water utilities distribute less than 1 million m³ per year and another 20 % between 1 and 5 million m³. Only 2 % of the water companies distribute more than 10 million m³ per year.

For more than 30 years, extensive international research was conducted on economies of scale in the water sector, and methods have been developed to assess the efficiency of the sector as a whole. "Studies from a significant set of countries show economies of scale [...] in populations of 100,000 to 1 million (or in some cases covering many millions), with population densities of up to 250 inhabitants per square kilometre, or with volumes up to 100 million to 200 million cubic meters per year." (Ferro, Lentini and Mercadier, 2011[6])

In an attempt to determine the optimal size for the aggregation process, a feasibility study has been conducted to characterise the efficiency of the Croatian WSS sector using a Data Envelopment Analysis (DEA). Results concluded that the efficiency of the sector could be partly improved through economies of scale. Moreover, the analysis demonstrated that the median volume of water production of the most efficient Croatian water companies is approximately 3.1 Mm³ per year and therefore this minimum value was considered the starting point for aggregation process.

Based on this result, which validated the rationale (made the case) for the aggregation reform, three different aggregation models were examined:

- a light aggregation approach through a strategic alliance between utilities,
- a medium approach through a partial integration between utilities, and

- a full horizontal and vertical integration

Each option was assessed against 17 criteria taking into account the service quality, the water price, the management and operation conditions of the service or the control over the service delivery and the utility. The full merger option emerged as the best ranked solution. Among the assumed benefits of the full merger were a better access to international funding and loan conditions, an improvement of operations due to more effective management and organisation. Important non-financial benefits would derive from the ability of large companies to establish increased service levels, hire better educated and skilled staff and effectively use management tools such as benchmarking in order to continuously improve efficiency and effectiveness.

The next analytical step consisted in the definition of the most appropriate scale of aggregation. To do so, a GIS-tool was developed, and three different aggregation scale strategies were studied:

- Gravitating cities: larger towns would merge with the surrounding municipalities also taking into account gravitational aspects of waterways, leading to an important and manageable economy of scale.
- Minimum of 3 million m^3/year: a minimum water production of 3 million m^3 per year is to be achieved, corresponding to the results of the DEA. This scale is considered the minimum from the point of view of economic benefits.
- River basin approach: this strategy would adopt river basins geographical boundaries for new utility companies, reflecting the Water Framework Directive approach. This would result in six very large companies, with important geographical distances within the future utility service delivery territory.
- The "gravitating cities" strategy was chosen as the best option as it would allow creating sufficiently large utilities through a manageable merger process.

Key foreseen practicalities for the aggregation reform

Asset

According to the Croatian legal provisions, WSS utilities are and should remain publicly owned by local governments, and the WSS asset is owned by WSS utilities that are to take the legal form of limited liability companies.

Shareholding allocation

Three options were considered in order to allocate shares among shareholders:

- according to the population of each municipality,
- according to the value of the current asset of each municipality, or
- according to the value of total asset (current and future infrastructure).

The allocation of shares based on the population was chosen as the most pragmatic and least complex option for Croatia.

Supervisory Board

Members of the supervisory board are appointed by the shareholder assembly, with one member of the supervisory board appointed by the workers of the new water utility company (according to article 163 of the Labor Act). The supervisory board should consist of specialists/practitioners of the water sector. The supervisory board is not intended to reflect the composition of the shareholders assembly. It is advised to appoint a small board of supervisors as to shorten the decision making process and to decrease bureaucracy. The supervisory board will appoint the Executive managers.

Possible options to overcome political resistance

In the preparatory phase of the reform, some measures were contemplated in order to overcome political resistance at local level, to resolve potential unwillingness to implement aggregation and to enforce compliance:

- withholding national funding and/or assess to EU funds, central government takes over;
- prescribing fines (penalties) to heads of local self-government units for non-compliance with the aggregation laws and dead-lines.

Difficulties and obstacles with the aggregation reform

The water utility aggregation process was initiated as a central government–driven, top-down reform, with the country divided into water service areas, mostly defined by county boundaries, using the principle of "one service area, one service provider, one tariff". It was planned as a two-stage process, where in the first stage WSS services were corporatised, where necessary, while in the second stage they were to be aggregated into new WSS utilities.

After completion of the first phase, in early 2015, aggregation design was completed along with the required legislative framework. However, owing to the sensitivity of the political situation at that moment (2015 was an election year) and potential backlash from local authorities, it first was delayed and then lost political support following the change of the central government. The reform had been driven largely by technocrats within the line ministry, who failed to acknowledge that they lacked the political champion and national government power to impose the reform process over the concerns of local stakeholders.

The reform stalled but was never fully abandoned. On 28th June 2019, the Croatian Parliament adopted three amendments to framework laws in the water sector:

- Amendment to the Water Services Act

This amendment stipulates the obligation to integrate existing public suppliers into a single public supplier in a given service area, around the largest existing public supplier. According to the text, all existing utilities will be merged into 35 to 40 regional utilities, each covering a service area with more than 2 million m3 of water sold annually. It also prescribes that a unique water price is adopted per service area; price that is regulated by the Water Services Council, to prevent monopoly and high tariffs, but also undervalued tariffs. Finally, the amendment states that water services shall remain public entities.

- Amendment to the Water Act

Following the amendment passed on the Water Services Act, subsequent amendments to the Water Act had to be adopted.

- Amendment to the Act on Water Management Financing

Following the amendments passed on the Water Services Act and to the Water Act, subsequent amendments had to be adopted for harmonization purposes.

These amendments are currently being challenged at Constitutional level.

On-going Mandatory Aggregation Reform. Romania

Table A A.4. Key data on aggregation of water utilities in Romania

Number of municipalities	Average population by Municipality	Level responsible for WSS provision	Number of WSS utilities	Average population served by WSS utilities	Aggregation index[1]	Formal policy or legal reform supporting aggregation	Predominant scale of aggregation	Predominant scope of aggregation	Process of aggregation
3,284	5,894	Regional	283	42,407	92%	Yes (2007)	Administrative boundaries	Services & functions	Mandated

1.The Aggregation Index measures the degree of fragmentation of service provision of the water sector in a country, using a simple normalized index based on the number of local governments and the number of service providers.

Key drivers of the aggregation reform

Historic perspective on aggregation

The water sector in Romania has followed a contrasting evolution over time, fluctuating between fragmentation and aggregation. Before the 1990s, Romanian water services were supplied at the county level by companies that also provided other public services such as solid waste collection, heating, and the like. Water infrastructure investments were entirely subsidized by the central government budget and operational costs were subsidized by local authorities or funded through cross-subsidies, with industries paying a higher tariff than institutions and domestic users. Immediately after the fall of the socialist system (1989), the operating areas of these services started to narrow down as each local authority wanted to have its own public service operators. As a result, hundreds of WSS utilities were then created.

In a reverse movement, a comprehensive water sector aggregation reform was designed in 2005–2007 and implemented during the five following years. This regionalization consisted of a top-down mandatory process incentivized by EU investment grants—Sectoral Operational Program Environmental (SOP E) funds—which were allocated only to projects led by a regional operator. These financial incentives shaped to some extent the aggregation implementation. As an illustration, the scale of aggregation of Raja Constanta Water Company was shaped by the SOP funds, as the utility chose to expand in municipalities that benefited from those funds, whether they belonged to Constanta county or not. As a result, Raja Constanta Water Company accessed an overall amount of €278 million in investment subsidies (World Bank, 2017[1]).

Scale of aggregation

From an institutional perspective, the regionalization was generally performed through the reorganization of public services operated by the capital city of the county. The process had two stages. First, it concentrated the operation of services provided to a group of municipalities at the county level. Some flexibility was introduced in the aggregation process as utilities had the choice to aggregate following their own pace and according to their preferred scale (see examples given for two water utilities in Table A A.5. The second step, which has not been achieved yet, aims to concentrate these county utilities into river basin utilities.

Table A A.5. Trends in aggregation for Brasov and Raja Constanta Water Companies

		2007	2008	2009	2010	2011	2012	2013	2014	2015
Number of Municipalities	Brasov	9	9	10	12	13	13	13	14	15
	Raja Constanta	47	52	61	83	102	108	114	133	134
Number of Connections (000')	Brasov	17	17	17	22	24	30	33	35	36
	Raja Constanta	75	82	109	117	122	126	127	136	137
Population Served (000')	Brasov	254	254	281	291	317	317	341	345	346
	Raja Constanta	498	502	608	626	691	695	706	739	731

Source: (World Bank, 2017[1])

Governance of aggregation

The overall aggregation reform is based on three key institutional elements (Figure A A.4.):

- an Intercommunity Development Association (IDA),
- a Regional Operating Company (ROC), and
- a contract of delegation of services.

The ROC is a commercial company, owned by the IDA member municipalities, to which the management of the water and wastewater service is delegated through a delegation contract. The ROC is thus appointed to manage, operate, maintain, upgrade, renew, and expand, where appropriate, all public assets designated in the contract. It collects the invoices paid by customers, in accordance with the contract provisions. The IDA acts as the sole interlocutor of the ROC, representing the common interests of its member municipalities regarding water and wastewater services, especially with regard to general strategy, investments, and tariff policy.

Figure A A.4. Aggregation institutional framework, Romania

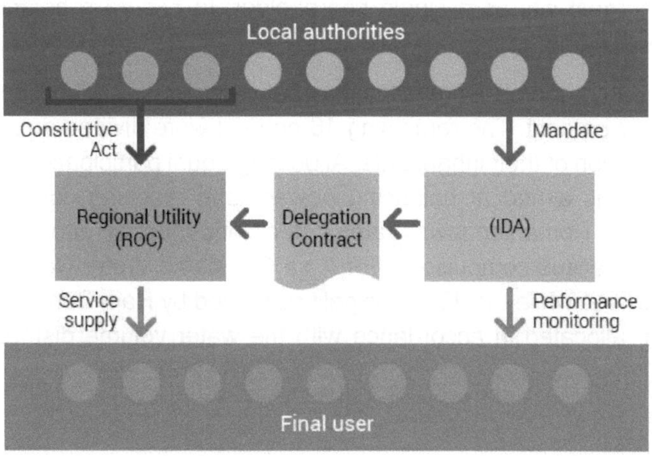

Source: (National Regulation Agency for Public Services, 2015[7])

Purposes of aggregation

Despite the compulsory requirement to aggregate in order to receive EU funds, the official Romanian Guide of Regionalisation states that the purpose of aggregation is the "improvement of sector performance by a better management and professionalism, as well as benefiting from scale economies." However, in the views of the European Commission and the Romanian government, the regionalisation process was also a means to promote integrated water resources management in order to comply with EU directives and generate environmental benefits, especially since the reform was finally intended to turn county utilities into river basin utilities. It was also a way to set up financial solidarity through cross-subsidies at the county level, and to offset decreases in water sales. Service quality and technical capacity enhancement were also targeted, especially as large investment projects were planned.

Key practicalities of the aggregation reform

Corporatisation of utilities

The aggregation process involves the creation of a new, separate, organizational entity that is accountable to more than one stakeholder. As such, the reform turned utilities into corporatized commercial companies that brings along many benefits. Corporatization gives financial autonomy to water utilities, as they have their own budget, duly separated from municipal budgets. Moreover, water companies make their own economic and financial decisions, especially regarding tariff policies, thus aiming at financial sustainability and resisting political interference.

Corporatization brings efficiency improvements as utility managers and staff behave in a more business-like fashion. Indeed corporatization is a way to modify the incentives of the WSS utility and make it act in a more customer-oriented way. In Romania, where water operators were turned into commercial companies, executive management staff must meet a number of objectives and performance indicators that are monitored continuously by the Board of Directors, the General Assembly of shareholders, and the inter-municipal body.

Share-holding and decision-making

A balanced institutional arrangement in which reaching consensus is embedded as a practice is key to align local interests and ease decision making in aggregated utilities. This alignment is generally done through decision-making arrangements and voting rights allocation.

In Romania, ROC share-holding arrangements among local authorities varies widely across IDAs and ROCs. In most cases, the power-sharing arrangement is done in such a way that it does not provide exclusive power to the largest city as a single shareholder, to ensure a balance of power and create incentives for consensus building.

For Brasov Water Company, shares were allocated between Brasov Municipality and Brasov County Council, each receiving 42 percent. The remaining 16 percent were divided among six other localities, in accordance with the proportion of their inhabitants. Allocating equal participation to Brasov County Council and Brasov Municipality was aimed at balancing powers and reaching consensus to avoid unilateral decisions. In addition, under Romanian law, strategic decisions must be adopted by a vote of two-thirds, which in Brasov made consensus compulsory. For Raja Constanta Water Company, the County Council holds 97 percent of the shares while the 33 municipalities served by Raja Constanta Water Company hold the remaining 3 percent, allocated in accordance with the water volume distributed in each settlement (World Bank, 2017[1]).

Exit and entry rules

Exit and entry rules set out the technical and financial conditions under which a service can join or withdraw from the aggregation. Those conditions mainly refer to the value of the assets being transferred. In addition, these rules also include governance arrangements that apply to newcomers. In Romania, during the aggregation reform, little emphasis was put on the definition of entry and exit rules. The exit rule boils down to the reimbursement of all amounts invested by the operator minus the depreciation costs already paid.

Tariff

The oversight and coordination of tariffs is generally done by the shareholders of the public companies in charge of service provision (most often local government representatives), in general assemblies. In Romania, the economic regulator for the water sector (National Regulatory Agency for Public Services, ANRSC) reviews and approves the tariff proposed by the utility after shareholders' approval. Hence, tariffs are voted on by the IDA General Assembly representing all local governments.

Financing

Fundamentally, the cost- and revenue-sharing arrangements depend on the legal form of the aggregated entities. In Romania, where corporatized entities have been created that merge all of the previous operations, costs and revenues are being consolidated and decisions on budget and investments are made for the overall utility through the shareholder assembly.

Asset

In Romania, WSS assets remain the property of local jurisdictions and are handed over for operation to the aggregated utility under a concession contract. The aggregated operator pays a lease fee to the WSS asset owners that is set aside into an asset management fund.

Liabilities

Liabilities for staff, suppliers, and financiers can represent important transaction costs (see Annex) for aggregating utilities. As such, they must be covered, either during the aggregation by the aggregated utility or separately from aggregation by the local government budgets. In Romania, the newly aggregated operator taking over services did not take on any liability from the previous operators. No debts or claims were undertaken. However, in some cases, local authorities had to extinguish former debts using their own budgets before the aggregation was completed. Furthermore, in Romania, the delegation contract model for the regionalization reform prepared by the Environment Ministry advocates for transferring all staff to the incumbent.

Achievements and difficulties of the aggregation process

57% of municipalities have joined an IDA

The regionalization process has progressed gradually over the past decade, and is not completed yet. Indeed the creation of a regional WSS operator does not imply the fulfilment of the reform. It should rather be considered as a preliminary step towards the achievement of the aggregation purposes, i.e. efficiency gains and effective investment strategy. The ANRSC has estimated that, by 2015, only 57 percent of municipalities had joined an IDA, but no data was reported on the proportion that effectively transferred WSS services to a ROC. According to a World Bank survey (2017) covering 85 percent of all Romanian municipalities, 65 percent of rural communes have joined IDAs but only 35 percent have effectively transferred their WSS services to ROC, while for another 6 percent the delegation was in process. As a result of this situation, only around half of the municipalities that joined an IDA are currently benefitting from the professionalized services that ROCs can deliver and from access to large-scale EU funds for investment. In addition to those municipalities that have still not joined an IDA or are in the process of doing so, there are many cases of rural municipalities that withdrew from an IDA due to either dissatisfaction with the lack of service improvements and investments, the tariffs which they perceived as excessive, or a change in mayors following local elections.

A positive evolution of water and sanitation services coverage

According to ANRSC data, the total population connected to potable water services in 2015 was of 12.6 million inhabitants, corresponding to an overall connection rate of 63.7 percent. Most of the unconnected population lives in rural areas: the connection rate to potable piped water in urban areas in 2015 was 93.8 percent while in rural areas the connection rate was 28.7 percent. Back in 2008, the total population connected to piped potable water services was estimated at 11.4 million (connection rate of 53.1 percent) thus showing about 10 percentage points increase over the last 8 years (Figure A A.5.). A large part of this improvement growth is due to the construction of piped water and sewerage systems in rural municipalities previously unequipped thanks to the expansion carried out by regional operators. Between 2008 and 2015, the number of urban localities equipped with piped water system remained stable at 317, while the number of rural localities equipped went up from 1,806 to 2,157. For sewage collection systems, the number of urban localities equipped went up marginally, from 309 to 313, while the number of rural localities went up from 451 to 809 (World Bank, 2018[8]). According to ANRSC data, the population connected to sewerage networks in 2015 stood at 9.5 million inhabitants, with an access rate of 47.7 percent (64.2 percent in urban areas). This represent less than five percentage points increase since 2008 (Figure A A.6.).

Figure A A.5. Water service coverage evolution, Romania

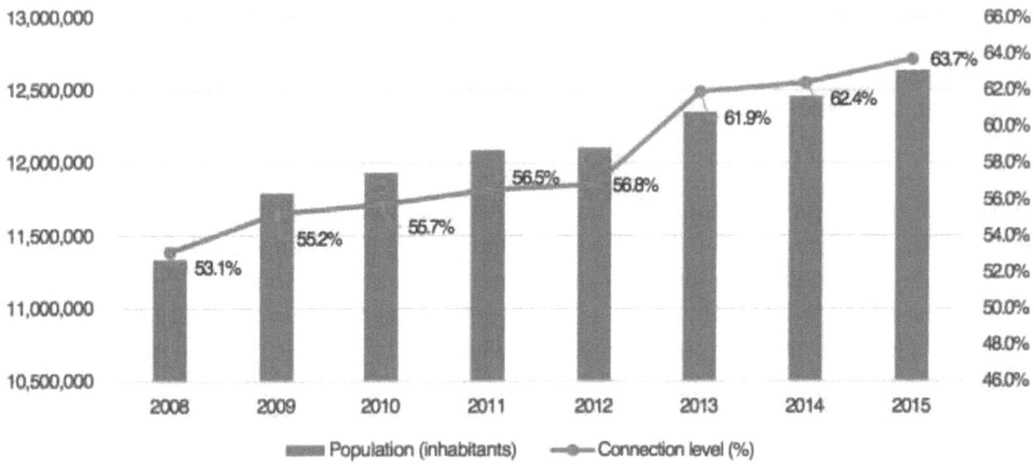

Source: (Romanian Water Association, 2016[9])

Figure A A.6. Sanitation service coverage evolution, Romania

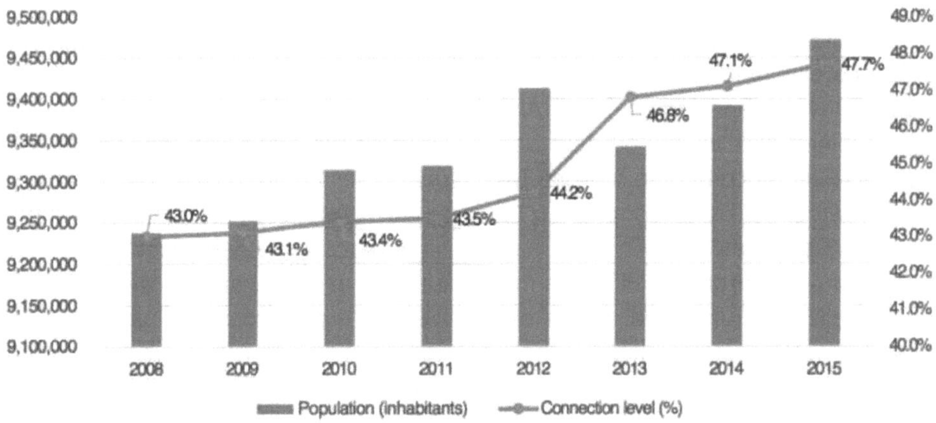

Source: (Romanian Water Association, 2016[9])

Moderated efficiency gains

The efficiency and performance improvements are much more limited. For instance, there was little evolution in the average percentage of NRW of ROCs in the past 5 years (Figure A A.7.). This is due to the fact that regional utilities have gradually incorporated small rural systems that were in very poor conditions. Still, the level of losses expressed with the m3/km/day shows some improvements, mainly because of the networks expansion and rehabilitation performed in the last years and financed through SOP Environment—the total length of newly expanded and rehabilitated water networks during that period was 3,100 km and 1,850 km respectively (World Bank, 2018[8]).

Figure A A.7. Evolution of water losses in regional operators, Romania

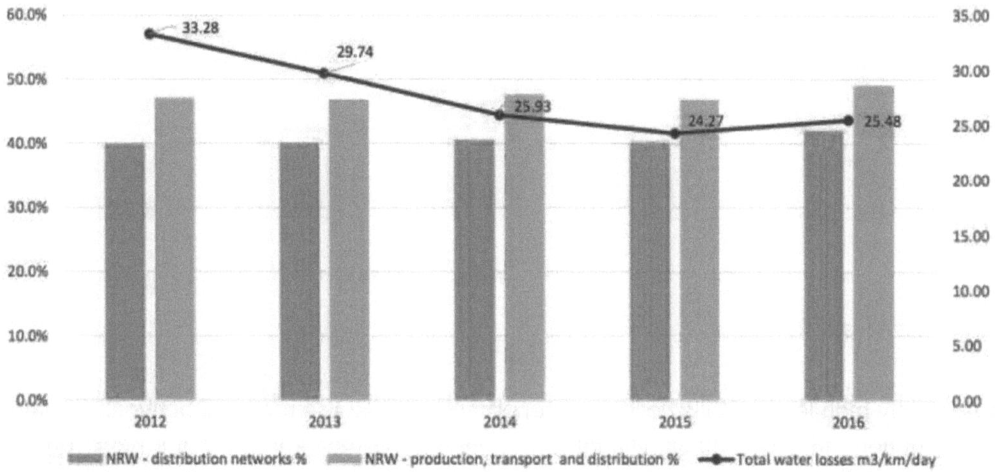

Source: (BDO Business Advisory, 2016[10])

Although the staffing level of ROCs is relatively high, at 6.5 staff per 1,000 connections on average in 2016, it decreased from 7.6 in 2013. This high level is due to a combination of factors. First, Romanian ROCs are well behind Western EU countries, where subcontracting is widespread (and often accounts for up to half of total labour); the degree of outsourcing of operational activities is close to zero. Second, relatively low salary levels in the country make it less economical for utilities to push for more automation. Third, as part of the regionalization process, many ROCs have incorporated employees working previously in the municipal services. There are nonetheless large differences between utilities, with some achieving ratios of 3–4 staff per 1,000 connections, and others with ratios as high as 12 staff per 1,000 connections.

The energy efficiency of ROCs remained stable in recent years, at about 0.85 kWh/m3 for water supply (per m3 billed). Nonetheless, the energy efficiency for sewerage services has gone up significantly, reflecting the development of wastewater treatment plants (Figure A A.8.).

Figure A A.8. Energy efficiency evolution, Romania

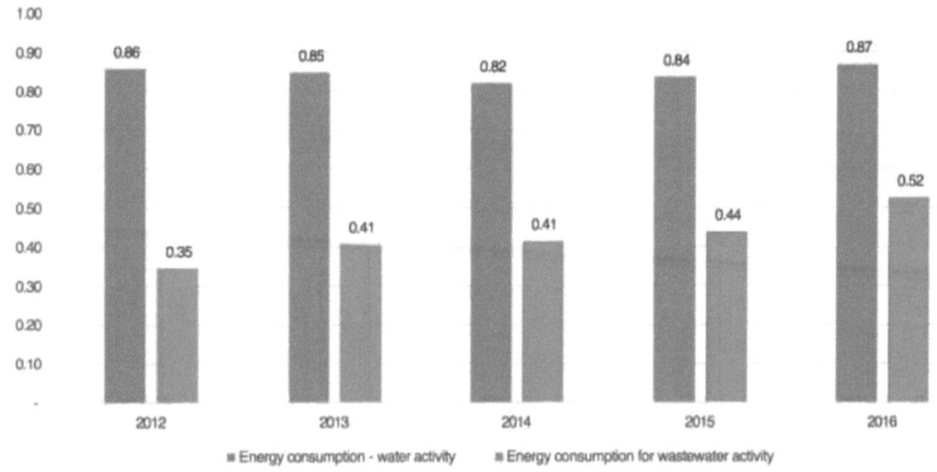

Source: (BDO Business Advisory, 2016[10])

Despite a relatively high level of bills collection period amongst ROCs reported between 70 and 80 days, the financial situation of ROCs has significantly improved in the past 4 years, with many regional utilities now recording a profit and being cash-positive. In 2016, the national average for the operating cost coverage ratio stood at 1.15, and for the net profit at 8.3 percent. It is important to highlight though that this improvement is mostly due to gradual tariff increases together with delays in implementation of the investments financed from SOP Environment, rather than efficiency gains. Thus, the overall profitability of the sector is currently sufficient to assure the coverage of operating costs and the repayment of the co-financing loans for investments. Furthermore, the impact of regionalisation showed a particularly salient improvement in the operational profitability of utilities (as measured by earnings before interest, taxes, depreciation and amortization, EBITDA), and the reduction in per capita consumption as a result of the generalization of metering together with steep tariff increases (price elasticity effect). While water consumption decreased significantly from 119 to 91 litres/capita/day over the last decade, the EBITDA almost doubled from 13.5 to 25.7 percent (BDO Business Advisory, 2016[10]).

Nevertheless, despite these positive impacts of the regionalisation process, several difficulties and impediments emerged.

Staff liabilities and transaction costs

Aggregation brings along the issue of staff transfer from former municipal structures into the newly aggregated utility. This generally creates large transaction costs (see Annex), which translate into labour cost increases and can hamper to some extent the financial sustainability of aggregated entities. In Romania, as stated in the previous section, the model of delegation contract for the regionalization reform prepared by the Environment Ministry advocates for transferring all staff to the incumbent. In the case of Raja Constanta Water Company aggregation process, all employees from the former operators were transferred into the new aggregated operator and no redundancy were made during the first two to three years of operation. However, as the services taken over were overstaffed, the number of employees in the aggregated utility increased by nearly 50 percent while salaries almost doubled (Figure A A.9.). The OPEX structure evolution for Raja Constanta Water Company shows the increasing share of labour costs throughout the aggregation process, rising from 30 percent to 36 percent. In 2013, the company launched a restructuring plan to adjust the number of employees, using a human resources consulting firm. Some 626 employees were dismissed (25 percent of total staff). Social protests were avoided, and only eight legal actions—all unsuccessful—were filed by former employees (World Bank, 2017[1]).

Figure A A.9. Evolution of labour costs and number of staff in Raja Constanta Water Company, Romania

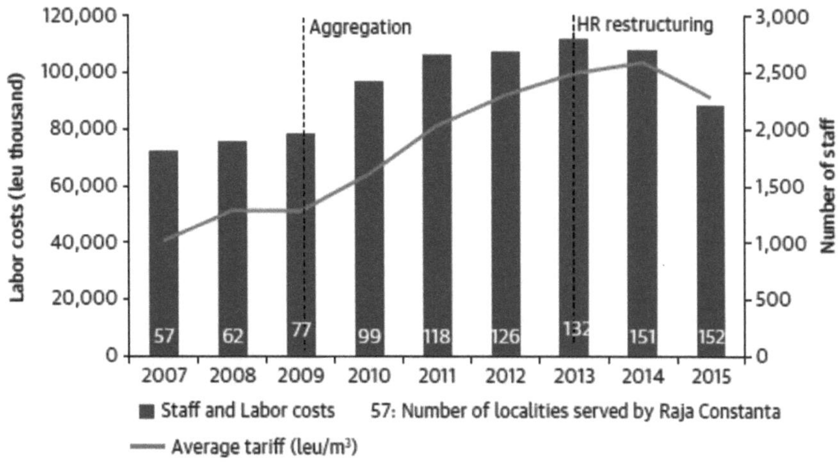

Source: (World Bank, 2017[1])

Engaging stakeholders to align interests at all levels

When mandated, aggregation is generally designed at the national level. Nevertheless, systematic consultations with local stakeholders should still be organized early in the process to ensure information about the process and better align interests of national and local levels. Such an early engagement helps build stakeholder ownership of the reform. It allows implementers to tackle potential problems or resistance, and diffuse their potential impacts, thus improving conditions for success.

In Romania, the alignment of national and local interests was an important issue during the regionalization process. Since 2005, Romanian local authorities, whether at county or municipality levels, have been questioning the regionalization reform designed by the central government. Owing to the pressure to absorb EU funding, the reform was passed quickly, which did not allow for proper information and engagement with local authorities and citizens. The government prepared master plans for each county and did not have time to complete them with more comprehensive technical and economic data, informed by local governments. As a result, the whole process was perceived as a top-down takeover of water services, with hostility from local authorities and citizens escalating when tariff increases were applied (World Bank, 2017[1]).

From cherry-picking to withdrawal practices

Over the regionalization process, IDAs have generally accepted all municipalities that wanted to join the existing ROC by signing the delegation contract. But some of them experienced difficulties in expanding their activity as quickly as needed to provide necessary and adequate services in the small settlements that they took over, often because of the lack of qualified personnel or financing. As such, IDAs were not "excluding" municipalities; however, they were to some extent cherry-picking[3] (Franceys and Gerlach 2008) municipalities that would bring along a source of financing and extended their operating areas in towns where EU funds were granted (World Bank, 2017[1]).

As a result, some municipalities now react by either rejecting or withdrawing from the aggregation, moves that may also derive from local political issues or other vested interests.

The municipalities that do not wish to join regional IDA and its ROC have applied for the renewal of their water operating licenses. Although these municipalities have hardly any access to funding for water supply improvements, they prefer to remain independent than join the ROC and see their tariffs go up without any perceived benefit. There are even cases where municipalities have joined the IDA and ROC, and are presently withdrawing. For instance, in Neamt County, six communes left the IDA in 2015. The main reasons for withdrawal are much higher water fees for households and delayed extension or rehabilitation of water supply network/sewage systems. To prevent such issues, withdrawal procedures must be thoroughly justified and approved by the IDA General Assembly. In addition, withdrawing municipalities must repay investments made by the ROC in their territory and/or WSS systems (World Bank, 2017[1]).

On-going Mandatory Aggregation Reform. France

Table A A.6. Key data on aggregation of water utilities in France

Number of municipalities	Average population by Municipality	Level responsible for WSS provision	Number of WSS utilities	Average population served by WSS utilities	Aggregation index[1]	Formal policy or legal reform supporting aggregation	Predominant scale of aggregation	Predominant scope of aggregation	Process of aggregation
35,357	1,897	Municipal	29,374	2,283	55%	Yes (2015)	Administrative boundaries	Services & functions	Mandated

1.The Aggregation Index measures the degree of fragmentation of service provision of the water sector in a country, using a simple normalized index based on the number of local governments and the number of service providers.

Key drivers of the aggregation reform

Horizontal fragmentation of water and wastewater services

In 2018, there were 12,096 water services, 14,355 wastewater services and 2,919 non-collective sanitation services in France. Eighty-two percent of water services integrate all water stages while the same proportion of wastewater services encompass all sanitation stages. Hence, although the French water and wastewater sector appears fragmented horizontally, it is quite integrated vertically. Currently water services are under the responsibility of 7,739 municipalities and 4,357 inter-municipal authorities, respectively serving 18% and 82% of the population. Wastewater services are under the responsibility of 10,873 municipalities and 3,482 inter-municipal authorities, respectively serving 22% and 78% of the population. Non-collective sanitation services are under the responsibility of 1,363 municipalities and 1,556 inter-municipal authorities (Table A A.**7.**). These services ensure mandatory missions, such the zoning of existing installations, or the control of installations. Forty percent of these services also ensure additional non-compulsory missions such as installations maintenance, construction and rehabilitation works, or waste material treatment.

Table A A.7. Water and wastewater services, France

	Responsible bodies	Number	Population
Water services	Municipalities	7,739	12,400,000
	Inter-municipal bodies	4,357	54,841,262
Wastewater services	Municipalities	10,873	14,400,000
	Inter-municipal bodies	3,482	50,380,936
Non-collective sanitation service	Municipalities	1,363	3,816,563
	Inter-municipal bodies	1,556	NA

Source: (EauFrance, 2021[11])

Purpose of aggregation

Taking stock of this important fragmentation, a law was passed in 2015, called NOTRe law (New Territorial Organisation of the Republic), to rationalise the French water and wastewater sector. Among the 136 provisions of the law, the articles 64 and 66 state the transfer of "water" and "sanitation" service provision from municipalities to inter-municipal authorities (*communauté de communes*, and *communauté d'agglomérations*) on a mandatory basis on January 2020. The objectives of the law are clearly set out in its explanatory memorandum: "The targeted evolution of water and wastewater services reflects the necessity to reduce the atomisation of competences while generating economies of scale. Public water and sanitation services suffer from extreme dispersion, which affects both their quality and their sustainability. The transfer of water and sanitation competences from municipal to inter-municipal authorities by 2020 make it possible to effectively pool together the necessary technical and financial resources in order to ensure an efficient management of water and sanitation networks. It will also allow improving water and sanitation services financial base, while paving the way for a comprehensive approach to water resource management, through enhanced performance and management, thus promoting the improvement of service quality provided to users."

Hence the objectives of the NOTRe law are threefold:

- It seeks to further pursue a movement of competence transfer from the municipal level to the inter-municipal level, which is deemed more relevant to manage public network services and achieve economies of scale.
- Furthermore, this transfer of competence will allow inter-municipal entities to have the financial and technical skills to undertake the significant and necessary investments to renew and upgrade WSS infrastructure in the coming years. The report of the General Auditor (French General Auditor, 2015[12]) has highlighted the ageing nature of some networks and the need for future investments. According to cost recovery study, 45% of the total drinking water network and 28% of the total wastewater network are installed in rural areas. This represents an asset of about 80 billion € and a renewal need of about 1.2 billion €/year for rural networks. In addition, 60% of the water services in France serve on average less than 1,000 inhabitants. As such, these small rural services fail the means to ensure an effective asset management. In this context, the aggregation at inter-municipal level should make it possible, through urban-rural solidarity mechanisms, to improve services' performance and carry out, among other things, investments that cannot be scaled down.
- Finally, it seeks to rationalize the number and variety of inter-municipal authorities by integrating further water and wastewater competences. In its annual report dated 2015, the General Auditors underlines the dispersion, the heterogeneity and the complexity of the territorial organization of public water and sanitation services.

By pooling resources together, the reform aims at reaching economies of scale and achieving investment capacities which are crucial to meet the challenges of asset management, renewal and upgrading.

It should be noted that the French aggregation reform mandates the transfer of WSS competence from municipalities to *communauté de communes*, and *communauté d'agglomérations*. By law, the *communauté de communes* shall gather a minimum of 15,000 inhabitants on a territory of one piece and without enclave, while the *communauté d'agglomérations* shall gather at least 50,000 inhabitants with a large city of more than 15,000 inhabitants, on a territory of one piece and without enclave. Thus, the reform rationale is to promote inter-municipal forms of cooperation where the implementation of cross-subsidies among settlements can balance differences between urban and rural water systems, which do not have the same production costs. In such configurations, larger urban utilities act as the nuclei around which less populated, less profitable, and less well-performing service providers aggregate. The nuclei help surrounding service providers to improve.

Key practicalities of the aggregation reform

Scope

The NOTRe law of August 7, 2015 provides that water and sanitation competence transfer will be done in "block":

- drinking water competence should be transferred as a whole (production, transport and storage);

- collective sanitation competence should be globalized together with non-collective sanitation competence.

Hence the scope of the aggregation process encompasses all stages and functions for both water and sanitation services. As such, the NOTRe law clearly seeks a full vertical integration of water and sanitation services. Nevertheless, it should be noted that the financing and accounting of the water service, the collective sanitation service and the non-collective sanitation service remain distinct; as each service having its own separated budget. Hence, cross-subsidies between water, collective sanitation and non-collective sanitation services are not possible.

Asset & investment planning

The transfer of a competence *de facto* entails, on the date of the transfer, the free hand over of the asset and equipment necessary to the service delivery and the substitution of the inter-municipal authority to the municipality for all rights and obligations associated with the infrastructure handed over (article L 1321-1 of the CGCT and following). Consequently, investment planning is thereafter done and decided by the inter-municipal authority on the basis of a yearly official deliberation jointly voted by the representatives of all municipalities. Investment programmes are not a consolidation of individual investment plans proposed by each municipality. As such, they require consensus among all municipal constituencies. They are funded through the water and sanitation invoices collected by the inter-municipal operator. Moreover, the inter-municipal authority becomes the sole contact point of the local River Basin Agency.

Budget consolidation

When proceeding to a competence transfer, the budget of the former water or sanitation service must be closed, and assets and liabilities are reintegrated into the municipality's main budget. Once this accounting operation is done, all assets necessary to deliver the water or sanitation service are then automatically handed over by the municipality to the inter-municipal authority through a specific accounting procedure. As such the asset of each municipality remains clearly identifiable, and the asset of aggregating entities is handed over (not merged) to the aggregated entity. The surpluses and / or deficits as stated in the budget of the former water or sanitation service can be transferred into the water or sanitation budget of the inter-municipal authority based on a common decision taken by the inter-municipal authority and the municipality.

Tariff

The final objective of the inter-municipal aggregation is to create a pooling of services and therefore harmonize the water price throughout the service delivery territory to ensure an equal treatment of public services users. This harmonization aims at creating a solidarity mechanism between urban and rural municipalities within the boundaries of the inter-municipal entity. Nevertheless, the French law allows for tariff differentiations between water users are possible as long as one of the following three conditions is met:

- a law authorizes it,
- differences in users situations are clearly appreciable,
- tariff differentiations corresponds to a need of general interest in relation to the purpose or the operating conditions of the service (EC, May 10, 1974, Denoyez and Chorques).

In the context of inter-municipal aggregation, it is possible for the inter-municipal authority to set differentiated tariffs across its territory, especially if there is a diversity of initial conditions between aggregating services in terms of service performance, for instance. In the longer term, however pricing must be unified in order to comply with the principle of equality of treatment. It should be noted that the deadline for water price harmonisation is not clearly defined in the law. It is therefore possible to achieve it over any given period although extending this delay increases the risk of litigation.

Management mode

The rationalisation of water and wastewater services targeted by the NOTRe law also foresees the harmonisation of management arrangements (in-house, delegated management) throughout the service delivery territory to ensure equal treatment of users. However, it is possible to have differentiated management arrangements for a transitional period: But, as indicated above, the eventual need to harmonize tariffs can also imply a harmonization of management arrangements.

Contracts

The French law establishes the principle of continuity of contracts. Thus, the inter-municipal authority replaces the municipality as the contracting party until the end of the existing and on-going contracts. This implies the substitution of the inter-municipal authority in all rights and obligations formerly born by the municipality. It also implies the substitution of the president of the inter-municipal authority in place of the mayor of the municipality without amending the contract. Nevertheless, the co-contractor must be informed of this substitution.

According to the principle of freedom of the parties to contract, the parties (inter-municipal authority and co-contracting party) may consider a revision of the contractual conditions before the expiry of the contract or even an early termination of the initial contract. In the latter case, the conclusion of a new contract must however be preceded by a lawful and compliant call for tender.

Achievements and difficulties of the aggregation process

Limited but steady decrease in the number of utilities

In order to monitor the progression of the aggregation process, an inter-municipal management rate is calculated and reported yearly by the French Biodiversity Agency. It is defined as the proportion of municipalities having transferred all their water and sanitation competence to an inter-municipal authority.

This rate amounted to 59.9% in 2018. Since 2013, its evolution shows a steady increase of 1 to 1.5 percentage point each year, and a sharper increase of 4.5 percentage point in 2017 and 2018 (Figure A A.**10.**), thus illustrating the transfer of competence from municipalities to inter-municipal authorities.

Figure A A.10. Inter-municipal management rate evolution, France

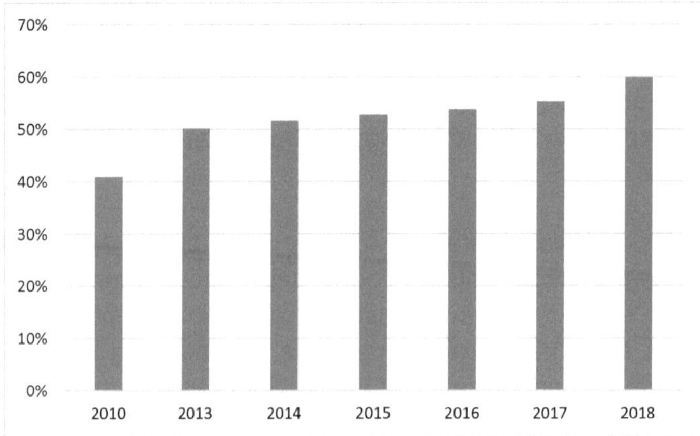

Source : (EauFrance, 2021[11])

The rate is currently higher in the North and South-West of France, while it is relatively lower in the South east (Figure A A.11.).

Figure A A.11. Inter-municipal management rate, France

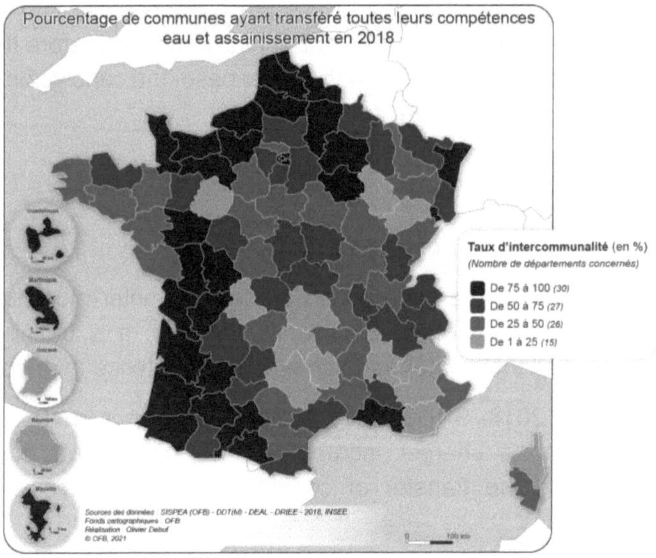

Source: (EauFrance, 2021[11])

Postponement of the aggregation deadline

The 2015 version of the NOTRe law provided for a mandatory transfer of water and sanitation competences to inter-municipal authorities on January 1, 2020. However many mayors were reluctant to lose their power in the field of water and sanitation provision. Following the adoption of the law, they engaged into extensive discussions with the Central Government to postpone the mandatory competence transfer deadline, which was then rescheduled to 2026. This new deadline was chosen as it corresponds to two terms of municipal office. It is also posterior to the forth-coming presidential and parliamentary elections, which makes it all the most hypothetical.

Presumably, this postponement should only concern 40% of all municipalities (ie, the ones that have not already carried out the transfer). "More than half of these municipalities will have to switch to the inter-municipal level anyway as they will not be able to meet efficiently water quality standards requirements nor and network and asset investment needs" (communication from the Association of French Mayors, 2017). Furthermore, municipalities that have already transferred their water and sanitation competences to an inter-municipal authority will not be able to reverse their decision.

This postponement was officialised as part of the Article 1 of the Ferrand law dated August 3rd 2018 which introduced a blocking minority mechanism vis-à-vis the competence transfer. With this Ferrand law, it is thus possible for municipalities that are members of an inter-municipal authority to oppose the competence transfer in 2020, if the following two conditions are met:

- the competence is not yet exercised by the inter-municipal authority,
- before June 30th 2019, at least 25% of the municipalities that are members of the inter-municipal authority representing 20% of the population pass such a "blockage" deliberation.

Under these conditions, the transfer will only take place on January 1st 2026.

Easing of the mandatory aggregation

The practicalities for the transfer of water and sanitation responsibilities were further loosened on December 27, 2019, under the law relating to engagement and proximity. This law introduced a mechanism allowing an inter-municipal authority to delegate all or part of the water and / or sanitation competence to one of its member municipality. The delegation takes place through an agreement between the inter-municipal authority (the delegating authority) and the municipality (the delegated authority). The agreement specifies the duration of the delegation, its scope and provisions. Following this new amendment of the original NOTRe law, the expected evolution of the rationalisation of water and sanitation services will probably be slower and less significant than initially expected.

On-going Mandatory Aggregation Reform. Italy

Table A A.8. Key data on aggregation of water utilities in Italy

Number of municipalities	Average population by Municipality	Level responsible for WSS provision	Number of WSS utilities	Average population served by WSS utilities	Aggregation index[1]	Formal policy or legal reform supporting aggregation	Predominant scale of aggregation	Predominant scope of aggregation	Process of aggregation
7,914	7,619	Regional	2,100	28,713	79%	Yes (1994)	Administrative boundaries	Services & functions	Mandated

1.The Aggregation Index measures the degree of fragmentation of service provision of the water sector in a country, using a simple normalized index based on the number of local governments and the number of service providers.

Key drivers of the aggregation reform

Fragmented and inefficient water and sanitation services

At the beginning of the 1980s, the Italian water sector was fragmented with almost 8,000 utilities operating mainly at municipal level. These utilities were also characterised by a low efficiency, low performance, low operating cost recovery, lack of investment and low coverage rate. This situation was typical of a low level equilibrium (Box A A.**2**).

Box A A.2. Low-level equilibrium concept

As described by Savedoff and Spiller (1999), the water and sanitation services sector in many developing countries is stuck in a so-called low-level equilibrium. In such situations, low tariffs are associated with low quality, low service expansion and general operational inefficiency. The term equilibrium indicates that without a reform of the sector's set up, there is no movement toward improved water services.

This phenomenon originates in incentives for governments to behave opportunistically. By lowering tariffs or resisting tariff increases, they can reap short-term political benefits such as electoral gains, so they will support the status quo over costly political actions that might involve increased water rates in the short run and yield diffuse benefits in the longer term. Moreover, consumers are relatively dispersed and too disorganised to assume an active role in holding the water authority accountable. They also are unwilling to spend more on poor quality services that are seen as wastefully managed. In turn, this creates incentives for water companies to operate inefficiently regardless of whether the services are provided by a public or a private company (Figure A A.12.).

Figure A A.12. Low level equilibrium

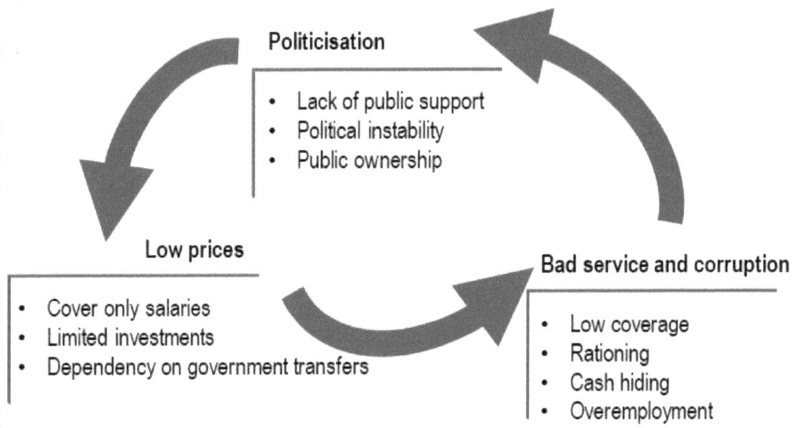

In order to get out of the low-level equilibrium, various strategies can be implemented, such as improving the regulatory environment or limiting government opportunism. Following the low-level equilibrium trap theory developed by Nelson (1956), large investment programmes can act as a "big push" that enables underdeveloped sectors to get out of the low-level equilibrium trap and embark on a development path.

Source: (World Bank, 2017[1])

Investments were typically financed through government subsidies, while operating costs were covered by tariff revenues. Tariffs were much lower than in other European countries. Because of high debt levels, local governments were less and less able to provide the subsidies necessary to maintain the existing infrastructure and to improve service quality. The asset was in a particularly poor state in Southern Italy where water supply was often intermittent. Furthermore, wastewater was often being discharged without treatment or with insufficient treatment.

Purpose of aggregation

In order to comply with the EU Wastewater Directive dated 1991, considerable investments in wastewater treatment were necessary in addition to investments needed to maintain the ageing infrastructure. These investments were to be financed by the service providers using their own resources instead of government subsidies. In order to do so, on the one hand tariffs were to increase. On the other hand, service providers were to become more efficient, reducing recurrent costs and non-revenue water so that a higher share of their revenues would become available for investments to maintain and improve service quality. Investments in wastewater treatment and bulk water supply were to be planned in a more rational way within the boundaries of river basins. Furthermore, fragmented service provision was to be consolidated into regional utilities that were expected to be more efficient. Local governments were reluctant to give up their responsibility for water supply, and mayors were also reluctant to increase water tariffs. In such context, the national government prepared a law to make municipalities regroup and form regional utilities, as well as to achieve cost recovery from tariff revenues. Under the planned law, regional governments would have an important role in setting the geographic boundaries of the new regional utilities.

The first aggregation laws of 1989 and 1994: towards the implementation of the Optimal Territorial Areas

As early as the mid-80s, the issue of optimal scope (level of integration) and scale (i.e., number of consumers supplied) of WSS provision was extensively discussed. On 18 May 1989, the law n. 183 was passed allowing for the consolidation of water services on a voluntary basis. However, this law did not trigger much interest from municipalities and no real consolidation of WSS municipal services happened. Moving from a voluntary to a mandatory approach, a more prescriptive law was passed shortly after, in January 1994, that completely reshaped the Italian water sector. The so-called *Galli* Law n. 36 introduced key clear-cut changes in the institutional and regulatory framework of WSS provision:

- an integration of the WSS service encompassing all stages of the water and wastewater cycles;
- a geographical aggregation for the service provision called Optimal Territorial Areas (*Ambiti Territoriali Ottimali*, ATOs) managed by autonomous authorities with a legal status; each authority should designate a single operator for each ATO;
- a tariff covering all the costs of the service and, in so doing, overcoming the practice of cross-subsidies among utilities at municipal level. Following a 1996 Decree, a "Normalised Method" was thus elaborated which defined the cost components to be used to determine the reference tariff. It fixed a standard of 7% for capital remuneration, a level that may have been appropriate at that time before the introduction of the Euro and falling interest rates. However, that rate was never updated after the introduction of the Euro in 1999, and its high level contributed to make the capital remuneration clause of the law unpopular among those that were primarily concerned with keeping tariffs low and affordable.
- a national committee in charge of monitoring the sector (*Comitato per la Vigilanza sull'Uso delle Risorse Idriche*, abbreviated into *Conviri*) and of an observatory for data collection on the sector (*Osservatorio sui Servizi Idrici*).

To implement the law, the 20 Italian regional governments were required to define "Optimal Territorial Areas" that would be serviced by the new regional utilities. Each ATO would comprise a group of municipalities, and in each ATO, an authority called AATO was to be created to set tariffs, establish an investment plan as well as a business plan, and award a concession to a public or private service provider. The AATO would monitor and regulate the single service provider in its area.

In August 2000, financial support from the EU was approved to support the implementation of the sector reform, and financial incentives were provided only to operational ATOs.

Heavy and complex technical provisions resulted in low enforcement of the Galli Law

Nevertheless, the implementation of the Galli Law proved difficult as it was based on a technocratic vision that was in many respects at odds with the Italian reality. According to the Law, once the AATO has been settled by the regional government, a survey on the existing WSS infrastructure should be conducted, and a business plan established based on this information. On these grounds, the single operator supplying the ATO could be appointed. The necessity to go through these preliminary steps before appointing the service provider resulted in important delays and blockages of the reform. There was also an obligation to run an investigation every three years to verify whether any differences in projected values for tariffs were due to end users or operators (e.g., reduced consumption and cost inefficiency, respectively). In general, the implementation of this obligation was highly unsatisfactory, and it resulted in numerous disputes between consumers (unwilling to pay for investments planned, but not started) and service operators (asking for full recovery of actual costs). In 2004, ten years after the Law's adoption, only 38 of the 91 planned AATOs were effectively set up (Figure A A.13.). Among these 38 ATOs, 25 mixed joint-stock companies were appointed as operators, 12 fully public joint-stock companies, and only one concession contract (*Conviri* Report 2005). Furthermore, the implementation of the Galli Law diverged from the original plan as most ATO boundaries of utilities were drawn along administrative boundaries and not along river basins'.

Figure A A.13. Water sector institutional framework, Italy

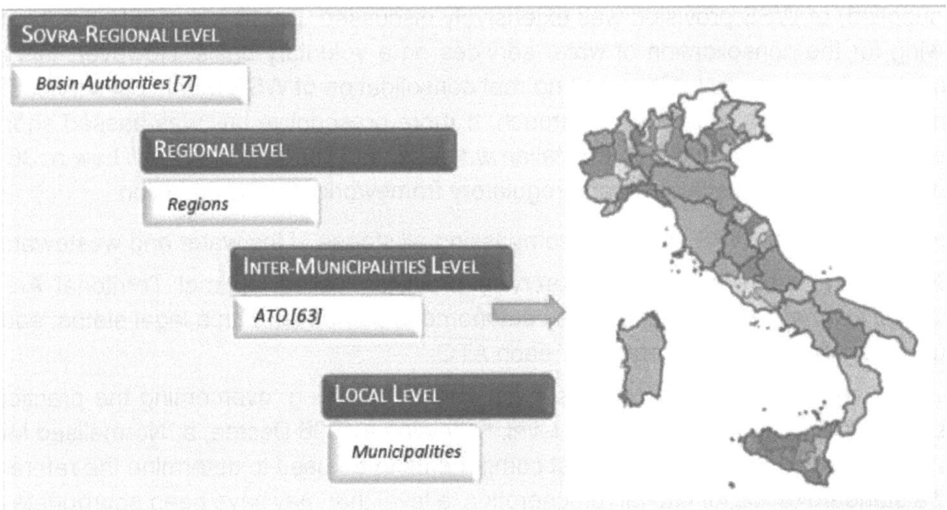

Source: (Porcher and Saussier, 2019[13])

Difficulties and obstacles in the aggregation process

Social and political resistance weakening the aggregation legal framework

In 2009, amendments to the Galli Law were passed including a safe rate of return on investments harmonised at national level. In 2009, the *Ronchi* Decree required municipalities and provinces that manage water through public companies to put the service out to tender, and it required mixed public-private companies to reduce the share of public capital to 30% by 2015. These changes launched a fierce social and political opposition, as they were perceived by opponents as an attempt to privatize WSS services. This opposition eventually led to a referendum, held in 2011, where the 2009 amendments were abolished. Furthermore, the referendum results stipulated that:

- a fair rate of return should not be included in the water tariff calculations and
- the obligation either to partially sell 100% publicly owned companies or to award concession contracts for the water service through auction procedures was to be abolished.

All these elements contributed to increase the uncertainty over the legal framework of the Italian sector, leading both private and public decision-makers to adopt an inertial strategy.

Second wave of reform: reinforcing mandatory aggregation through improved local regulation

In 2014, the so-called *Sblocca Italia* law was passed, and stated mandatory rules for establishing *Ente di Governo di Ambito* (EGA), which are local territorial governments acting as local Regulators, responsible for appointing one service operator per ATO. Hence, the *Sblocca Italia* law reaffirms the aim to reap off the benefits of economies of scale and scope that are seen as key to foster new investments in the sector. However, the same Law also defines a transitional period during which more than one operator could be active in the ATO. In addition, municipalities as participating authorities of EGAs retain a say in the decision to appoint operators. Because of these two factors, several operators are still found in some ATOs. The largest part of the EGAs in the North-East, the North-West (with the exception of the Valle d'Aosta Region), and in the Centre of Italy already appointed the operator(s). On the contrary, in the South of Italy and the Islands, a limited number of EGAs have chosen the water operator(s), thus underlining the long-lasting and well-known "Italian divide" phenomena between the North and the South.

Key practicalities of the second aggregation reform

Governance of aggregation

The EGA should also choose the governance arrangement of the water service among the three following options:

- a joint-stock company to which the service is awarded by a competitive tender,
- a mixed joint-stock company in which the private firm is chosen by a competitive tender, and
- a fully public company, that is, the so-called in-house option (Box A A.3).

Box A A.3. Management models of water services in Italy

The Italian water services are locally provided in 48% of cases by in-house operators; 29% of cases by joint-stock companies, of which 12% are in the stock exchange; in 2% of cases by concessionaires; and the remaining cases, which are largely located in the South and Centre Italy, are managed through simplified forms inherited from the past regulatory settings (Figure A A.14.).

Figure A A.14. Management models, Italy

Source: (Porcher and Saussier, 2019[13])

Tariff setting and regulatory framework

Finally, the EGA[4] should present a water tariff proposal compliant with the new regulation to the National Regulator ARERA.

In November 2011, the Law n. 214 designed a new institutional framework reform (Figure A A.15.) and assigned the following regulatory functions for the water and wastewater sector to the already existing and independent Italian Regulator for electricity and gas (*Autoritá per l'Energia Elettrica e il Gas*, AEEG—now ARERA):

- revenue and tariff calculation
- contractual quality discipline
- technical and infrastructural quality regulation
- unbundling and information feedback
- consumer protection
- enforcement, monitoring the conditions under which the services are provided, with powers to demand documentation and data, applying sanctions, and determining those cases in which operators should be required to provide refunds to consumers.

Figure A A.15. Water regulatory framework, Italy

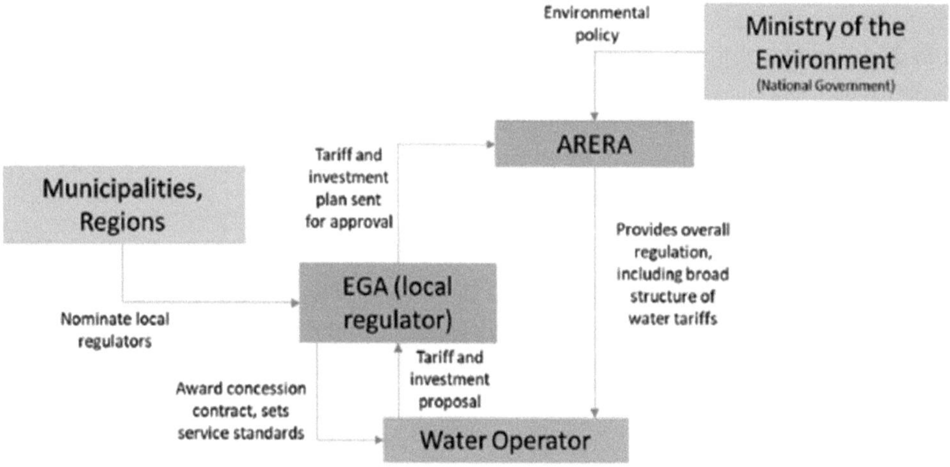

Source: (Centre on Regulation in Europe, 2019[14])

In this new regulatory framework, ARERA, EGAs and water operators are all involved in the price setting review and approval process (Figure A A.16).

Figure A A.16. Tariff decision-making process, Italy

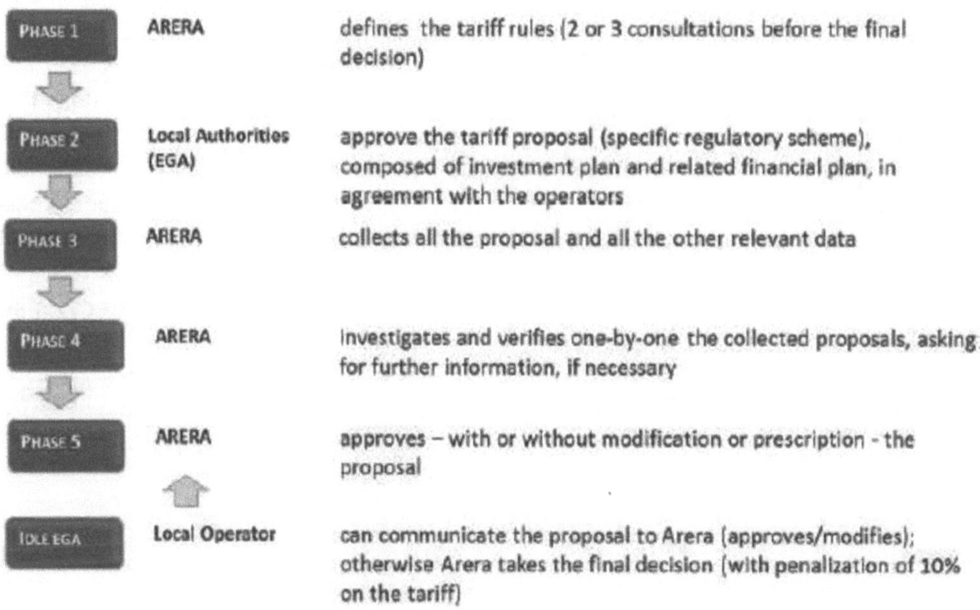

Source: (Porcher and Saussier, 2019[13])

Achievements and current status of the aggregation process

Reduced number of EGA and single operator model in place in half of them

EGAs have been substantially rationalised and improved, bringing about a reduction in their number (they have decreased from 91 in 2011 to 63 in 2017). In so doing, in many cases (i.e., in 12 out of 20 regions), the model of one EGA per region has been adopted with the aim to reinforce its institutional functions and competences and to upgrade the quality of each EGA's technical staff.

Water operators have been restructured, with their numbers decreased from more than 2600 in 2011 to nearly 2100 in 2017 (most of them, about 1300, are still present in the South of the country), within a process of continuous rationalisation and acquisition of infrastructures and their direct management. Such restructuring process leads to the vertically integrated supply (i.e., only one operator supplying the water services); as for the remaining not-restructured provisions, according to the Law, mergers among local suppliers of the water services should be planned in the short run.

Overall limited improvement in technical and economic efficiency

A report by Global Water Intelligence (Global Water Intelligence Report, 2018[15]) shows that the change in performance for Italy since 1990 appears relatively weak (Table A A.9.). Italy is the only country of the sample to see the proportion of non-revenue water increase (by 10.4%) and the percentage of households whose wastewater is treated fall (by 3%) since 1990.

Table A A.9. Evolution of selected performance indicators since 1990, Italy

	% change since 1990	Absolute value (2017)
Water quality	+0.06%	99.57%
Wastewater treatment connection	-3%	57.80%
Non-revenue water	+10.40%	34.71%
Average price/m3	+15.14%	€1.5

Source: (Global Water Intelligence Report, 2018[15])

The Global Water Intelligence report also shows that capital expenditure per capita in Italian water and wastewater sector is generally the lowest among the six European countries with only Spain having similarly low capital investment. Indeed, the other four comparator nations have capital expenditures per person consistently more than double the level in Italy (Figure A A.17.). The Italian water association has estimated that in order to close the gap with the best performing OECD countries, investment levels would need to reach about €80 per capita, while planned investment is only at €54.6 per capita, leaving a gap of €25.4, suggesting a need to increase investment by 46%. Where water services are directly managed by municipalities, the investment gap is much higher.

Equally, operating expenditures per capita in Italy are also among the lowest for the six nations considered (Figure A A.18.).

Figure A A.17. Evolution of capital expenditure in selected European countries (per capita)

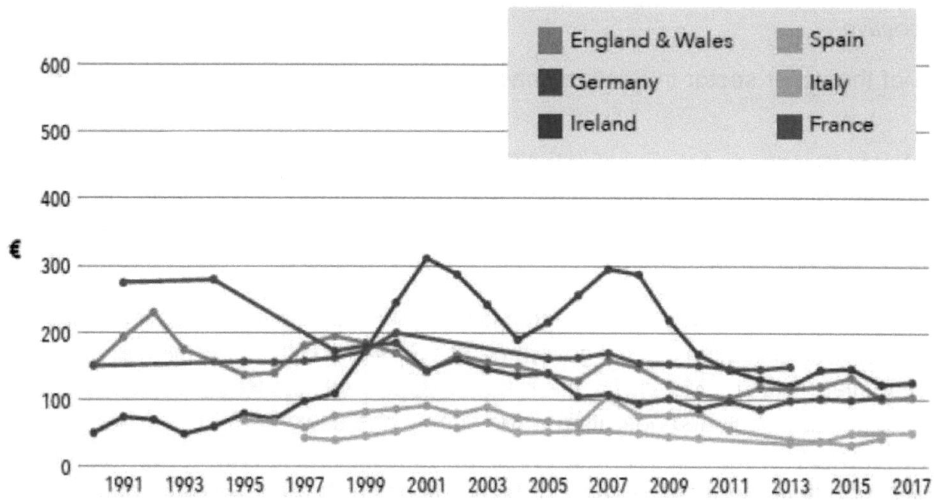

Source: (Global Water Intelligence Report, 2018[15])

Figure A A.18. Evolution of operating expenditure in selected European countries (per capita)

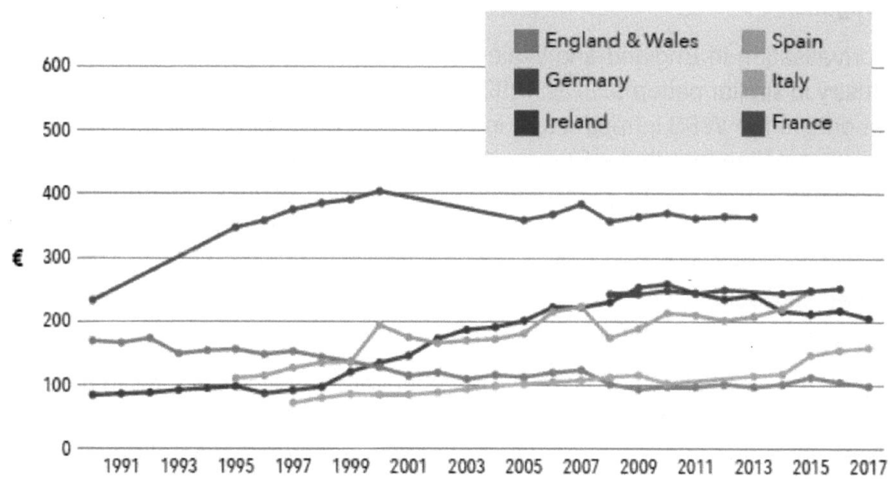

Source: (Global Water Intelligence Report, 2018[15])

Completed Mandatory Aggregation Reform. Scotland

Table A A.10. Key data on aggregation of water utilities in Scotland

Number of municipalities	Average population by Municipality	Level responsible for WSS provision	Number of WSS utilities	Average population served by WSS utilities	Aggregation index[1]	Formal policy or legal reform supporting aggregation	Predominant scale of aggregation	Predominant scope of aggregation	Process of aggregation
655	8,237	National	1	5,395,000	100%	Yes (2002)	Administrative boundaries	Services & functions	Mandated

1.The Aggregation Index measures the degree of fragmentation of service provision of the water sector in a country, using a simple normalized index based on the number of local governments and the number of service providers.

Key drivers of the aggregation reform

Historic perspective

The structure of the water sector in Scotland has undergone significant transformation over the past 40 years.

In 1967, the Water (Scotland) Act consolidated the Scottish 210 water authorities into 13 large Regional Water Boards, separate from local government, and responsible for the provision of water supply only. Whereas the 1967 Act brought a considerable concentration of water supply operations, it left aside sewerage, which remained fragmented.

Following a recommendation by a Royal Commission in 1973, the Local Government (Scotland) Act introduced a major reorganisation of local government in Scotland with a new two-tier structure (Edinburgh Council 2004). Implemented on May 1975, this reform established nine Regional Councils and three Island Councils whose functions included operating water supply and sewerage. The responsibilities of the nine Scottish Regional Councils were similar to those of the 10 English and Welsh Regional Water Authorities, with the significant difference that they did not hold responsibility over water resources management at local level, and that funding and tariff setting prerogatives remained in the hands of local governments. Capital expenditure was undertaken by the Regional and Island Councils and subject to the approval of the Secretary of State.

Purpose of aggregation

After the 1989 privatisation in England and Wales, the Conservative government intended to restructure the Scottish industry in similar patterns. In its 1992 consultation paper, the government explained the need for large investments in the WSS infrastructure in Scotland in order to bring it up to European standards. The cost to ensure compliance with the European Directives on Drinking Water (80/778/EEC) and Urban Waste Water Treatment (91/271/EEC) was estimated at 5 billion pounds (Sawkins and Dickie, 1999[16]). Another reason for the government proposal to reform the sector was the position, put forward for many years by water professionals and especially academic water engineers, that the Scottish water industry was too fragmented and lacked principles such as integrated river basin management, which were in place in England and Wales (Sawkins and Dickie, 1999[16]).

In November 1992, the Scottish Office launched a consultation exercise on the future of Scottish water services, encompassing eight options, which was concluded in March 1993. As part of the exercise, a consultation paper "Investing in our future" was issued with the background of government proposals to reorganise local government in Scotland. The drivers for the reform process as proposed in the document were related to the rising requirements to improve water quality and pollution control in Scotland. Under the new Water Supply Regulations dated 1990 (which translated the EC Drinking Water Directive standards into domestic legislation), about half of the water supply zones in Scotland did not achieve the required standards for parameters such as aluminium, microbiological quality, lead, trihalomethanes and iron (Scottish Office, 1992).

Water pollution control was the second driver for reform. The requirements of the EC Bathing Water Directive and the EC Urban Waste Water Treatment Directive had significant implications for local authorities, with an estimated capital expenditure needs in the water and sewerage industry to £5 billion (€5.8 billion) over 15 years, with half of that assigned to maintenance and replacement and the other half to quality improvement.

The report also argued in favour of larger units in order to meet greater efficiencies and economies of scale and to meet the growing complexities of the industry in the future. In addition, the report looked at the separation of the role of service supplier and the role of inspector and regulator.

In April 1996, a second major reorganisation of local government took place where 29 single-tier councils replaced the 53 district and 9 regional councils while the three island councils remain unchanged. The 32 councils were responsible for all local government services which were carried out by the old councils with the exception of water and sewerage that became the responsibility of three public water authorities - North of Scotland, West of Scotland and East of Scotland Water Authorities (Edinburgh Council, 2004) (Figure A A.19.).

Figure A A.19. North of Scotland, West of Scotland and East of Scotland Water Authorities, Scotland

Source: Water Industry Commission of Scotland, 2015

The three authorities were created mainly along the line of existing supply and disposal networks, and the boundaries of previous local authorities of Scotland. The three new Public Water Authorities (PWAs) were created as public corporations under the Secretary of State for Scotland (before devolution of powers to a Scottish Parliament in 1997), who was responsible for the efficiency of the industry. The PWAs operated on a commercial basis. At the same time a Scottish Water and Sewerage Customers Council (known as the Customers Council) was created. This was a national body with three area committees corresponding to the water authorities, financed by a levy on the three water authorities, with the role of representing consumer interests and handling complaints. It was also given the role of approving the tariff proposals of the water authorities.

Key practicalities of the aggregation reform

Full aggregation into a single operator

By 2002, water operating costs of the PWAs were double those of the best performing private companies in England; service levels lagged 67% behind leading companies south of the border (Water Industry Commission of Scotland, 2020[17]). Prices were higher than the rest of the United Kingdom, despite the presence of natural, rich, water resources.

Taking stock of this situation, the Water Industry (Scotland) Act was passed in 2002, and the three former Public Water Authorities in Scotland were merged into one body, Scottish Water. A single authority was thought to be better placed to avoid regional price disparities, finance capital investment, and maximise economies of scale. The Water Industry (Scotland) Act 2002 also addressed the issue of consumer representation, by creating five regional Water Customer Consultation Panels.

Tariff setting and regulatory framework

In order to regulate this drastically revamped environment, the Water Industry Commission of Scotland (WICS) was created in 2005, taking over from the Water Industry Commissioner for Scotland. This slight change in name was meant to reflect a fundamental shift in the attributions of the regulator. Indeed, the new WICS is now in charge of:

- Setting prices on a 6 year period,
- Facilitating the newly-established competition for the business sector, and
- Monitoring performance of Scottish Water in the areas of customer service, investment costs and leakage.

Prices are set for a 6 year period, with the third cycle (2015-2021) concluding this year. The determination of charges process is highly iterative, involving a yearlong back and forth between the Scottish Ministers, WICS, Scottish Water, but also other agencies such as the Scottish Environment Protection Agency, the Drinking Water Quality Regulator, and Citizens Advice Scotland. The process is started by the Ministers, who establish guidelines and principles; a basis upon which WICS proposes its methodology for prices setting for the period. The different stakeholders are then consulted, which results in a draft determination by WICS. Following another round of consultation with the Scottish Ministers, WICS publishes its final determination that sets out the maximum charges Scottish Water can levy on consumers during the regulatory period. Since 2002, household water charges in Scotland have fallen by 10 %, while it increased by 19 % on average in England and Wales. In 2019, charges are 16 % lower than in the rest of the United Kingdom, relative to 2002.

Charges are based on five “High-level principles” encompassing values of sustainability and equity while ensuring that the utility is effective, economic and efficient:

- Stable - stable and certainty in charging.
- Level of Charges - do not rise by more than inflation, as measured by the Consumer Price Index, across the period.
- Full Cost Recovery - cover the full costs of providing services to customers.
- Harmonised Charges - charges should, for similar services provided to customers of a similar category, be the same for each customer in that category regardless of location in Scotland.
- Cost Reflective Charges - charges for given services to particular customer groups should beset to recover the cost to Scottish Water nationally of providing that service to that group as a whole.

WICS adapted price cap regulation (RPI-X) to the situation of Scottish Water via a process called a ‘Strategic Review of Charges (SRC) (WAREG, 2019[18]). Each price review includes a review of Scottish Waters objectives, which are Scottish Ministerial industry objectives, on water quality, environmental performance and customer service. WICS price limit determination for the utility is based on Ministers objectives and set at the lowest reasonable overall cost for the customer and capped. At the start of each price setting period, a written regulatory contract is signed by Scottish Water which ties managerial incentives to performance against the contract. An improvement target framework is also set with progress monitored and reported (WAREG, 2015[19]).

Traditionally, Scottish Water provided a detailed Business Plan to WICS outlining how much public borrowing is needed to fund confirmed investment outputs. The regulator comments on the draft plan, and approves tariffs if the plan is agreed to by the stakeholders (WICS, 2020). The plan includes the utility’s view of the price cap which WICS reviews and comments on (WAREG, 2015).

Households are generally unmetered with no volumetric component. Charges are collected together by local authority (municipality) billing. Tariffs are uniform across the whole country, but depends on the Council Tax band of the property’s location (WAREG, 2015[19]); the higher the band, the more the resident pays for water services. Reductions are available for vulnerable groups, generally those in receipt of welfare benefits, and reflect discounts available in council tax charges. Over 50% of customer charges cover the utility's operational costs, service provision, and improvement. Scottish water charges include water supply and treatment in public and private settings (Scottish Water, n.d.[20]).

In comparison, non-households are metered and their charges are made up of six elements:

- a fixed charge for water
- a volumetric charge for water
- a fixed charge for wastewater
- a volumetric charge for wastewater
- property drainage
- roads drainage

Following the outbreak of COVID, WICS introduced two schemes to support non-household customers adversely affected by the virus. These schemes give customers the option to prepaid bills refunds, or request a temporary deferral of wholesale changes depending on circumstances (House of Commons, 2020).

Achievements of the aggregation reform

The costs of the restructuring leading to the creation of Scottish Water were important. "Our first task was to carry out probably the most complex merger which has ever taken place in Scotland as we joined together the former regional authorities – East of Scotland Water, West of Scotland Water and North of Scotland Water. We inherited 300 IT systems, which we reduced to 80. We inherited terms and conditions that varied massively across the country and within 18 months brought them together. We inherited three different charging systems, three different billing systems, three widely different cultures and three entirely different sets of standards and procedures." (Scottish Water, n.d.[20]). Considerable efforts were made to enhance efficiency. Between 2001-02 and 2009-10, operating costs were reduced by almost 40% (Figure A A.20.). Around 1500 staff left the merged business.

Figure A A.20. Operating expenditure evolution (2012-2013 prices), Scotland

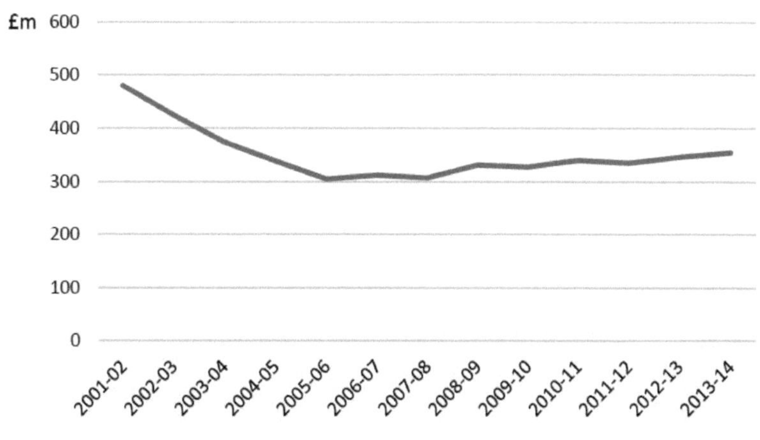

Source: (Water Industry Commission for Scotland, 2015[21])

The level of leakage at Scottish Water has declined from 1104 megaliters per day in 2005–2006 to 544 megaliters per day in 2014–15 (Figure A A.21.).

Figure A A.21. Evolution of selected water performance indicators, Scotland

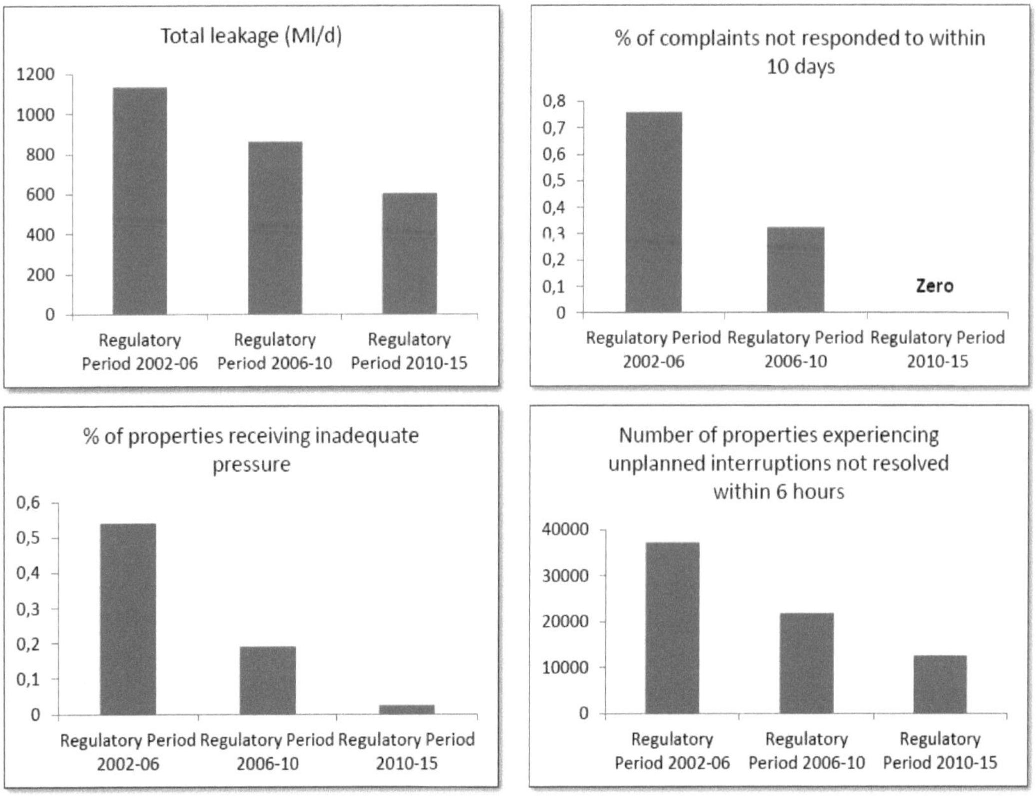

Source: (Water Industry Commission for Scotland, 2015[21])

The entire Scottish Water budget supports the programme of investment by Scottish Water. This budget is around £3.6 billion for the current regulatory period 2015-2021 (Scottish Government, 2019).

References

BDO Business Advisory (2016), *BDO Business Advisory Financial Survey for WSS Utilities and State of the Reform 2012–2016.* [10]

Centre on Regulation in Europe (2019), *Water sector ownership and operation, an evolving international debate with relevance to proposals for nationalisation in Italy*, https://cerre.eu/wp-content/uploads/2020/05/cerre_report_water_sector_ownership_operation.pdf. [14]

EauFrance (2021), *Observatoire des services publics d'eau et d'assainissement, panorama des services et de leur performance en 2018*, http://www.services.eaufrance.fr/panorama/rapports. [11]

Ferro, Lentini and Mercadier (2011), "Economies of scale in the water sector: a survey of the empirical literature", *Journal of Water, Sanitation and Hygiene for Development*, Vol. 1/3, pp. 179-193. [6]

French General Auditor (2015), *Rapport Public Annuel 2015*, https://www.ccomptes.fr/fr/publications/le-rapport-public-annuel-2015. [12]

Global Water Intelligence Report (2018), *International Comparisons of Water Sector Performance*, https://www.water.org.uk/wp-content/uploads/2018/12/GWI-International-sector-performance-comparisons.pdf. [15]

Kommunalkredit Public Consulting (2009), *Report on measures to cope with over-fragmentation in the water supply and sanitation sector*, http://www.danubis.org/files/File/utility_resources/user_uploads/final_report_overfragmentation.pdf. [3]

National Regulation Agency for Public Services (2015), *Annual Report.* [7]

ÖVGW (2015), *Austrian Association for Gas and Water.* [2]

Porcher and Saussier (eds.) (2019), *Facing the challenges of water governance*, Palgrave Macmillan, https://doi.org/10.1007/978-3-319-98515-2. [13]

Romanian Water Association (2016), *Report on the State of the Water and Sanitation Services.* [9]

Sawkins and Dickie (1999), *Regulating Scottish Water*, pp. 233-246. [16]

Scottish Water (n.d.), , https://www.scottishwater.co.uk/. [20]

WAREG (2019), *Tariff regulatory frameworks in WAREG member countries*, https://www.wareg.org/download.php?id=341. [18]

WAREG (2015), *Institutional Regulatory Frameworks, A Comparative Assessment.* [19]

Water Industry Commission for Scotland (2015), *Performance Report 2010-15*, https://www.watercommission.co.uk/UserFiles/Documents/Performance%20Report%202010-15.pdf. [21]

Water Industry Commission of Scotland (2020), *Strategic Review of Charges 2021-27*, https://www.watercommission.co.uk. [17]

World Bank (2018), *Romania Water Diagnostic Report*, https://openknowledge.worldbank.org/bitstream/handle/10986/29928/W18010.pdf?sequence=2&isAllowed=y. [8]

World Bank (2017), *Joining Forces for Better Services? When, Why, and How Water and Sanitation Utilities Can Benefit From Working Together*, http://hdl.handle.net/10986/28095. [1]

World Bank (2015), *Water and wastewater services in the Danube region, Austria country note*, https://sos.danubis.org/eng/country-notes/austria/. [4]

World Bank (2015), *Water and wastewater services in the Danube region, Croatia country note*, https://sos.danubis.org/eng/country-notes/croatia/. [5]

Notes

1 The definition of "services and functions" is given in Annex, under the sub-section "Scope".

2 The remaining 33 percent of aggregation had no predominant scale.

3 Service providers naturally prefer to extend services to wealthy populations for cost recovery reasons, and to easy-to-reach areas where infrastructure already exists. By doing so, they select (or "cherry-pick") solvent customers for good revenue collection and seek to avoid sunk investment costs and associated OPEX increases.

4 The local operator(s) can directly communicate decision about tariff proposal to the Regulator if the EGA does not act, i.e. if it does not proceed with the tariff proposal and the related investment/ financial plan. In addition, if even the local operator(s) does (do) not act, the Regulator can move on the decision-making process and also apply a 10% penalty on the tariff.

Annex B. Definitions

The following definitions are borrowed from the World Bank report on *Joining Forces for Better Services?* (World Bank, 2017[1]).

Definition and basic concepts

Aggregation is defined as the process by which two or more WSS service providers consolidate some or all their activities under a shared organizational structure, whether it implies physical infrastructure interconnection or not, and whether the original service providers continue to exist or not (WB study to reference). It can encompass a large variety of situations, which can be distinguished according to their purpose, scope, scale, governance, process.

Purpose

The main purposes of WSS aggregation are:

- Economic efficiency, which seeks lower unit costs, through economies of scale or economies of scope or more effective investment strategies;
- Performance improvement, which covers technical and managerial aspects of service quality and considers customer satisfaction;
- Professionalization, which targets technical capacity enhancement and addresses bottlenecks caused by scarcity of human capital;
- Environmental benefits, seeking integrated water resources management by sharing sources or reducing pollution;
- Solidarity, to cross-subsidize investments between regions or social groups to extend coverage and/or recover operation and maintenance costs.

Scale

The scale of WSS aggregation can vary widely. It can cover a group of local jurisdictions following administrative boundaries, whether these jurisdictions are contiguous or not. It can also cover a whole region or the entire national territory. Aggregation can also be implemented at the watershed level, following water catchment boundaries.

Scope

Aggregation can cover few or all functions associated with WSS services, or they can cover few or all stages of WSS services. Functions can encompass, for instance, operation, administration, customer relationship, investment or finance. Stages can encompass, for instance, production of water, distribution of water, collection of wastewater, or treatment of wastewater.

Process

The process can be mandated—and thus top-down driven—and initiated by national authorities which design a legally binding legal framework for aggregation. It can be mandated and supported financially by national or supranational entities. It can be voluntary and incentivized by public subsidies, external funding, or technical assistance stemming from national or supranational stakeholders. It can be voluntary, deriving only from a bottom-up initiative, stemming from utilities or local actors without a national framework to encourage it.

Transaction costs and aggregation

Awaited benefits from aggregation do not always materialise, and there can be many reasons for such drawbacks. Some of these reasons derive form the existence of one-off and long-term transaction costs.

One-Off Transaction Costs (Linked with the Aggregation Process)

In the framework of an aggregation, one-off transaction costs encompass the following three broad categories (Dahlman, 1979[1]):

• Before aggregation, research and information costs incurred to find and gather information on the service providers to aggregate with. For instance, the entire design phase of the aggregation would fall in this category.

• During aggregation, bargaining costs corresponding to the negotiations necessary to reach an agreement among aggregating utilities and translate it into legal provisions and binding documents, as described in the list of aggregation governance aspects[2]. This might lead, in concrete terms, to suboptimal solutions, such as the commitment to take over unnecessary staff or liabilities to make the bargain more palatable to the various parties.

• After aggregation, enforcement costs corresponding to the costs necessary to implement aggregation and make sure that all aggregating parties comply with their commitment and duties. They could, for example, entail the harmonization of salaries to a higher level or the costs of setting up new systems and procedures.

Long-Term Transaction Costs (Consequences of the Aggregation)

Several long-term transaction costs can be distinguished (Canback, 2003[3]) and applied to aggregation situations:

- Bureaucratic insularity: As utilities grow, senior managers are less accountable to the lower ranks of the organization and to shareholders. Particularly in large utilities with well-established procedures and rules, individual rent seeking is possible. This relates also to the frequent finding that managers in large organizations tend to emphasize size over profitability.
- Motivational aspects ("atmospheric consequences"): Increasing size brings increasing specialization, which in turn leads to reduced commitment from employees. Employees in large organizations often have a hard time understanding the purpose of corporate activities, as well as their individual contribution.
- Communication distortion due to bounded rationality[4]: As utilities grow, complexity increases. Hierarchical layers are added to manage the increasing complexity. Inevitably, these layers distort the flow of information. This limits the information available to executives, which Williamson (1975[5]) called a loss of control.

In addition to such "classic" diseconomies of scale, which can arise as a single utility grows, aggregations add complexity to the organizational structure, thereby adding to transaction costs. Among the most important characteristics that change through consolidation:

- Dealing with fragmentation of ownership: The fact that an aggregated utility serves several municipalities requires the formulation of decision rules for the shareholders and the allocation of voting power. Various schemes for the distribution of voting rights are possible, but in all cases, the distribution requires additional bureaucratic procedures and mechanisms to deal with multiple instead of single owners.
- Heterogeneous initial conditions and heterogeneous preferences: Municipalities for which service is bundled through an aggregation might have widely varying initial performance, service quality, and states of infrastructure. This raises questions about whether to apply the same policies to all utilities and how to prioritize investments and service improvements. To some extent, local preferences with respect to service provision may differ. How the management of the aggregated utility responds to these challenges might vary from case to case, but the utility needs conflict resolution mechanisms to align interests and arbitrate between those that diverge. This adds again to organizational complexity and decision-making costs.
- Complicated cost- and revenue-sharing mechanisms: As more municipalities are involved in an aggregation, possibly complicated cost- and revenue-sharing systems must be set up and adapted over time. Apart from the administrative burden, such a system also reduces transparency between service delivery and the price paid for the service, particularly if cross-subsidization between municipalities is pursued. Cost-sharing mechanisms give each municipality an incentive to attract as much investment and expenditure (public work contracts) as possible, regardless of whether or not the investment is sensible. These so-called common pool problems become more pronounced, the larger and more complicated the cost-sharing mechanisms are.

Overall, it is important to measure the outcome of a given aggregation primarily against its original purpose, which may or may not involve economic efficiency. In some cases, it might be necessary to accept a permanent transaction cost in return for an important externality; for example, a cross-subsidy between low- and high-cost service areas or an environmental benefit.

References

World Bank (2017), *Joining Forces for Better Services? When, Why, and How Water and Sanitation Utilities Can Benefit From Working Together*, http://hdl.handle.net/10986/28095. [1]

Notes

[1] Dahlman, C. J. 1979. "The Problem of Externality." Journal of Law and Economics 22 (1): 141–62.

[2] When aggregating utilities, various governance aspects have to be dealt with. The main ones relate to institutional elements; financing, assets, and liabilities; and harmonization of processes and practices.

[3] Canback, D. 2003. "Diseconomies of Scale in Large Corporations." Technical description, Canback Dangel Predictive Analytics Advisors, Somerville, MA.

[4] Bounded rationality conveys the idea that individuals have a limited rationality when making choices.

[5] Williamson, O. 1975. Markets and Hierarchies. New York: Free Press.

9 789264 713727

Printed by Libri Plureos GmbH in Hamburg,
Germany